Richard Krebs' past subsequent to [...] also to such a scandal within th[...] feared head of the FBI, was oblige[...]

After Krebs' death there were [...] determine how much was true in [...] written about the monstrous shadow world behind the facade of the worldwide communist movement. Peculiarly, such studies were only paid attention in the country of his birth when five essays on the events of *Out of the Night* had already been published in Scandinavia.[6] This was presumably due to the respective immediacy of the events in question and also to the fact that many of the protagonists of the autobiographic novel were still alive at that time.

However, that the key to the most controversial part of his life, namely his cooperation with the Gestapo, was there in these papers, there, in the desperate last letter from 'Fitsch' – this was overlooked by all those who later consulted these writings. All of them were no doubt looking for a unevivocal answer to the question: Was the author of *Out of the Night* a shameless liar or a profoundly honest man? In the face of Richard Krebs' life such a formulation, misses the point entirely. The truth, as so often, is more complex.

PART I The young Seaman

A Captain's Son and the Revolution

Richard Krebs was born on the December 17, 1905, the second of five children. Hugo, his father, was a captain of the North German Lloyd in Asia.

Hugo Krebs was from Silesia and of upper-class origin. According to his 1936 *Ahnenpass*, a document that served as proof of ancestry in the Third Reich, his father, Richard's grandfather, had been the vice-manager of the Gothaer Public Mortgage Bank and Silesian general agent of the Magdeburg Life Insurance Company. He was appointed Royal Prussian *Kommissionsrat* in 1880, an honor bestowed on businessmen who had been exceptionally successful in their field.

Born in Breslau, Hugo Krebs left Silesia before he turned eighteen and moved to the *Waterkant*, the North Sea coast of Germany. He attended the Merchant Marine Training College in Bremen and worked for North German Lloyd from 1885. He was a captain in the West Indies and the South Pacific and was appointed senior inspector in 1902. Why Hugo Krebs pursued what must have been a somewhat unorthodox career for a member of the Silesian upper-class can only be speculated upon; perhaps there were tensions within the family, or perhaps he was simply adventurous – a trait that would be particularly pronounced in his son's character.[7]

Even if Hugo Krebs rebelled against a proscribed life in his youth, by the time his own son was born in 1905 he had made peace with the world. A photo from this period shows a proud lieutenant of the reserve, a pillar of Wilhelminian society, staring self-confidently into the camera's lens.

Pauline, Richard Krebs' mother, was born in Sweden, but her family was from a South German family of priest and scholars. The parish rooms of the principal church of Heidelberg are named after one of their relatives, the protestant author Julius Schmitthenner.

As Pauline was still a child, she moved with her mother back to South Germany. There they were to live in Darmstadt, near Frankfurt, and there she was to complete studies at the Teacher's College. At the age of twenty-eight, considered somewhat late in her day, she married Captain Hugo Krebs and went with him to sea. A first child was born to them on board while their ship was in Antwerp harbor, but it was soon to die. Their next child, Richard's elder sister Annemarie, was born in 1904 in Hong Kong. Pauline Krebs returned to her mother in Darmstadt to give birth to Richard.

The one time Comintern agent, who was to see the inside of the grimmest penitentiaries of Germany and the USA, kept his origins secret for the whole of his life. After all, an upper-class background was not a calling card well received by the communist movement; and, again, there would have been every reason for fearing the worst if the diverse police and secret police authorities interested in him had caught up with his family.

For this reason, the autobiographical novel *Out of the Night* contains only few words about the mother of its hero, Jan Valtin. These consist of fact and admixture — Pauline Krebs had three, not four sons — and are indicative of the relationship between their hero's life and that of his creator: "My courageous and deeply religious mother had a dream of her own: a house on some hill, with a garden and a sprinkling of birches around, a friendly anchorage to which her four sons, all of whom were destined to follow the sea, would flock for a holiday after every completed voyage. She was a native of Sweden, and she shared the natural hospitality and a respectful love of all growing things which seem to be the characteristics of the Swedish."[8]

The only other information about the relationship between Mother and Son comes from his second wife, who recalled the little that her husband described of his childhood. In his account, Richard felt neglected in favor of his later-born siblings, and, for this reason, became all the more attached to his grandmother in Darmstadt. This woman was remembered by the Krebs family as a strict, devoted protestant matriach.[9]

After Richard's birth, Pauline Krebs remained for some time in Darmstadt and then followed her husband to Hong Kong where, in 1907, she gave birth to Richard's favorite sister, Caecilia, known as Cilly. After Hugo Krebs' transfer to Singapore with concomitant promotion into the Inspection Service of North German Lloyds, then one of the world's largest shipping companies, Richard's brother Julius was born.

In 1911, whilst the elder children remained in Asia, their mother returned again to Darmstadt where Richard's younger brother Hugo Junior, (or Peps), was born. The family were reunited a year later in Genoa where Hugo Krebs had a new post as an inspector.

Two decades later Richard Krebs was to have his hero Jan Valtin describe the results of this itinerary life thus:

"One result of this nomadism was that by the time I was fourteen I spoke, aside from my native language, fragments of Chinese and Malay and had a smattering of

Swedish, English, Italian and the indomitable Pidgin-English of the Waterfront. Another upshot was that I had acquired early a consciousness of inferiority towards boys who had the privilege of experiencing their boyhood in one country. In the face of the challenging bigotry of those who had taken root, — 'This is my country; it is the best country,' — I felt a certain sad instability. I retaliated by regarding with a childish contempt the healthy manifestations of nationalism."

When Italy declared war on Germany in 1915, the family was obliged to return to their homeland. This time their destination was not Darmstadt but Bremen, the seat of North German Lloyd. For the first time in conscious life, Richard Krebs was in the country of his birth. For Jan Valtin this was a sobering experience:

"In school my marks were below average. The haphazard training I had received at the foreign schools did not enable me to meet the rigid requirements of the German educational system. My teacher, a man named Schluter, had lost both his sons in France whereupon his wife had killed herself with gas. He reacted to his own misery by beginning and ending his days at school with most brutal beatings of his pupils. At the slightest provocation he used to haul them his desk, in front of a class of fifty, and flog them until they were unconscious. I became his frequent victim because my heroes were neither Bismarck nor Ludendorff, but Magellan, Captain Cook and J.F. Cooper's 'Red Rover' – foreigners all as, indeed, I was myself."

Richard Krebs' second wife also recalled an incident from her husband's school days that in retrospect seems almost prophetic. The pupils had been given an essay to write on the theme of sea travel. The young Richard Krebs, having spent his childhood on the sea, presented a story on the sinking of a ship that was so accurate in its description of shipbuilding technique and of such verisimilitude that his teacher, convinced that it must have been written by an adult, returned it to her pupil unmarked. Hugo and son were pleased to jointly compose a 'real' children's story for the self-satisfied pedagogue as countersign.

This story, recalled by an American woman some eighty years later and several thousand miles away, is all we know of the personal relationship between Father and Son. In *Out of the Night* the high-ranking reserve officer and employee of North German Lloyd figures as a class-conscious social democrat who, despite the position of inspector that he holds, is made all too aware of the Wilhelminian class system.

In his book the author and trained agent doesn't just veil some aspects of his past but intentionally doctors them, particularly those that regard the social standing of his family: "In an atmosphere of equatorial heat and British world domination I first became aware, shamefacedly, of the vast gulf which separated me, the child of a worker, from the sons and daughters of colonial officials and the white merchants of the East. I had no access to their parties, and the bourgeois arrogance of their parents made them shun the humble home of my family. We had but two Chinese servants, while they had fifteen and twenty." There can be no question of the son of a former captain and senior inspector of North German Lloyd having been treated as the child of a worker. Nor is it credible that the Lieutenant of the reserve "believed in an active socialist internationalism and workers' solidarity above and beyond the borders of nations", and therefore, "condemned the socialist leaders of Germany when they declared a social truce and voted for war credits in August, 1914."

Whatever political opinions Hugo Krebs might have held, it is hard to imagine that a man working in an elevated position for North German Lloyd since 1915 was a social democrat. It is, however, quite likely that the widely-traveled former captain, like many of the inhabitants of the North German Hanseatic League cities, was aware that a war against the leading naval powers could not be won by a Reich limited to the European continent.

The longer the war went on in Germany, the greater the dissatisfaction became among the population. The lack of farm laborers caused by the war and the Allies' blockade of the sea channels led to the 1916-1917 Famine in which several hundred thousand perished.

1917 saw the first of the uprisings and strikes of the era, although a combination of sweeteners and violence successfully subdued them. More dangerous to the Kaiser's rule was the growing tension within the Navy, where the first cases of desertion and insubordination came in 1917 rather than 1918.

"The men, crammed into narrow quarters a thousand and more on a single ship and ridden by hunger, hated the officers for their arrogance and the champagne and butter they consumed. The *Kulies* of the Fleet wanted more than an end to the war; they talked of revenge for all the degradations of the past. On several ships secret action committees of the sailors and stokers had been elected. The latrines in the shipyard became the centers for clandestine revolutionary meetings. Desertion increased; sailors sold their uniforms and decamped inshore. Several ringleaders from the warships had been court-martialed and executed by imperial firing squads."

By the end of September 1918 it was clear in Berlin that the war was no longer winnable, and that its continuation could only lead to a humiliating defeat for Germany and, finally, to its occupation. The first overtures of peace, namely the end of submarine war, were announced on the twentieth of October.

During this same period the German Naval Command decided to send its military cruisers and destroyers – the very pride of the Wilhelminian age — into a senseless final battle against the superior forces of the British Navy. Officers had champagne served in their messes, to be drunk one last time before their 'heroic sacrifice.' This was too much for the sailors who, unconsulted, were to be sent to their graves.

The long-brewed rage of the starving sailors turned now on their gluttonous superiors and spilled over in mutinies which began in Wilhelmshaven near Bremen and spread through all naval posts. Deserters and mutineers of previous years were liberated from prison, officers were disarmed and their stripes removed. The movement spread like fire from the coast inland. In one town after another, councils of workers and soldiers took power, and on the ninth of November the Republic was declared in Berlin.

The young Richard Krebs, in accordance with the expectations he was born to, was attending high school[10] as the insurrectionary sailors from Wilhelmshaven reached Bremen. His proletarian hero Jan Valtin, whose father, it goes without saying, had been elected to one of the soldier's councils, described the experience as follows:

"That night I saw the mutinous sailors roll into Bremen on caravans of commandeered trucks – red flags and machine guns mounted on the trucks. Thousands milled in the streets. Often the trucks stopped and the sailors sang and roared for free passage… I saw a man lose his life. He was an officer in field grey who had come out of the station the minute it was surrounded, and was seized by the mutineers. He was slow in giving up his arms and epaulettes. He made no more than a motion to draw his pistol when they were on top of him. Rifle butts flew through the air above him. Fascinated, I watched from a little way off. Then the sailors turned away to saunter back to their trucks. I had seen dead people before. But death by violence and the fury that accompanied it were something new. The officer did not move. I marveled how easily a man could be killed."

Richard Krebs has Valtin mock the High School pupils among whom he himself numbered with the words: "Young sons of the bourgeoisie who had been sporting sailors' caps now left them at home."

Whilst the population of Bremen were suffering a further winter of famine due to the continued blockage of the water channels — only to be lifted some months later — in Berlin bloody battles were being fought between the Social Democrats, subservient to the status quo and even prepared to bolster their numbers with members of the reactionary *Reichswehr** and the radical stalwarts of a Soviet Republic. The facts about how bitterly these battles were fought were soon to be suppressed. Who still remembers that the first bombs to land on Berlin did not fall during the Second World War, but were dropped in March 1919, by the *Reichswehr*? This was by way of assisting the white troops who, street by street, were taking the northeast quarter of the capital in battles with the reds. From Berlin, the white terror spread throughout Germany. Town for town, the worker and soldier councils were defeated and their supporters put up against the wall.

Thousands were killed. The journalist Sebastian Haffner described the events thus: "This civil war opened the gates to the insalubrious history of the Weimar Republic that was born of it, and, in turn, to the Third Reich, as it irrevocably divided the social democrats. It robbed the leftovers of the SPD of any hope of alliance with the left, made of them a perpetual minority, and created among the voluntary corps or *Freikorps*, who fought and won the civil war for the Social Democrats, the habits and mind-cast of the SA and SS that many of their number would later join."[11]

In Bremen, one of the first cities to be 'cleansed,' the struggle was comparatively mild, but the little that Richard Krebs witnessed must have left a strong impression upon him; he has his alter ego Valtin experience it all the closer as bicycle courier for the revolutionaries:

"The Noske guards stormed the bridge. As they ran, they shouted. And abruptly the machine guns opened in merciless bursts. I saw many soldiers fall. Death was commonplace… I mounted my bicycle and rode away, unaware at first of the direction I was taking. Dead men sprawled grotesquely here and there, and in many places the snow was splotched with blood".

Perhaps these repercussions of the November Revolution would not have taken on such dimension for Richard Krebs if his life had not been abruptly altered by the death of his father a year later, in March 1920. His father died a few months after his appointment as manager of the nautical department in North German Lloyds, one of

---

* German National Defence Forces

the highest posts within the shipping company's hierarchy. In this capacity he had directed the logistics of the business of shipping, allocated captains to ships and ships to voyages, and was known to all employees of the company. The fact that Lloyd was later to support the rebellious and politically radical son of this man bears witness to the stature with which he was accredited.

Presumably in response to a request by Pauline Krebs the board of North German Lloyd sent the following testimonial to the administration of San Quentin: "The above man, who, we regret to learn, is an inmate of your Institution, is… the son of a former member of our Staff who held a good position and was well respected. The son has had a good education, and, like his father, adopted the sea as a profession… He is the type of man who needs strict discipline, and even in his youth showed signs of a rebellious nature, which, unfortunately, after the death of his father and the extreme weakness of his mother, was allowed to gain the upper hand.

We consider him to be a thoroughly capable man, and one who, provided he is kept under rigorous control, is able to give a good account of himself."[12]

Apprenticeship at Sea

The death of the father left the family reliant on the widow's pension of the mother. This, together with her savings, would in other times have been sufficient for both herself and her children, but in the post-war period inflation made a mockery of such a sum. The family, to be seen in one photo taken prior to the war posing before an automobile – a possession that in those days was for most prohibitively expensive — embarked after the war on an irresistible decline.

This had probably already began in 1921 as Richard Krebs, at the time only fifteen, left his high school without intention of changing to another. As he told the American Military more than twenty years later, he was a mediocre scholar who only achieved good grades in one discipline, namely French.[13]

With the help of his mother he found a berth as ship's boy aboard the Magdalena Vimmen, a sailing ship of North German Lloyd's. The latter had only just started to rebuild their fleet, decimated by the conditions of the Treaty of Versailles, and was therefore obliged to fall back upon such craft.

His experiences aboard the Magdalena Vimmen were to form the background to the story *Afloat* that was first published in the San Quentin prison magazine.

"What is life like during the first days at sea? Ask any man who has sailed with a foremast gang on a squarerigger... he will tell you... it is hell; and more than that, if he happened to be the youngest man in the fo'c's'le!

Four o'clock in the morn... a burly chap in boots and peajacket stood massively in the centre of the fo'c's'le. Out of their slumber he whipped the watch below with hoarsely bellowed fragments of a saltwater chantey.... I opened my eyes... weary... every bone in my carcass ached from the rope-tugging ordeal of the previous evening... I stretched, turned over, closed my eyes...

The barque lurched with a corkscrew motion. I heard the slam of the sea — and the rattle of flying spray as it struck the deck. I heard the wind moan through the rigging... Something struck the edge of my bunk with a crash and clattered to the floor... I shot up — alive!

Someone had flung a wooden-soled sandal at me. Across the dingy, flickering space sat an uncouth seaman-swathed in salmon pink underwear. He was bony and stubby of body, but the legs that dangled over the rim of his berth were rangy. He glowered at me.

"Hey, you! Go'n'get coffee!"

"Huh?"... I remembered that an old tar had once told me that one must be hard-boiled.

"Get your own coffee," I muttered.

The seaman glared. Agile and lumbering, like a great ape, he sprang from his bunk. He leaped across the forecastle. Without ado, he tore me out from my covers. His bony fist shot out, connected with my nose, and sent me sprawling under the table. Someone laughed loudly.

"That's right, Claussen-teach him manners!"

He of the pink underwear bored me with burning eyes. "Don't get smart here," he advised darkly. As an afterthought he punctuated his remark by kicking me in the belly.

Painfully I scrambled to my feet. The ship heeled with a racing sea. I slipped and fell-overturning a heavy bench. A seaboot came whizzing through the gloom. It struck the side of my head... the world reeled." [14]

His journey was interrupted at the Chilean port of Antofagasta. Hazy from his experiences in a world unknown to him and a bottle of *vino tinto* that he had emptied with one of the girls from the harbor, he missed the dawn sailing of his ship.

The Chilean police soon arrested the young vagrant and told him to "choose between forced labor in the Chuqui copper mines or a swift disappearance on the vastness of the Pacific," as he wrote in an unpublished manuscript on stowaways. Richard Krebs chose the second of these options, and swam across to the Annie:

"A Norse barque hulked deeply loaded and ready to sail. Barefooted and half-naked I swarmed aboard over the chain cable and disappeared in the rusty murk of the chain locker.

Four days out the pot-bellied cook caught me stealing a chunk of salt fish from the galley. He booted me from the forecastle to poop and back, told me the Annie was bound around Cape Horn to Marseille, and put me to work.

Daily I crawled into the ship's pigsty and cleaned it. It was a sacrilege to let the porkers roam out over the holystoned deck. Forced to remain in their cage they squealed bitter protest against my intrusion on hands and knees, doing their part to roll over me with the sudden heave or pitch of the ship. At the Horn, with breakers foaming over the decks, this act became a devil-dance and soon the crew called me "The Stinker".

The Skipper had a dog. Her name was Magdalena and she had the habit of easing nature through the coiled-up braces. So, when the wind changed, the yards were trimmed and the watch strung out at the braces, I chanced to listen to the most ferocious hand-wiping and curses I have ever heard. I was assigned to 'dog turn': whenever Magdalena showed her intention to settle down among the ropes, the mate on watch would shrill his whistle and roar: "Ho, the dog squats in the braces!" Whereupon it was my task to assault Magdalena with a belaying pin and chase her below into the captain's saloon."[15]

At some point on his journey along the coast, probably in Buenos Aires, Richard Krebs managed to escape from dog turn and to disappear. For a whole year thereafter he vagabonded from harbor to harbor and lived from casual labor. His travels took him as far as the south of North America, where he found work with a black laborer. His days as a vagabond were to mark the rest of his life. He made the acquaintance of all sorts of people in this time, from smugglers and petty criminals to bent employers, some of who were later to appear in his novels and short stories.

"When my friend Singapore Joe, who has long ago sunk his scruples where the ocean is deepest, wishes to make a deal in opium, diamonds passports or guns, he invites a thirsty seaman from that ship to a drinking place in sailortown. What happens is simple. While the victim snores in some cellar or police station, the ship leaves port and Singapore Joe is aboard as a stowaway. Two days out he provokes discovery on the now short-handed ship and is given the lost man's berth, while the latter, marked as a deserter, has forfeited his accumulated wages, which makes most skippers feel fine.

Joe's method is not new. In Callao lives one Mr. Kugelman. He lives by selling jobs to sailors. When no jobs are available, Mr. Kugelman makes jobs. He sends out his assistant, a skinny hellion named Akerly, to slug a mariner on shore-leave and deposit him on a buoy in a remote reach of the anchorage to wonder how he got there. Then Mr. Kugelman sees to it that his customer is deposited on the marooned man's ship shortly before she heaves her anchors to steam seaward."[16]

In his travels along the coast of North and South America he also came across many German seamen who had deserted in droves and preferred to somehow struggle by in South America than to return to their homeland. From the Fatherland they brought the chaotic ethos of the time and the memory of the successful mutiny in the Kaiser's fleet. As the German Consulate reported with disgust at the time, they had the reputation in the harbors of South America of causing trouble wherever they went. The maiden voyage of a German vessel after the lifting of the Allies blockade on Germany itself gave rise to an international scandal.

In Hamburg, 1920, the Lucy Woerman, a Woerman line ship, took on board hundreds of unemployed seamen. These were supposed to man and sail ships to

Germany that had been left in South America due to the war. Almost none of them had the intention of carrying out these orders, however, because almost none of them intended to return to Germany. The fact that the seamen were no longer prepared to suffer the old regime on board contributed to the ensuing mutinies. The *Seemansordnung*, the naval code of the imperial regime, was draconian to the point of allowing a captain to dispense all forms of punishment short of the death sentence to his crew. Strike, even when the ship was in harbor, was considered mutiny and was punishable by imprisonment. As was to be seen, however, in the events on board the Lucy Woerman, the old guard had been vanquished. The German consul in Chile sent the following missive to Berlin on the seventeenth of September1920:

"The steamer arrived at seven o'clock. After the harbor authority's formalities... I went on board. The captains of the sailing vessels also came to collect their crews. No sooner was their ship moored than the crew started to make contact with the German ships and to distribute political tracts.

Captain Pohlig and Captain Bock reported that they had had a terrible journey; that the crew, together with the officers, had gone over to the soviet system. Furthermore, that the ten percent of bad men aboard had incited the whole crew and taken control of a ship that was not only carrying several stowaways but also several women who had sneaked on board in Hamburg: in short, that terrible things had come to pass. The crew wasn't prepared to keep the terms of their contracts, and... some even wanted American rates of pay."[17]

The case of the Lucy Woeman was by no means unique. On the Priwin, a sailing ship also bound for South America, the crew set up a council that forcefully took over the matter of food distribution from the captain and doubled the men's rations. No wonder that another German consul reported, "German seamen are known to be so radical that their mere arrival in another land brings with it the fear that extremist politics will be fostered."[18]

The disorder brought by the Germans to South America and the news of the revolution in Russia contributed to the feeling spreading the globe that the old order had had its day. With this came the growth of socially revolutionary movements such as the North American IWW, the Industrial Workers of the World. In 1920, the South American branch succeeded in bringing Buenos Aires' harbor under their control for several months and squeezing out of the ship building and harbor companies hitherto unheard of improvements in social conditions for their workers.

In spite of such successes, the work of a sailor in those days was badly paid and dangerous. The conditions in part really resembled the description in B. Traven's classic *The Death Ship*. Traven, who himself left Germany in the 1920's for Mexico, describes this existence through the eyes of a stoker who suffers inhumane exploitation on board and then vanishes along with his deathtrap somewhere on the Atlantic. A union man from Hamburg recalled how once a group of rich and leisured travelers were being shown a ship by the captain and inadvertently came into the crew's quarters, which in general were studiously avoided. A lady asked the 'good cap'n' whether men were really lodged here and received the reply "No, Madam, that is for the stokers."[19]

A run-in with one such slavedriver was to be the cause of Richard Krebs' return to Europe: "One of my shipmates had broken a leg off Tierra del Fuego. The captain refused to have the injured man transferred to a hospital. There was a near mutiny on board in which I had a hand. To avoid arrest by the Chilean harbor police, I deserted at night in the captain's gig and repaired to familiar haunts in Antofagasta. Christmas Eve of 1922 found me celebrating with other stranded sailors on the green lawns of Plaza Colón, toasting Mrs. Bready, the chesty female shipping officer of Nitrate Coast, who generously had supplied a keg of wine. The following day the manager of the Hotel Washington in Antofagsta, a smooth-tongued cosmopolite of Russian extraction, hired me to act as his agent on incoming ships. I soon discovered that my employer dealt in narcotics, and that wretched young peasant girls whom he had lured from southern valleys by promises of positions as chambermaids were as much part and parcel of the furnished rooms he rented as were the beds and mirrors. I was sufficiently naïve to pick a quarrel on that score. The Russian manager called the police and accused me of having broken the peace of his house. I fled."

The ship on which he escaped was the skiff Obodrita, which arrived in Hull, Great Britain in 1923.[20] This, comparatively speaking, was a mere stone's throw from Bremen, where Richard Krebs ended the first of his voyages.

Richard Krebs turns Communist

As Richard Krebs returned to Germany in spring 1923 he was seventeen years old. He arrived in Bremen with a few dollars in his pocket and the dream of becoming an officer like his father. Given his 'proper' upbringing and his family's support, he might well have become a novelist-captain, who some day would have written the flamboyant history of his youthful travels, complete with decorative descriptions of rebellious German sailors – at least, if the times had been willing.

The land to which he had returned was falling into disrepair. The French government had occupied the *Ruhrgebiet* to ensure the payment of reparations. The German government called for passive resistance and printed money to support strikers there and those of its citizens who had been forced out of the French zone. Hyperinflation was the net result, which even swallowed up all that the middle-classes had put aside since the war. In January 1922 a dollar was worth two hundred marks; in July, five hundred; and in January 1923, eighteen thousand marks. The pinnacle was reached in November 1923, with the dollar at 4.2 billion marks. Savings accounts, federal loans and all forms of debenture bonds were decimated. The British Ambassador wrote, "The systematic expropriation of the German middle-classes' wealth, not by any socialist government, but by a middle-class government which campaigned under the banner of protecting property, is an occurrence without precedent. It was one of the grossest cases of pillage in history."[21]

Among the victims was the widow Pauline Krebs. The few dollars that Richard had brought back from America were quickly taken from him to buy food for his younger siblings. There could be no talk of marine training college under such circumstances.

To not draw on his mother's resources, and because he could see no future in Bremen, Richard Krebs moved on to Hamburg in the hope of finding a berth. The shipping companies' employment offices were, however, overfilled with older and more-experienced men, all of them as intent as he was on finding a foreign ship on which to earn hard currency.

In October 1923, the high point of inflation, the day's wages of a skilled worker wouldn't quite buy a pound of margarine, and a pound of butter was worth two days' work.

For Richard Krebs the return to Germany was like a return to a nightmare. In *Out of the Night* he offers a devastating portrayal of the impotent rage of the people and the demoralizing effect of poverty; there an old refugee-woman offers the body of her daughter for a place to spend the night, and there, when the police attempt to confiscate a bag of stolen flour from a stevedore, a riot ensues.

Political chaos was on the increase. The right-wingers, veterans of the war, blamed the war's failure on left-wing sabotage. The men of the *Freikorps* who wanted to be rid of the loathsome republic, and the monarchists who dreamt of the pre-war order, all worked away at plans for a putsch. Their time was not at hand. Hitler's failed putsch in Munich, November 1923, bears witness to the fact.

The left wing still cherished the hope of profiting from the chaos in order to reverse the defeat of 1919. This time though, it was no merry mixture of disappointed SPD* men, anarchists and what-have-you reformists who were constructing the revolution, but the special envoys of the Russian Revolution who, with the members of a party of Bolshevist inclination, the Communist Party or *Kommunistische Partei Deutschlands* (KPD) were trying to organize the coup.

A coup, a revolution, the annihilation of the hated order: for the captain's son Richard Krebs, after all his experiences in Hamburg and in the desperate straits he found himself after his return to Germany, this was nothing less than the solution. Having failed in his attempt to leave Germany legally, Krebs tried again as a stowaway. He was discovered in Cuxhaven, taken from the ship and, along with the steady influx of looters and harbor-rioters, put in the overflowing Hamburg Prison.

There he made the acquaintance of a Communist who showed interest in him and who gave him the address of his sister. On release he visited her, and while staying with her grew acquainted with the literature of the Communist Movement.[22]

---

* Sozialdemokratische Partei Deutschlands: German Social Democratic Party.

The KPD that Richard Krebs was soon to join was an organization formed subsequent to the bloody repression of the workers and so. The November Revolution took place under Marx's dictum that the power of the proletariat, qua socially progressive class, would come framework of a mass movement and would, as if subject to some natural initiated from below. This was to be understood as analogous to the events French Revolution of 1789, where the socially progressive class, the bourgeo drove the nobility from power. These articles of faith, which had also been significance to the pre-war SPD, were severely shaken in 1919. In industrialized Germany, among the many world-leading industrial manufacturers, the proletarian classes had proven themselves quite helpless. All eyes were therefore on Russia, where a quite different concept of revolution, the Leninist concept, had been successful. A strictly regimented, fairly small group of conspirators had appointed themselves vanguard to the masses and, with the help of a fanatical secret police, the Extraordinary Commission for Combating Counterrevolution and Sabotage (or Cheka), had founded the dictatorship of the proletariat in bloody civil war.

Rosa Luxemburg, figurehead of the German Revolution, had criticized Lenin's concept and prophesized that it could only end in a dictatorship of state bureaucracy. In the eyes of many of her comrades history had not vindicated this stance. Reactionary soldiers took the hesitant and overly scrupulous Luxemburg and killed her.

The poet Ernst Toller, one time chairman of the Munich Soviet Republic of 1919, reported how the prestige of the Russian Revolution took on ever-greater tragic-comic dimensions as the incompetence of the German revolutionaries grew ever more apparent:

"Some Russians are accorded substantial political influence simply on the strength of their soviet passports. The great work of the Russian Revolution gives these men such allure that experienced German communists are in awe of them. Because Lenin is Russian, these men are credited with comparable powers. The words: 'We did it differently in Russia` overturn all political decisions.

The same fateful influence is possessed by some women, who, having passed a few weeks in Soviet Russia, draw on their tourist experiences and claim that the glance they caught of a realized revolution lends them all the necessary qualifications for leadership of all revolutions to come. And men that have been working for years within the socialist movement bow down without hesitation, yes, with even a disconcerting pleasure, before their slogans and commonplace proposals."[23]

The logical consequence of all this was the foundation of a party modeled on the Bolsheviks, the KPD, who were to hone themselves for the next round of the class struggle.

The fact that the KPD could quite quickly become the most important radical left party in the early 'twenties was due not only to the altered situation but also, and in no small measure, to the power and financial support of its patron, the Bolshevik Party. Moscow hoped to exploit the disorder in Germany so as to found there the longed-for sister state. In 1923 a certain Comrade Thomas came from Soviet Russia bearing great wealth with which to finance the desired 'German October.' Red Army officers, ienced in the waging of civil war, came to Germany to help their comrades along way. The professional revolutionary Victor Serge, who was little short of a one-n vanguard, recalled thirty years later how in the Berlin Police Headquarters he ught a residence permit for ten dollars and a few cigars. As he wrote in his emoirs, the chaos in Germany gave rise to even the wildest hopes:

"One breathed in the air of a collapsing world. Everything was just in its place: people were unassuming, kindly, industrious, bankrupt, wretched, debauched and resentful. Right in the middle of town, beyond the dark Spree and the Friedrichstrasse, a huge railway station was being built. Bemedalled cripples from the Great War sold matches outside night-clubs in which girls who had a price like everything else, danced naked among the flower-decked tables of the diners. Capitalism was running riot, apparently under the inspiration of Hugo Stinnes[*], and accumulating immense fortunes in the midst of insolvency. Everything was for sale: the daughters of the bourgeoisie in the bars, the daughters of the people in the streets, officials, import and export licenses, State papers, businesses in whose prospects nobody believed. The fat dollar and the puny, puffed-up coin of the visitors ruled the roost, buying up everything, even human souls."[24]

The leadership of the KPD was less than convinced of the viability of the Russian model for the 'German October'. Only a minority, the so-called radical left, was full of enthusiasm for the plan. At the 'Headquarters of the World Revolution' in Moscow, however, all reservations of the majority were ignored since Zinoviev, leader of the Communist International, had come to the conclusion that "The proletarian coup in Germany is inevitable, ye, close at hand."[25] Berndt Kaufmann and his co-authors, who evaluated archives that had been closed to the public until 1989, give in their standard work on the intelligence service of the KPD the following description of its efficacy: "In an incredibly brief period an illegal operation had been brought to life whose feelers spread across the length and breadth of Germany. Its envisaged purpose was to assure that within a large-scale military operation power might be seized and held. Some three hundred and fifty paid and probably several thousand unpaid soldiers were at its service. The number of proletarian *Hundertschaften*, squadrons of fighters one hundred-strong, rose to 1331 by the twenty-first of October. Furthermore, three hundred partisan groups were formed. At least ten of the leaders of this operation were soviet citizens, sent to Germany by Moscow's general staff specifically to this end."[26]

Richard Krebs was thus a small cog in a large machine, whilst those at the wheel were half-heartedly preparing for revolution on someone else's orders.

At the time, though, this was a matter entirely beyond the scope of his vision. Much more pertinent for the moment was the troop of billstickers and watchword painters to which he had been assigned, a group perpetually dogged by police attention.

In the early 'twenties the area around the Hamburg harbor was characterized by its narrow cobbled streets and the timber-framed houses built on several stories along the narrow canals. Along these canals connecting the main harbor with its subsidiaries

---

[*] Hugo Stinnes was an industrialist widely reviled for acquiring distressed assets

— many of which have now been filled in — one could still see barges propelled forward between the houses by muscle power. Although the tiny apartments were full to the point of overflowing, in the crisis years their inhabitants were obliged to rent their beds by the day to casual laborers and seamen. This dark and unhygienic accommodation was beloved of none, and life was led in the streets and alleyways and along the canals. There children and door-to-door salesmen, women in search of food for their families and sailors of all nationalities were all to be found, the latter group outnumbering by far their contemporary counterparts; the days of the heavily manned sailing ship were not quite over, and on the steamers legions of stokers and other machine workers were employed until the diesel engine was introduced. Loading and unloading was a long process, sometimes lasting weeks, and in the crisis periods of the 'twenties and 'thirties ships often rested at anchor for months without loading a cargo. The boundary between the wayfarers, who in any case were often there for the long periods at dock, and the residents was eroded. If the seamen had money, particularly if they had the dollars so highly prized in the inflationary periods, then temporary marriages often ensued.

The harbor quarter in Hamburg was a world onto itself that had more in common with the sailortowns of the world's other harbors than with the rest of the German *Hinterland*.

Its very language – a wild mixture of Plattdeutsch and sailor's English — distinguished it from the adjacent areas. In the harbor district there were seamen's homes and boarding houses, canteens and soup kitchens, bars and *Bierkeller*, employment offices and bordellos, Seamen's Churches and union buildings. Everyone in any way related to seafare came here to meet, to drink, to seek women and to buy or sell stolen or smuggled goods. Smuggling and theft of cargo were extraordinarily popular among the workers of the sea and were considered an established right, a reasonable form of recompense for the vicissitudes of seafaring and of the German currency, which effectively devalued pay in foreign ports.

The streets were rough. The hard conditions of work on the docks and the ships set the tone for behavior and manner. The harbor was a man's world, and traits such as physical strength, stamina, brutishness and robustness were what counted.

The authorities feared and hated this foreign world. A National Socialist sociologist wrote that the inhabitants were "extremely antisocial and, as such, well known to the police. They seldom feature in police records, however, because they, in true antisocial spirit, settle their affairs between themselves."[27] The social historian Hartmut Rübner writes that: "The inhabitant of the port didn't reserve their unconcealed aggression for the representatives of the law alone, but treated all outsiders of bourgeois standing to it. In times of crisis the situation became even more severe, that, according to the police themselves, the harbor region was in a 'perpetual state of latent civil war' and could therefore, 'only be policed by double patrols.'… In times of strike or similar conflict the quarter served as a haven offering protection from the police. In the harbor quarters of German ports on the North Sea there were repeated uprisings in 1919, and in 1920 there were numerous cases of looting and food riots led by striking workers and radicalized unemployed, styled 'proletarian self-help'".[28]

The harbor men had no great love of the landlubber's SPD and its affiliated unions. The leading organizations here were the KPD and their allies the German Shipping Union.

Richard Krebs must have been made conspicuous by his precocious eloquence, his enthusiasm and his strength of will — the traits that would characterize him as a man — for he was soon to be introduced to Albert Walter, the man responsible for political agitation in the Hamburg harbor milieu.

Albert Walter is described in *Out of the Night* as "a thick-set, jovial, highly energetic Bolshevik of international caliber... bronzed, [and] barrel-chested... [his] small brown eyes always seemed on the alert." He was chairman of the German Shipping Union and played a key role in the International Propaganda and Action Committee of Transport Workers (or IPAC-Transport), a cadre under orders from Moscow to infiltrate the world's seamen's unions.

Walter, a long-serving social democrat unionist, had been arrested in New York after the Americans joined the war in 1917 and had remained in prison for its duration. After the October Revolution he founded in the detention center a series of Bolshevik circles among Germans POWs. The renown this won him was such that Lenin invited him to Moscow and employed him in the construction of the Propaganda Committee.

In the early 'twenties the union work of the Communist International was not directed at founding an independent organization, but at influencing existing ones. IPAC-Transport was to collect workers with Communist leanings in all branches of transport and to direct their work on behalf of the Party within extant unions. It was no coincidence that a German was given such a key role in this operation. In the 'twenties the Comintern was essentially a joint Russian-German enterprise, with the Russians providing finance and having final say, and the Germans representing the Comintern to the outside world — not least for reasons of geographical proximity. In the case of IPAC-Transport it was Albert Walter who was the main representative whilst a succession of Russian functionaries gave the orders.

IPAC-Transport was only one of the several IPAC's that were named after the varied branches in which they operated. There was IPAC branches in mining, municipal services and rail transport, etc. IPAC-Transport was not only the most successful of these committees, but also had another function that kept it hand in glove with the soviet secret services: from among its membership agents were recruited to the OMS, the top secret contact and information service of the Comintern.

The OMS was so secret that even within soviet bureaucracy its very existence was restricted information. Unlike the funds for the secret police, its monies were never shown as such but instead transferred to 'innocuous' sources. [29] This is unsurprising, as it was to play a vital role in the supply of money, weapons and ammunition for the 'German October' of 1923 and for various attempted coups across the world. Another reason for the secrecy was the dirty secret of the Comintern; one which grew dirtier the longer it existed: Moscow's interference in the internal affairs of its sister parties. This may have initially amounted to no more than manipulative scheming, but over the years was to become nothing less than the systematic issuing of orders.

Neither the governments nor the proletariat of these lands were to be initiated into the secret that the leader of the Communist Party in their land was nothing but a marionette for Moscow.

Complete bureaucracy, the apotheosis of this process, was still unforeseeable back in 1923. Like the whole of the communist movement in its infancy, the OMS was an improvised affair that lived from the enthusiasm of its workers and the lawless temperament of those seamen who created IPAC-Transport.

The arduous nature of travel and the difficulties of reliably disseminating information that were commonplace features of life in the 'twenties are now almost unimaginable. There was no transatlantic air service, and even international broadcasting was still in its naissance. Information and freight that today would be sent electronically or by air transport was mainly distributed by ship up to the late 'thirties. The OMS was therefore reliant in the main on shipping to sustain its worldwide connections.

After war and revolution the Soviet Merchant Marine was not in prime condition and, in any case did not lend itself to OMS purposes, as the Soviet Government could not risk being compromised. For this reason the OMS resorted to using seamen with communist leanings, mostly of German and Scandinavian origin, to guarantee delivery of their communiqués. The OMS no doubt benefited from the fact that smuggling and harboring stowaways had counted as established rights since time immemorial.

The man who dovetailed the interaction of IPAC-Transport with the OMS, and who organized these transports from Leningrad, was a figure destined to play a decisive role in Richard Krebs' life. According to a CIC file description written several years later, Knüfken was a man with sharp features, not tall but strong, who was economic of word and gesture. Apart from German, his mother tongue, he also spoke fluent Russian, English, "Scandinavian" and probably bits of many other languages.[30]

Known also as the 'Captain Kidd of the Comintern,' Knüfken was the archetypal revolutionary German seaman; his hijacking of a fishing ship off Hamburg with which he sailed to Soviet Russia made him into a legend.

Hermann Knüfken, born in Düsseldorf, 1893, of poor parentage, signed up at the age of fourteen for work on a fishing ship and was drafted into the navy on the outbreak of the First World War, at the age of twenty-one.

Knüfken, a radical socialist, was repulsed by the enthusiasm with which the old reservists greeted the war. When the morale of the men on board his ship darkened from eating rutabaga whilst watching officers feast, Knüfken and three comrades decided to hijack the ship and to sail for Denmark.

The plan failed and Knüfken fled to Denmark alone. In his memoirs he writes: "We were no pacifists. The Germany of the Social Democrats made us vomit. We spent no time discussing the whys and wherefores of responsibility. We knew who was guilty in this war. We wanted a *tour de force,* although, regrettably, this became a rout."[31]

In Denmark Knüfken worked with agents of the British Secret Service; "We shared the same goal: the military defeat of the German powers."

In August 1917, after the Kaiser had declared an amnesty on deserters and he had made arrangements with the 'friends' in the British Secret Service, Knüfken returned to Germany. On a further attempt to enter Denmark illegally he was arrested and held in custody on a charge of treason, then a hanging crime. He was saved by the "intellectual impoverishment of the German counter-espionage service" who believed they could "tap in to connections between Germany and the foreign enemy."

In November 1918 he was freed from Kiel Naval Prison by a sailor uprising, joined the revolutionary sailor's councils and took part in the battles of March 1919 in Berlin. In April 1919 he went to the Baltic States on business of the Sailor's council, was arrested by men from the *Freikorp* and had a foretaste of the coming Nazi scourge. It was his first meeting with "organized German brutality."

By means of bribery he was able to escape their clutches and to return to Denmark via Copenhagen.

In Cuxhaven he was among the leading activists. A police report described him as "an extremely radical, proactive Sparticist."[32]

There the voyage began that was to bring him fame. The writer Franz Jung and the worker Jan Appel were elected by the founding congress of The German Workers Communist Party (KAPD) to go as party delegates to the Second Comintern Congress in Moscow. The KAPD, with its insistence on freedom of speech within the party, its direct revolutionary activities and its dream of a democratic Soviet (i.e. council) Republic, can be seen as the true heir of the 1918 Revolutionary spirit. It stood in complete contrast to the KPD, who had adopted Lenin's undemocratic doctrine of the "revolutionary vanguard."

Knüfken signed up on a fishing trawler and smuggled the two delegates on board. The ship had scarcely left the harbor before Knüfken had taken the bridge, pistol in hand, and assumed command. The ship sailed for the soviet port Murmansk. The Russians were deeply impressed by this act. Here at last was a German Communist who was also a man of action. Lenin himself awarded Knüfken the title 'Comrade Pirate.' The ideas of the KAPD proved somewhat less popular, but the Russians generously overlooked this fact. Knüfken returned to Germany entrusted with a mission: to check the feasibility of hindering Allied weapon deliveries to Poland. After some success – the locksmen of the canals between the North Sea and the Baltic refused to let further munitions deliveries pass — he was arrested on charges of piracy and sentenced to five years in a Hamburg prison.

His sentence was an ordeal for the prison governor, one of the social reformists of the Weimar Republic. Recognizing the good intentions of this man, Knüfken later wrote – by way of half-hearted apology – it was simply the duty of a revolutionary worker "to be a bad prisoner." He claimed that his watchword was "never give up, never conform, always be prepared for new activities."[33] Knüfken incited the other prisoners and started one hunger strike after the other. His greatest coup was the barricading of his own cell from inside; the cell door was so strong and so well blocked that the warders could not break it down. A compromise was reached: for Knüfken's promise to call the strike off he was to be given a more comfortable cell in a psychiatric ward. Once there he started a further hunger strike that caused such disturbances in the harbor quarter that the exasperated senate freed him in 1923 on condition that he leave the country.

Knüfken went to the Soviet Union, where he was given a hero's welcome. He moved to Leningrad and worked for IPAC-Transport and built up the International Port Bureau, which, in combination with its swiftly founded Hamburg counterpart, was soon to become the model on which the world-wide chain of Seamen's Clubs was based. At the same time, according to his unpublished memoirs, he was working for the OMS.

"The reader will appreciate the significance of IPAC-Transport if I describe more closely its structure and the functions of its departments. Soon after the founding of IPAC-Transport a decision was taken to organize Port Bureaux, entrusted with the commission of establishing Seamen's Clubs in which and by whom ship's crews from around the globe were to be exposed to propaganda. Onboard cells and inside-men on board were organized. Simultaneously, infiltration of the reformist unions was undertaken by and in these Clubs. The Comintern, or rather Abramovitch[*] and Piatnitzki were aware of how to exploit this apparatus for the Comintern once it had been created. The inside-men on board who had originally done little more than smuggle propaganda material had to be turned into postmen. There was always something that was unsuitable for diplomatic bags and which couldn't be sent or, more importantly, received over the regular mail. Such things were taken by the seamen, and it is astonishing, how far and how safely these missives traveled. A ship arrived in the port and the inside man delivered the letter to the recipient awaiting him. Letters for India continued on their way a few days later with a Hansa steamer bound for India. Post for North America was transported on a Hapag or Lloyd ship. Any mail for Spain, Portugal or North Africa went on a Neptun or an OPDG Ship. For shorter journeys the regular tourist ships were used.

There was always something to do, particularly when the insider was considered particularly dependable. Not all mail left the Russian ports in this manner. The Central European Profintern[*] office and the West European Comintern office made free used of European ships for their purposes, and they therefore required the cooperation of people in the employ of the Port Bureau at the intended destination.

Where at all possible, Russian ships were not to be used for this work. These were to avoid coming under suspicion at all costs. Comintern agents and other parties who had been in Moscow and who, for one reason or another, couldn't travel by plane or train with forged documents, sailed safely to small harbors where there were no passport controls.

Certainly... IPAC-Transport had very important work to do, and no one understood this better than the Russians. This was why for IPAC-Transport the Comintern was, from the very beginning, a more important authority than the Profintern."[34]

---

[*] Abramov-Mirov, Alexander Lasarevitch

[*] Profintern: Red international of Labor Unions. The union equivalent of the Comintern

The German October

From the nicknames "Neptune's great uncle" and "father of the seamen" that Richards Krebs gives Albert Walter in *Out of the Night* it is plain that he was more to him than just a superior. The man who was his first sponsor in the communist movement also went some way to replace the father he had lost. The first thing Walther did was to employ Krebs on the waterfront. Richard Krebs has Jan Valtin describe the early days of his work for IPAC-Transport so:

"Each morning the harbor 'activists' gathered on various concentration points along the waterfront. There the leader of each brigade assigned his men to certain docks and ships, and supplied them with leaflets and pamphlets, and with the slogans of the days. So armed, we slipped into the harbor and boarded the ships and set out to win over their crews. Most ships were guarded by officers or company watchmen, and a wide range of dodges and tricks had to be employed to board the ships in spite of the guards. Often we swarmed aboard over the hawsers. At times we slunk aboard disguised as hawkers of neckties or as laundrymen. We distributed our leaflets, sold newspapers and pamphlets, launched discussions, and endeavored to enlist the young militants among the crews in the Communist Party...

Returning ashore at the end of the end of the day each 'activist' wrote a detailed report on the ships he had visited that day. At headquarters these reports were copied and filed. These shipping files contained detailed data on practically every ship in the merchant service, permitting Albert Walter and his aides to obtain at any time an accurate picture of available forces before deciding on any major action. This system, known as the 'Hamburg method,' was later adopted by communist waterfront organizations on all continents."

Besides this agitation of ship's crews Richard Krebs also took part in the preparations for the 'German October' — under orders from the party he smuggled alcohol to Scandinavia. Given the worthlessness of the mark on the one side and the restrictive North European laws at the other, this was an extremely lucrative business. So much so, in fact, that it wasn't the exclusive province of the KPD, but was pursued by all Germans who got the chance. The smuggling of alcohol took such dimensions that in 1923 it became a diplomatic affair that was even discussed in the Reichstag. In one comical passage in *Out of the Night*, Krebs describes how in those months the locks of the Kaiser Wilhelm Canal were swarming with bank representatives and all forms of petty businessmen, trying like pirates to board ships from Scandinavia in the frantic hunt for hard currency. "It was no unusual sight to see agents from leading banks pursue a grimy stoker through a ship when they knew that he had obtained a few dollars or pounds through smuggling or the sale aboard of objects pilfered from the cargo."

The party also employed the as-yet unsuspected new member, Richard Krebs, as courier for the preparations for the 'German October.'

Exaggerating in his inimitable manner, Krebs made his hero privy to the Communist assassination plans on Germany's most powerful man of the time, the chief of General Staff Von Seeckt. Like the author and courier, Valtin left before the members of his group — a so-called T or Terror Group — were caught and their plans foiled. In reality the seventeen year old was nothing more than a member of the courier apparatus whose recruits were mostly young people.

The only account of Krebs' activities in this period that reasonably be given credence is to be found in American CIC files. These were built up after the Second World War during weeks of interviews that ensued from the contents of *Out of the Night*. During this process the matter of the Daul sisters was pursued. In Krebs' book they were alleged to have played a certain role.

"Both girls were plump, blond, dressed like working girls... [and] spoke excellent German. In spite of a slight accent, they could easily pass as German. ...[They] maintained an apartment in the Venusberg district which was a contact point (Anlaufstelle) for conspirative [sic]work. They were in touch with Hugo Marx, and with higher party echelons.

During the fall of 1923 KREBS was doing minor courier work for the combat organization (Rote Marine) in the harbor area, once was ordered to conduct an unknown man to the DAUL apartment. [*sic*] When he arrived with the man he was instructed to stay overnight in the apartment, apparently for security reasons. He left the next morning, has never seen them again."35

Krebs' wasn't entirely wrong in his presumtions, as the CIC were later to confirm: "In February 1925 they were sentenced to 15 and 17 months in fortress arrest as accessories to a treasonable enterprise in connection with the political leadership of the 1923 HAMBURG revolt"36

A Communist uprising in Hamburg was the only visible result of the 'German October'. The KPD chairman Heinrich Brandler had already revoked the Moscow-made plans because of their probable failure when the uprising broke out. How this all came about is still a moot point. According to one version, the Hamburg Communist Party chairman Ernst Thälmann had a choleric fit in the middle of the relevant session and sent a courier to give the order, the latter disappearing so swiftly that he was then no more to be stopped. Another version of the story is that the date had already been set, but the courier bearing the message of its cancellation didn't arrive in time. Whatever the truth of the matter, the Hamburg uprising in late October was an affair that lasted only a few days, a footnote to the post-war chaos, soon to be forgotten in the 'golden 'twenties.'

In a later internal report of the KPD's military command, it was claimed that the Hamburg uprising was no mass act but a putsch: "As the fighting began the arsenal consisted of thirty-five rifles and several pistols. Not even all KPD members could be mobilized. Although the KPD had around eighteen thousand members in Hamburg at the time, there was fighting in only three suburbs of the city. Along the front lines there were no more than one hundred and fifty Communists, whilst about one thousand worker built barricades, organized munitions and treated the wounded."[37] There was no sign of the German coup being "inevitable, ye, close at hand," as Zinoviev had put it. The 'Headquarters of the World Revolution' had erred greatly in its estimation of the German masses' morale. The man who was to pay the price for this was the Communist Party chairman who had acted against orders from 'headquarters'; he was relieved of his post.

The uprising was followed by a wave of arrests, and some months later the KPD itself was declared illegal. Thousands of its supporters ended in prison. For Richard Krebs the dream of the revolution had temporarily come to an end. Like so many others, he had to make for cover. He fled to Belgium and went to ground in the harbor quarter.

! First Commissions

Krebs took no time to find his way around the Belgian port. The docks and the moles stuffed full of foreign freight were all as familiar to him as the sounds and smells of the sea. Also, it was easy to beg a meal among the sailors from all lands who were to be met in the harbor bars. Here, in the windows and on the streets of the red-light district, scantily clad women awaited financially well-disposed men, and here Krebs met Mariette, a hooker with a 'heart for revolutionaries.' We only know of her from *Out of the Night*, yet he must have come across her or the woman she was modeled on during this time. She was the first woman in his adult life to make a deep impression on him.

Krebs, like all seamen with a half-decent wage, must have had a good number of women by this time. There was the girl in Antofagasta with whom he had drunk a bottle of *vino tinto,* and for whose sake he had missed the Magdalena Vimmen's sailing. There was the fat landlady of the Corkfender, the sailors' bar in Antwerp, whose attentions had caused a punch-up at four in the morning. This incident provided material for an autobiographical story he would write three years later. Perhaps he also met the heroine of his first novella, *Juanita.* Juanita was a South American beauty and a *femme fatale* over whom a fight was fought to the death in a South American harbor town.[38]

Mariette was a special figure in Richard Krebs' life. Neither in his autobiographical novel nor in his short stories is another character described with such love and attention. "Small and trim, she had luminous coal-black eyes... The girl was draped in white silk. Her bare feet stuck in white sandals studded with coloured beads. The grime of Antwerp was blotted out."

Selfless, she offers him her help, because, as she says "'Were I a man, I'd be a revolutionist...but a woman, what can she do. People give me plenty of money because I'm a pretty whore. I don't care. I like revolution. When a revolutionist comes to me, I help him.'"

The beautiful revolutionary was more than a fleeting encounter for Richard Krebs, and perhaps he fell seriously in love with her. Certainly he confesses in *Out of the Night* "I came to know her for only a few brief hours, but inexplicably she persisted in haunting my memory during later prison years".

Girls like Mariette weren't unheard of in the ports of the early 'twenties. The most famous was the communist Kenny Guttmann, who founded a union of prostitutes that comprised most of the girls of Hamburg and Altona working in this trade.

Kenny Guttmann published a paper called *Am Pranger (In the Stocks)*, which, if Hermann Knüfkens memoirs are to be believed, was the best selling Hamburg paper of its day. When the love of the revolutionary and experimental died down into what Knüfken calls the "normalizing ...bourgeois morality" of the mid 'twenties, the paper was banned. As the liberal era was also over in Russia, the party was ordered by Moscow to distance itself from Ketty Guttmann – an order that the party obeyed "with new-found righteous indignation," as Knüfken mockingly remarked.

Mariette introduced Jan Valtin to the Ukrainian Bandura. Krebs' familiarity with this man has been attested to by other sources.[39]

"He looked the part of a tight-lipped, picturesque brigand; a boned, starved looking man with angular Slavic features. He wore brogans, a reeking old overcoat and a smeary sixpence cap from under which protruded the fringes of matted yellow hair turning grey... Bandura was the typical representative of those itinerant waterfront revolutionaries I have since met in every port of call. One and all, they were fugitives from the political police of their own lands. Few had passports. Thus deprived of all chance to obtain a lasting refuge and steady work, they vagabonded from one country to the next, often voluntarily, more often hounded as dangerous undesirables."

Bandura was an anarchist polyglot who wrote inflammatory flyers, littered with orthographical errors, in virtually all European languages and distributed them on ships. His band of harbor activists were loosely associated with the anarcho-syndicalist workers' organization the Industrial Workers of the World or IWW. This American-based association, with supporters as far afield as in Germany, was the only organization that Bandura didn't categorically reject. Bandura gave Richard Krebs the job of checking the ships on the harbor to see what the chow was like. Where it was bad, he was to incite the crew. Bandura wanted to verify that Krebs was an active combatant rather than a union official or 'mutton thief' as he put it.

After several weeks in Antwerp, Krebs took his leave. With Bandura's help he signed up on the tramp ship Eleonora, bound for San Pedro in California. On his eighteenth birthday in late December he was already on the West Coast. He rode goods wagons across the country and did casual work, ending up back in Los Angeles. Here he was arrested during a routine check and held for several days for having no entry permit.

He then moved on to Hollywood where he worked as film extra and stuntman. The three films he played in have the lyrical titles *The Sea Hawk*, *The Lost World* and *The Covered Wagon*.[40]. Krebs was in the process of finding his place in the Californian sun. Admittedly his status as illegal immigrant could have had unpleasant consequences, but in the U.S.A. in those years there were hundreds of thousands of illegals there, a fair amount of whom were refugees from Germany, hoping to profit from the next general amnesty and to build themselves a better life.

Krebs, however, already had a home, and this was in the Communist Party. A comrade reminds his alter ego of this fact in *Out of the Night*:

"He showed me letters received from party members in Germany. The German courts were grinding out wholesale sentences against communists for treason, insurrection, rioting, conspiracy and murder. Many had been sentenced to death but all such sentences had been commuted to life imprisonment. Among those who were condemned for life was one of my friends who had helped to storm the Eimsbüttel police station, Willhelm Willendorf, a big-boned, sad-looking, fearless militant… Inside I boiled with helpless rage, and with shame! Over there in Germany comrades went into dungeons for life, and here was I — well on my way to enjoy the Hollywood humbug… 'I'm going back to fight', I said."

Richard Krebs signed up on the Montpellier, which was to bring him back to Europe in 1924.[41]

The Montpellier's first port of call was Antwerp, where Richard Krebs worked again for a few days with Bandura and his men. Thence the ship sailed for Hamburg. In Germany the first wave of repressions was already receding, and Albert Walter and company were again able to continue semi-publicly in their labors. Even Grigori Atschkanov, director of IPAC-Transport and leading figure in the Comintern, was to be found in Hamburg. The handwritten letters that he sent to Moscow in early 1924 can be found in the Comintern Archives there.[42] In these, the talk is principally of the difficulty of finding suitable cadres for the foundation of an organization in the USA. Most American activists of this time were of anarchist inclination and gave IPAC-Transport a wide berth because of its close links with Moscow. An attempt to merge the IWW with IPAC-Transport failed because of a lack of submissiveness on the part of the Americans.

It was this that brought Grigori Atchkanov to Hamburg in 1924; he was hoping to gain grassroots influence whilst circumventing the IWW. To this end he was visiting moored American ships. In early May he found his way aboard the Montpellier.[43]

Grigori Atchkanov was no apparatchik, but a former ship's engineer a, true seaman, and, according to Hermann Knüfken, "a true man, unlike so many."[44] The experienced revolutionary and original Bolshevik made a great impression on Richard Krebs, who remembered him as "a lively little man with a mop of gray hair and restless button eyes." Krebs saw in men like Atchkanov "Idealists who had behind them the overwhelming authority of the victorious Soviet Revolution." For his part,

Atchkanov recognized the intelligence and revolutionary enthusiasm of the young German.

He was, in particular, interested in Krebs' connection to Bandura and Bandura's links with IWW groups on the West Coast. During the course of long conversations Atchkanov, with the help of Albert Walter, persuaded Krebs to give up his bond to the Ukrainian anarchist. They claimed that Bandura's course of action had no future and that the world revolution could only succeed if everyone should submit to the dictates of the Communist International.

Having succeeded in persuading him of their arguments, they gave him the mission of returning as Trojan horse to Bandura. The plan was that Krebs should be Bandura's delegate on the West Coast, so as to meet with his IWW connection and to bring them into contact with IPAC-Transport. A great amount of propaganda material was put at his disposal and gradually smuggled aboard the Montpellier.

Making contact with the IWW was not all that was entrusted to Richard Krebs in Hamburg. If the words of Jan Valtin are to be credited, and there is no evidence to the contrary, then his task also included such requisites as these: "I was to attempt to find one "activist" in every port of call reliable enough to be supplied with money and instructions for the formation of activist brigades after the Hamburg model... I was to foster contacts with men belonging to the United States Coastguard, particularly with those who had gotten themselves into some sort of trouble, and forward their names and addresses to Albert Walter and Atchkanov. I was to 'test' – by bribes – certain official of the American Shipowners' Association in Los Angeles Harbor as to his willingness to place communists aboard American Ships. I was also to take close-up photographs and furnish a description of a new harpoon gun used by the waling ships ... I was expected to send in regular reports on all I could find out about the economic conditions and political attitudes of American waterfront workers, particularly those engaged in the vast lumber industry and on the tank ships of the Standard Oil Company."

This was an important mission, and today it appears almost unbelievable that a senior party member would confide such work to an eighteen year old, yet Krebs' subsequent rise in these circles seems to confirm that it was so.

Precocious Communist Party membership and the assumption of responsibility at an early age was not unusual in the early days of the Communist International, whilst the movement still depended on the revolutionary fervor of Communists across the globe and its bureaucratic apparatus had not yet been formalized. Some members were even younger than Richard Krebs. The Russian Secret Service officer Pavel Sudoplatov, who was to organize the assassination of Leon Trotski, was only fourteen when he worked for the Cheka as a telegrapher in the civil war. At the age of seventeen he already ran a ring of spies, and as he was twenty he was appointed to a position in the Ukrainian Cheka headquarters.

The meeting with Atchkanov was to be of enduring significance for Richard Krebs, for he became familiar not only with senior members of the Comintern but also with typical OMS-style commissions. An aspect of these was the smuggling of propaganda material, a task that was to bring him to the attention of the Soviet Secret

Police, the GPU* on two counts; one was the fact that the OMS cooperated with the GPU for the whole duration of its existence, and the other was that it functioned as a sort of foreign intelligence service until the mid-twenties, a fact that could be verified by one of the few relevant articles based on the KGB's archives that were briefly opened to the public in the mid-nineties.[45]

In addition to all the missions that Krebs was given by Atchkanov, he received a particularly sensitive, last-minute job: to smuggle a Comintern man aboard who was headed north under secret orders. This man was Michael Avatin, alias Lambert, alias Schmitt, a sailor of Baltic origin who, as presumed Soviet agent, has left traces in the secret service files of America and several European countries,[46] and who, in many respects, represents the recondite nature of Krebs' own Comintern activities.

Avatin plays the leading role in a number of historically particularly contentious passages in *Out of the Night*, where the action revolves around murder and the bloody settling-of-accounts with traitors and renegades. Valtin describes the elegant figure of the Comintern 'Triggerman' as having "steady grey" eyes and a "thin and hard" mouth.

The portrayal is, in short, of a fearless man for whom no job is too dangerous. In Krebs' description of Valtin's last meeting with Avatin he writes "He flashed a smile of recognition at me. With Avatin a smile meant nothing. He could smile at a man one minute and kill him the next". Nonetheless, in all descriptions of Avatin a certain unconcealed admiration for the 'man of action' who settles with his enemies without scheming but 'like a man' is apparent. In the unpublished story *Magellans in the bunker*, written before *Out of the Night,* it can be seen how much the young Richard Krebs was impressed by Avatin:

"In Rotterdam I met a man who is perhaps the world's master stowaway. His name is Alvatin. He hails from Riga, and his business is that of a traveling instructor for The Third International. He has journeyed to the coasts of all continents, always arriving at his destination with astonishing precision. For shorter excursions he chooses to hide in the space between the boilers in a steamer's stokehold. He enters it when the boilers are cold, remaining there until the ship is at rest and the boilers have cooled off again at his point of destination. Between these times the boilers become volcanoes of heat and power. There is no escape for Alvatin at sea, and neither a chance for any living man to intrude upon the stowaway's privacy. Meanwhile, Alvatin perspires, sleeps, and arrives with uncanny precision."[47]

Avatin personified the enigma central to Richard Krebs' life. Was he in some manner complicit in the work of Avatin? Were his relations to the mysterious figure, whose identity could never be ascertained by the Gestapo, other than those of simple acquaintanceship? Richard Krebs avoided answering these questions to the end of his days. Even in the autobiography of his fictive hero he avoided describing the exact nature of their relationship.

---

* The renaming of Cheka to GPU was one of the first of many renamings of the Soviet Secret Police. For simplicity sake the Soviet Secret Service is heretofore referred to as the GPU

Vanguard on the West Coast

In early May 1924 Richard Krebs left Europe to carry out the commission he had received from Albert Walter and Atchkanov in Hamburg.

He arrived on the West Coast with the Montpellier in June 1924. Any description of the one and a half years that followed must rely heavily on Jan Valtin's account in *Out of the Night*. Only the bare facts of when and where he stayed are certain, and this was because the relevant chapter of Krebs' book almost provoked a lawsuit. The captain of the Montpellier threatened to sue for libel. In *Out of the Night* Krebs wrote that it was no problem to smuggle propaganda material on board, as the crew were on the *Reeperbahn*, Hamburg's red-light district, and the captain had drawn the curtains of his cabin so as to sweeten his last night at anchor with two girls and copious amounts of wine. To defend the factual nature of his work, the author listed all the places at which he had stopped in his early years, the ships on which he had sailed and the companies to whom they had belonged, the ports at which they had called and the authorities with whom he had had dealings. These he cross-referenced with details of how these facts might be verified.[48] The captain withdrew charges.

The first port of call was San Pedro in California, where Krebs made contact with IWW men on the orders of IPAC-Transport. As the Montpellier continued its voyage along the West Coast a stowaway was discovered, who claimed to be an Estonian to the Shipping Commission in San Francisco. Avatin's discovery by the authorities had no repercussions for the IPAC-Transport delegate, as no link between the two was surmised.

In San Francisco he took leave of both Avatin, (who had no choice but to remain on board), and of the Montpellier, in order to pursue his campaign in the larger ports along the West Coast.

The USA in which the eighteen-year old Krebs found himself trying to establish the basis for a net of seamen and harbor activists true to Moscow was on the eve of the 'golden 'twenties'. There were no native cadres, indeed, it was the era of the babbits, the eponymous, apolitical, petty bourgeois of Sinclair Lewis' novel. The economic future looked marvelous, the stock market boomed, and the suburbs, filled with detached houses, were created. The introduction of the conveyor belt in Detroit's factories led to motoring for the masses. A feeling of self-satisfaction was prevalent and all forms of social criticism were rejected as malicious propaganda.

The Communist Party was small and internal struggle was rife within it. Furthermore, few of its members were 'real' Americans. The majority of them were immigrants from Central and Eastern Europe. To the minds of the ruling classes the most dangerous activists were the *Wobblies*, the traveling organizers of the IWW, to whom, broadly speaking, Antwerp's Bandura could be included. They dreamt of 'one great union' that would incorporate all workers and finally attain power. The structure of this organization was to be according to the council system principle and thereby avoid the authoritarian structure of traditional unions. This formula didn't sit comfortably with the 'democratic centralism' of the Bolsheviks.

When Richard Krebs arrived in the USA in 1924 the IWW's best years were already over. Inspired by the Russian Revolution, the *Wobblies* had, in times of crisis, managed to attract a considerable group of supporters for their radical program from among American seamen and harbor workers. The alarmed middle-classes reacted by the merciless persecution of all communists, real or putative. The *Red Scare* in America was of much severer consequences for the IWW than for the comparatively insignificant American CP. Its activists were imprisoned on false charges, tarred and feathered in western mining towns or simply shot while evading imprisonment. The most famous *Wobbly*, Big Bill Haywood was forced into emigrating to the Soviet Union.

The escaped activists that Richard Krebs met were easily persuaded that under such circumstances the only kind of operation that stood any hope of success was a tightly disciplined underground organization.

Richard Krebs acquired a license from the coast guard as lifeboat man before taking up the full measure of his activities, so as to have a document to show the immigration authorities if need be.

He then traveled up and down the West Coast. By night he distributed on ships the pamphlets he had received from Communists on German craft and met in ports with such small groups of activists as had survived the *Red Scare* and remained at liberty. At the same time he successfully attempted to bribe an employee of the American Shipowners' Association, responsible for the hiring of crew members, in order to henceforth alleviate difficulties in the employing of agitators on American ships. He also investigated the Seamen's Church Institutes, the cheap and well-equipped seafarer's boardinghouses essentially intended as shelters from radical influences.

IPAC-Transport had charged him with the task of finding out how to combat these institutes in order to prepare the way for the foundation of its own establishments, the Seamen's International Clubs or Interclubs.

Krebs was not paid for any of this. He lived from the wages he earned on the coastal freight ships that he took to the scenes of his activities. If he had no other alternative, then he followed the example of Avatin and stowed-away. On occasion, if Valtin's words are to be seen as his own, then loneliness overtook him and he wished for the security of domestic life or he would dream of rightfully standing on the captain's bridge. On one occasion, as he felt particularly miserable, he took a piece of wood and beat his own head with it so as to exorcise these petty-bourgeois thoughts.

In late 1924 he was given the command to travel to Hawaii. This was the first of four ensuing voyages. He signed on the freighter Calawai, as ever, smuggling propaganda material aboard.

Having returned to the West Coast, he compiled a comprehensive report that, fifteen years later, he was still able to recall with pride in his youthful success. The document, comprising several pages, reports on the mixture of races in Hawaii, their interrelations and their possible receptiveness to propaganda material. It apparently later fell victim to an editorial decision, but is preserved in its full length in the first edition of *Out of the Night*. It is easy to imagine how this report reaffirmed the impression in Moscow headquarters that Krebs was a promising young cadre.

Krebs' next step was to sign on a whaling ship in order to reconnoiter a new kind of harpoon gun. This kind of task, considered a proletarian duty in the Weimar Republic, was so commonplace that it went under the euphemism of 'industrial reporting'. In Germany 'industrial reporting' was the province of the KPD's intelligence service until, during the Weimar Republic's demise, soviet comrades took an increasing interest in the matter. Who was responsible for charging Krebs with this mission remains unclear.

If the report of Jan Valtin is to be believed, the next mission went wrong. Again he had been supposed to travel to Hawaii, this time in the company of a certain Comrade B, whom he knew from Hamburg. Once there, he was to make contact with Filipino plantation workers. Everything went well, according to Valtin, until a 'patriotic' crewmember noticed that the two of them were in cahoots and denounced them to the captain as *wobblies*. Valtin lost control of himself and gave him a good thrashing. In the summer of 1925 he again came to the attention of the immigration authorities. Krebs escaped and, having already once been arrested and having fled in 1924, left one and a half years later his second set of traces in the files of American judicial authorities. Towards the end of 1925 he returned to Germany.[49]

Leningrad to San Quentin by way of Shanghai

Richard Krebs returned to Germany in early fall, 1925, shortly before his twentieth birthday. On the sixteenth of August 1926, scarcely a year later, he was publicly arrested in the city of Los Angeles. Shortly afterwards he was given a sentence of one to ten years for assault with a deadly weapon.

The period between his return to Germany and his imprisonment is one of the most opaque times in the life of Richard Krebs. The only sure facts are that, in early 1926, he signed up on the SS Franken, a North German Lloyd ship that brought him to China in the summer. From there he traveled to Vancouver as a stowaway on the Empress of Canada. Eight days after its arrival and 1,250 miles further, he was taken into custody.

Krebs himself gave two accounts of why he traveled to Asia and why he suddenly appeared in Los Angeles. One was that of *Out of the Night* and one was in interview with American secret agents a few months before his death. The first, the literary one, was an apology for the life of his alter ego Jan Valtin, the second was given to help Americans in the battle against Communism whilst avoiding incriminating himself. For this reason the account is rather terse and dry. As the American minutes note, the only matter on which Krebs refused to comment was the origins of the attack.

Both accounts are in agreement on the matter that on returning to the USA, Richard Krebs reported to his paternal friend Albert Walter. Walter told him that he had been awarded the great honor of attending a course in the Soviet Union.

Although there is no record of it, it is almost certain that Krebs visited his mother and siblings after his return — by this time he would not have seen them for one and a half years. In the interim his elder sister had started working in a hospital. It is to be assumed that in Richard's absence this sister, who was never to marry, was the principal support of her mother.

Perhaps he spent a few days or weeks in Bremen, perhaps he even visited his beloved grandmother in Darmstadt who, just like his mother, would hardly have been delighted that her Richard had devoted himself to the godless communist cause.

Richard Krebs, who had read The Communist Manifesto with the same fervor as his maternal relatives had read the Bible, would not have been impressed by her reproaches. The extent to which he knew the most widely read work of Marx and

Engels was shown when American Immigration Officers interrogated the author of *Out of the Night* in 1941. On this occasion he was able to make them lose face through his detailed knowledge. The bourgeois officers asked questions intended to prove the *Weltanschauung* of Krebs to be communistic, as communists were strictly forbidden entrance to the land. To this end Inspector Elden P. McGlynn had, on the eleventh of April 1941, gone to the lengths of acquiring a copy of said work, the eleventh edition of April 1939. It was rhetorically asked whether this was indeed the same work referred to in conjunction with Jan Valtin's entry into the KPD — the officers' intention being to confront their famous victim with its choicest passages. The maneuver backfired. Richard Krebs responded in the negative, explaining point by point how the pamphlet that they had acquired by no means corresponded to the one he himself has read in 1923. Their copy, he claimed, was namely the abridged version of a text bastardized by Stalin. He listed every step and every detail of the falsification of the document and described how each 'corrected' passage corresponded to each congressional development of the Comintern. This was beyond the ken of the officers, who, speechless and frustrated, were forced to renounce their plan of discussing the text.[50]

In 1925 though, the October Revolution only eight years past, no one would have been able to envisage the possibility of such a conversation, particularly not a card-carrying Communist like Richard Krebs.

After a relatively short stay in Germany he left for Leningrad. The journey was the culmination of a long-cherished dream:

"I despair at describing my emotions [he later wrote in *Out of the Night*] when the first dim landmarks of the Soviet Union rose out of the mist, — Kronstadt, the outlying islands, and then the workaday contours of Leninport... I walked through the weary streets of Leningrad, and my steps were light and firm. Of the many strange towns I had entered in the course of my long vagabondage, Leningrad was the least strange of all. I was like a ragged wanderer coming home at last to see if things are as they should be. Gone was all the unrest, gone the accursed lust for action at any price. I was no longer a chunk of mutinous scum in enemy country. I was content to hold my head high and let my eyes drink in the expressions in the faces of simple men and women who had their place at the helm of the first Dictatorship of the Proletariat."

But what did the course that he had been selected for consist of? The two versions diverge entirely here. In *Out of the Night* the talk is of a course over several months at the Lenin School, a faculty belonging to the Comintern, at which chosen Communists from all over the world were trained as professional revolutionaries in courses lasting one or more years. Here there is a virtuoso description of the day-to-day life at the school, the contents of lessons – Clausewitz to Marx and Lenin, — of the fellow students and the teachers.

"Our job was destruction — utter, uncompromising destruction — of capitalist society and the capitalist state, an uprooting and overturning of all standards and values grown out of the basic conception of *my* Land, *my* house, *my* country, *my* wife, *my* factory or ship or mine or railroad."

But Krebs never was a student of the Lenin School, as a glance in the register of students at the Comintern archive in Moscow shows. There is no trace of his alleged teachers and fellow-students either.

That he was given some form of training in the Soviet Union is, however, as good as certain. His later, swift rise to Comintern functionary after his time in San Quentin is otherwise inexplicable.

As will be shown, the assault in Los Angeles itself hints at least indirectly at some form of training

So what did Krebs learn in Leningrad?

To the Americans he said no word about the Lenin School. In this version his training amounted to a six-week course for a future union cadre of IPAC-Transport. The features of his course, he claimed, simply involved the organization of workers, strike leadership and radicalization. Sea-transportation, however, was not even touched upon.

It is probable that here he was trying to conceal something. It is a fact that Krebs had belonged to the traveling cadres of IPAC-Transport in spite of his youth. It seems, furthermore, scarcely plausible that a course in the Soviet Unions biggest port, organized by IPAC-Transport had no relation to marine affairs.

The statement loses even more credence when *Out of the Night* is consulted, as there Valtin's contact man in Leningrad was one Comrade Ryan — a leading cadre of IPAC-Transport.

If the *Out of the Night* version is compared with the one offered to the CIC, bearing in mind the close relations – so acutely observed by Knüfken — between the OMS, the intelligence services of the Comintern, and IPAC-Transport, then the following picture comes to light: Richard Krebs was in Leningrad for some length of time between late 1925 and early 1926. There he was given further training in so-called faction work: the infiltration of unions and more particularly, seamen's unions. Beyond this, he must have been examined very carefully to ascertain his suitability for future employment — a consideration that must have represented a substantial aspect of the whole arrangement. Given the close cooperation between IPAC-Transport and the OMS on the one hand, and between the OMS and the Soviet Secret Police on the other, he must have come to the attention of either the GPU or the Naval Secret Service of the Soviet Union, whose headquarters were situated in Leningrad. Perhaps he came into contact with an individual from these circles without being aware of their identity — his close relations to Michael Avatin might have played a role in this. It is conceivable that under OMS orders, Hermann Knüfken himself verified Krebs for fitness of service. At the time he was, in effect, the most important contact man for IPAC-Transport in Leningrad.

In early 1926 Krebs reappeared in West Europe. In Rotterdam he hired aboard the Franken, a North German Lloyd ship sailing on her maiden voyage to the Far East. The voyage went via Genoa, the Suez Canal, India and Indonesia to Hong Kong, where Richard Krebs left the ship. From Hong Kong he traveled to Shanghai. There he boarded the Empress of Canada and sailed as a stowaway to Vancouver. Two or three weeks later he was arrested.

The phases of this voyage around the globe can be reconstructed from various sources.[51] Its cause or origin, however, throws up questions. It may well be that it is a sailor's job to voyage, but this hardly accounts for the fact that Richard Krebs left Shanghai as a stowaway instead of showing his papers and hiring aboard in a legal fashion. In spite of his two arrests he was not wanted by the American authorities.

To approach the reason for Krebs' journey around half the world, the two versions of Krebs' story may be cross-referenced.

In *Out of the Night*, the journey's impetus is a courier mission; Jan Valtin is supposed to distribute money and bags of unknown content to contact-men at the various stops on his journey. These are to identify themselves to him by secretive means, such as proffering the counterpart of a torn photograph in Krebs' possession. He succeeds in his mission and in Shanghai joins a group of Communists who are busy agitating among the seamen of the colonial powers. Whilst in Shanghai he receives a command to travel with all due haste to San Francisco, where further orders are awaiting him. As he cannot quickly get a berth, he stows away on the Empress of China, bound for Canada.

To the American CIC, Richard Krebs insisted that his travels in Asia had no relation to party business, and that the Party first contacted him in Shanghai. Only there, he claimed, did he receive the order in question. Although in *Out of the Night* the order came from an unnamed authority, Krebs claimed to the CIC it was actually from Hamburg.

The CIC source is essentially the more reliable of the two. After all, Krebs made all his statements freely in order to furnish America with as much information as possible at the offset of the Cold War.

Nevertheless, his statement gives rise to suspicion. Although not under orders, Krebs is supposed to have traveled around half the globe whilst maintaining permanent contact with Hamburg? As the American minutes note in an aside, the only matter on which Krebs refused to comment was the prelude to the attack on the shop owner in Los Angeles. The journey to Asia was part of this prelude. What was he trying to conceal?

Taking the premises of *Out of the Night*; namely that so soon after his time in Leningrad, Krebs was carrying out a mission as a courier, then the indication is that his training there had not been restricted to union affairs. The possibility presents itself that he was working with the OMS, the Comintern's network and intelligence service or, conceivably, with the Soviet Secret Service.

His trip as a stowaway to Vancouver was the last great adventure of his youth. It is verifiable both by records and by the statement of a passenger, a gambling man with whom, due to an extraordinary coincidence, he was later to share a cell in a French prison.[52]

As Jan Valtin he later described the impudent manner in which, with the words, "A telegram for Mr. Collins" he swiftly boarded the liner and disappeared from sight:

"Ships didn't puzzle me. I veered into a passageway, climbed a companion, ran along the promenade deck, climbed a ladder, and rushed for the Empress' third funnel. No smoke came from it. It was a dummy, put there for esthetic reasons. On a long voyage the inside of a funnel was a better place for hiding than a lifeboat."

On this long voyage he was to meet that very adventurer whom he was later to come across under such different circumstances. The latter was busily making his voyage worthwhile by gambling with a fellow. Together, the two invited the stowaway to their lavishly supplied table, a successful ruse that was pursued until a waiter compared the list of first-class passengers with the number of diners. Krebs was placed in an improvised prison on board, but didn't remain there for a long time. In Vancouver he jumped ship and made for California. He was arrested in August in Los Angeles.

What exactly took place? In the court the prosecuting attorney summarized the case thus: "The defendant on Aug 16, 1926, entered a store of Morris Goldstein in Los Angeles and proceeded to purchase merchandise. When Goldstein proceeded to wrap a package the defendant hit him in the head with a revolver. Defendant then pointed a gun at him saying: 'Hands up' Goldstein proceeded to cry out and throw merchandise at the defendant. Defendant, frightened, ran out of the store and up an alley when he was captured with a gun in his possession" A few lines later it concludes: "The accused confirmed the above description of the event and added only that an argument had preceded the attack," this being the only comment that Krebs is known to have made to the accusations.[53]

Richard Krebs was given one to ten for assault with a deadly weapon. Having pronounced the sentence, the presiding judge, Edwin F. Hahn concluded with the following brief summary: "There seems to be no mitigating circumstances justifying the attack and the court is rather impressed with the belief that the defendant is not entirely normal minded" [54]

Indeed, the details of the crime don't fit a man who an American detective was to describe seventeen years later as a "tough goon." He was a man who knew how to look after himself — his comrade Ede Nikolajczik would later admire Krebs' cold-bloodedness in a theatre house brawl with the Nazis.

If the judge's summary doesn't appear apposite, then the possibility of a concealed motive can scarcely be ignored.[55] In *Out of the Night* the lead up to the attack is summarized as follows: having left the Empress, Valtin illegally enters the USA and heads for an address in San Francisco that had been communicated to him in Shanghai. There a friendly female agent of the Soviet Secret Service gives him a place to rest and slowly acclimatize.

A few days later he is summoned to Los Angeles by telegram. A soviet intelligence agent that he only knows as 'Getsy' gives him the order to 'execute a traitor.' The young revolutionary waivers between blind obedience and his instinctive distaste for this killing. "It is one thing to shoot an enemy in barricade fighting. Shoot him in self-defence. Or in a red rage. An altogether different thing is a deliberate killing". Despite his despair he finally accepts the order: "Thousandfold worse than hanging was ostracism from the Party".

The peculiar nature of the attack, the use of the revolver as a bludgeon where the fist would have sufficed, the ludicrous flight from the shopkeeper when he fought him off by throwing a few items —all this testifies to the dilemma that Krebs later described in *Out of the Night*. For the dedicated Communist the half-hearted execution of the order was the only solution to an existential crisis.

One question is irresistible; American Secret Service men would certainly have posed it if Krebs hadn't refuse to comment on the whole matter: did the Soviet Secret Service truly entrust such a mission to an untried comrade? It seems extremely improbable, even given the fact that in 1926 the Soviet Secret Police had only recently been founded. Either the mysterious Getsy has sent the neither tried nor tested comrade on the off chance, or Krebs' superiors had already been advised that he was suitable for such missions. If this is the case, a prelude to this act must have taken place between the return to Germany and the arrest in Los Angeles. In all likelihood, this was in Leningrad where, presumably, soviet comrades in contact with Richard Krebs came to the conclusion that the young German might be employed in matters of an altogether more serious nature.

Autodidact in Living Hell

On the twenty-second of October 1926, Richard Krebs began a prison sentence of up to ten years. Prison terms of undetermined duration were – and still are— a speciality of the American Justice System, designed to help keep prisoners subdued. Prison term length is determined by a prisoner's conduct. How might the young seaman have felt on disappearing behind bars for an undetermined length of time?

In the 'twenties San Quentin was the biggest penitentiary on the American West Coast. It already had the reputation of being hell on earth, a 'Living Hell' as former inmate Johnny Cash was to put it after a spell there forty years later. In 1929 San Quentin had 4,883 inmates with 293 lifers and 16 on death row among them.[56]

All nationalities were represented among its populace. Beside the hundreds of prisoners of various European nationalities, there were Chinese, Indians, Africans and a couple of dozen Nippon.

In the autobiographic notes that were included in the short story collection *Bend in the River* (1942), Richard Krebs described the then new prison compound of San Quentin as "A huge rectangular block of concrete, hollowed out by long steel-and-concrete corridors and a steep array of tiers with breast high railings which gave the interior the semblance of an odd-looking warship built by a mad engineer. There were some eight hundred cells in this concrete colossus. Each cell was occupied by two prisoners. The walking space in such a cell was less than eight feet long and less than two feet wide."[57]

The newcomer Krebs was initially assigned to the trash brigade — sweeping the yard and collecting waste. A few weeks later he was transferred to the infamous jute mill, described in the following terms by a fellow inmate: "We heard about a thousand men toiling at back-breaking and heart-breaking labor, trying to produce an arbitrary minimum daily average of jute cloth from out-moded decrepit and bulky looms: where almost daily some guy on the catwalk around the sidewalls, shot into the crowd; where ricocheting bullets frequently wounded and sometimes killed some convict who was attending to his duties and unaware of the actual or imaginary violation of rules that caused the shooting."[58] Severe punishment was frequently distributed to "Those unfortunates who often, through no fault of their own were not able to 'make yardage': suspended privileges, no tobacco ration, no letter-writing, good behavior credits taken away — and sometimes they were thrown into 'The Hole,' that cellar of cubicles where chill dampness always prevailed and where the inmates were fed only bread and water, once daily, and – otherwise practically naked — were given naught but one thin and filthy blanket.

In the Jute Mill nerve-racked men had brawls and bludgeonings and near-riots. Physically, mentally and near morally undermined, they became beasts. Deafened by the continuous clangor and roar of ancient machinery, breathing in lint-heavy dust of the fiber that came from the disease-ridden Orient, many collapsed at their looms after having appealed repeatedly for opportunities to report at the hospital. One who claimed to be ill except at an appointed 'hospital hour' was subject to punishment for malingering."[59]

In his memoirs Gil 'Pat' Rankins, a man with literary ambitions and a fellow prisoner, reminisces about Richard Krebs, who in San Quentin was known as 'Skipper'. On being asked how he stood the Jute Mill, Skipper answered: "I lost thirty pounds... but sailors are tough, especially if they've sailed in European craft."[60]

Richard Krebs, physically robust and in possession of a broader *Weltanschauung* than the majority of his fellows, was able to suffer the hard conditions and had become proficient in his task. After the first three months he was completing the work of eight hours in four of five. The time he had spared he used for reading —an exercise not without peril, since a warder seeing a prisoner idly reading was permitted — after a cursory warning cry — to shoot at him.

"Most of my reading was done in San Quentin's Jute Mill. During those thirteen months I have read more than in any ten other years. I had never read books in English before that. I read English first and foremost, because that seemed to me the most sensible way of learning a language. I studied English to increase my understanding and appreciation for what I read. Why I did it, I do not know. It was a natural urge."[61]

He started with Jack London's *Call of the Wild*, and quickly devoured everything of his in the prison library. He moved on to Conrad, in whom he found a life-long literary model. Joseph Conrad, of Polish origin, had, like Krebs, learnt English on the open seas and become an undisputed master in what had been a foreign tongue. Conrad's themes — the sea, seafarers, the brutality of colonialism and the confrontation of the individual by a society foreign to him —these were pertinent to the German prisoner on whom self-reliance had been foisted.

In the evening, after the cells had been locked, the young prisoner made his first attempts at writing. A murderer employed in the prison carpentry workshop had made a large board for him that he set on his knees as a writing desk. He organized himself paper and pencils from the prison library, and after all the prisoners had been checked off, would sit on the toilet seat, the board on his knees, and write until a bell announced lights off.

After lights out, lying in bed, he would murmur words and sentences to himself to increase his vocabulary and practice fluency of speech.

Initially the inmates paid little attention to the German sailor who read in every free moment. The only prisoners with whom he had dealings in this period were the IWW activists, who had, in part, been condemned before the First World War in fixed trials. The most renowned of these was Jim McNamara, who had been condemned to life in a controversial trial for alleged participation in a bomb attack on the Los Angeles Times. This aging man was the first prisoner with whom Richard Krebs had closer relations.[62]

A feature of life in San Quentin was the frequent executions. As Rankins later wrote, the prisoners' mood became dangerously insurrectionary on those days.

"There came a 'Black Friday' in San Quentin. That meant a day of execution for some poor devil who has been taken out of his 'Death Row' cell on the middle deck of Old Prison Building No.1 and escorted down to Hooligan Alley to ascend the three flights of the northernmost of the three outside stairways that gave access to the upper stories of the great rectangular Manufacturing Building. The scaffold room was just beyond the north partition of *The Bulletin* office.

Hangings were always held on a Friday morning at 10:30 o'clock sharp. The victim was always taken from Death Row on Tuesday afternoon, right after lockup, and kept until Friday in a wooden cage in the north room adjacent to the death chamber. And at about nine o'clock on such Black Friday mornings, all convicts working in the Manufacturing Building, the Old Hospital, the Library, Educational Departments, and nearby structures were marched into the Big Yard and kept there in the open, rain or shine, until the 'necktie party' was over.

Black Fridays were frightful days — depressing, nerve racking. The convicts were in a vicious mood — a mood that required but a tiny spark to cause an explosion. Everything was tense, jumpy."[63]

As he later wrote in *Bend in the River*, Krebs was close to losing his self-control on those occasions:

"During the first five or six hanging days I experienced in San Quentin, the minutes between ten and ten-fifteen on Friday filled me with a tenseness and apprehension beyond description. They were hanging a human being and there was nothing I could do about it. I imagined myself in the condemned man's place. I went through all the agonies of being hung. In me, indignation and resentment mounted to an insane hatred against a system in which men could be strangled slowly and with pious serenity. Each hung man was I."[64]

He also writes that later he grew calmer, and that after the tenth or twelfth hanging he could sit in the overcrowded yard immersed in a game of chess. "Nevertheless [he writes,] the gloom persisted. I battled the urge to write about rebellion 'Don't give yourself away I admonished myself. 'Stick to the sea.'"

Towards the end of his time in the Jute Mill, Krebs' first story was published in the San Quentin Bulletin. It appeared not under his own name but under that of a wealthy fellow inmate, a bad seed of good family anxious to impress his fiancée. Unusually, for Krebs' early efforts, this was no seaman's story but a paean to the Prison library. He had written it in the hope of winning the responsible warder's affections to escape the Jute Mill and be employed in the library — his preferred billet. When it became apparent that he would be transferred for other reasons, he let his wealthy acquaintance have the story.

In Gil 'Pat' Rankin's San Quentin memoirs there is an impressive story about his first meeting with the fellow inmate and later friend Richard Krebs in the prison library:

"It was a raw foggy day in 1928. I was standing before a counter in the prison library... Several score of prison inmates were in the big room that occupied most of the main floor of the decrepit Old Hospital building facing the open square of the 'Garden Beautiful' so incongruously flourishing in that sordid setting. There was a buzzing of voices and a shuffling of feet as men chatted, moved about, entered or departed. Judson and I were discussing Warden Lawes' remarkable book about Sing Sing Prison in New York.

Behind me, from across the room, flared angry voices.

Scuffling followed. I jerked around and saw convicts surging away from the center of the disturbance in that spontaneous way that marks them as prison-wise. In a penitentiary, a fight is a bad thing to see, hear, know about, or be suspected of knowing about.

Men crowded out through the only exit. I was tense with desire to go away from there myself, but the trouble zone lay between me and the doorway. I started to edge around the sides of the room.

Three convicts were involved in the fracas. Nobody was near them five seconds after it started. A plump, apple-cheeked boy was clutching the Jacket of a burly fellow who held a vicious-looking knife in his hand and was endeavouring to shake off the kid to get at the third man, who was caught between wall and counter-end.

Then I met Skipper Krebs... through my feet... without seeing him.

First I felt the vibrations hit my soles, from the wooden floor, and shoot upward along my shinbones. Then I heard the mighty boom of the voice that shook the building like a deep-toned organ. It was a voice that sounded not loud — *but it felt loud*. Its indescribably deep timbre drowned all other sound; like the roar of distant thunder or the pounding of giant combers on a coral reef. It was booming music that commanded attention without hurting the ear-drums.

Even as my ears registered the sound, I saw something — a heavy reference book — skid through space twenty feet across the room with the precision of a rifle bullet, and strike the head of the burly convict with the knife. He slumped and the knife fell to the floor. Out of the corner of my eye at the right I saw a tall form sail vaultingly over the high counter and streak toward the fallen man. Somehow en route he scooped up the fallen knife — and my skin crinkled at the prospect of his entry into the fray so armed.

But I was wrong. The tall newcomer swept the burly one from the floor with the ease of an acrobat repeating an oft-practised act and bore him a dozen paces in long strides... out of sight into the private office of the Chaplain. A gasp of mingled astonishment and relief went up from the throats of the dozen or fifteen convicts who had not yet succeeded in escaping from the big room. There was renewed shuffling of feet and buzz of conversation as these few got into motion — but it stopped suddenly.

'Listen lubbers!' The bass-organ pipe spoke again. Everyone stood in his tracks and eyed the curly-haired giant that stood in the doorway of the Chaplain's office. His feet were planted well apart as a sailor stands, and he seemed to lean slightly forward as one leans against a stiff gale at sea.

'Listen' he repeated in a soothing rumble. 'Nothing happened here just now, savvy? No rumpus, no fracas, no shiv — nothing, see? ... And any swab stoolie that says otherwise is a liar — a goddam liar, understand?'

Nods and murmurs of approval signified assent. The big fellow threw his long arms up and out in a gesture of dismissal accompanied by a captivating grin."[65]

The transfer to the library was the beginning of a new life for Krebs. Resisting the pressure applied by his *wobblie* friends to preserve him from the 'the press' whoredom to capitalism,' Krebs enrolled on a correspondence course in Journalism run by the well-known journalist Arthur L. Price at the University of Berkley. In Arthur L. Price Krebs found a dispassionate critic and champion of his talents with whom he was to remain in contact for the rest of his life. Richard Krebs sent him piecemeal hundreds of pages on various matters for assessment and criticism. In his own opinion the majority was "ludicrously tempestuous and immature writing."[66]

Arthur L. Price was convinced of the talent of the German prisoner, although the latter didn't always keep within the parameters that he was set. "I wrote as a sailor about the distant sea instead of reporting, as a good would-be journalist should, on the more interesting aspects of my immediate surroundings: the Jute Mill, for example, or the Furniture Shop, or the fight to the death of two convicted pimps over the favors of a perfumed young boy known among us as 'The Queen of Sheeba.'"[67] Apart from his studies in journalism Krebs also pursued a whole range of courses offered by the correspondence college in California. In the two years up to his release he completed seventeen semester-long courses in Spanish, French, English, Russian, Mathematics, Astronomy and Map-reading. Arthur L. Price later wrote that in several subjects the German prisoner of San Quentin was at the time the best student in the history of the university.

After a year as prison librarian, Richard Krebs became languages and math teacher in the prison school. A writer for the prison journal was inspired to write a description of Krebs' lessons:

"As you enter the door, you are met by a flood of guttural German. The instructor of this class is a young German seaman with the stature and the spirit of wanderlust of the Vikings. His voice, thunderous from trying to outdo the volume of Cape Horn winds, rumbles shakily when he tries to throttle it down a bit. Glaring from under a mop of curling black hair, he reminds us of a corralled young bull ready to bellow defiance at his captors. His pupils laugh frequently at the vivid words and the lively pantomimes of their vociferous pedagogue…and his startling descriptions of strange places keep their enthusiasm at a poignant pitch."[68]

The German model prisoner who had succeeded to work his way up to the position of teacher in two years was evidently well trusted by the prison administration. He was drafted in by the overworked prison censor to help with the translation of letters written in Danish, Swedish, Norwegian and Dutch — an arrangement that by no means disturbed those of his fellow prisoners who otherwise would have received no mail. We know from papers left by Krebs that he took the opportunity to renew contact with Hamburg and Albert Walter, although what he communicated to them is not recorded.[69]

From the memoirs of Rankins it is evident that Krebs enjoyed general acclaim. The inmates crowded into his classroom, and once 'Skipper' started publishing his seaman's stories under his own name in *The Bulletin*, he rapidly became one of the most popular figures in the penitentiary and was often consulted for advice in diverse matters.

Inasmuch as this was possible in San Quentin, and in his own words even, Richard Krebs felt 'fine.' He was absorbed by his work and studies and repressed all other concerns. That he was nonetheless haunted by events around him is evident from the *Notes on San Quentin* that he compiled on the repeated request of his English teacher:

"Imprisoned preacher: 'Very few come out better than they were when they came in.'… The prison Jute Mill produces four million jute bags each year. Each summer about seven hundred San Quentin convicts suffer with dysentery. Then they fight like beasts for an open toilet seat in a crowded yard. The disease, the doctors said, is caused by some latent germ in the jute which comes to life in the heat of the Jute Mill…

The negro Sam Thomas was executed in March, convicted of killing a girl named Rose, and betrayed by a girl named Ruby — who herself was later murdered by unknown hands. As Sam Thomas stood on the gallows he begged the hangman: 'Please mister, let me kneel down and say a last prayer.' The hangman nodded. 'Sure Sam, go right ahead,' he replied. Sam bent his knees to pray, and in that instant the hangman gave the signal to drop the trap. It took Sam Thomas thirteen minutes to die at the end of the rope."[70]

From mid-1927, after the meeting of the parole board, Krebs knew that he could expect to be released at the end of 1929 as long as he didn't come to the attention of the authorities for the wrong reasons. As he wrote thirteen years later, his feelings were mixed. After three years San Quentin, seventeen correspondence courses and his first taste of success as a writer, his mental horizons had broadened dramatically. As *The Bulletin* noted "Krebs' travel and seafaring yarns published from time to time in *The Bulletin* have aroused much interest in literary circles — not only in California but in Chicago and New York."[71]

In the notes to *Bend in the River* Krebs wrote that the three years in San Quentin had been the three most productive and happiest years of his life.

"True, I had become thin, and my muscles which had been like wire hawsers, had become too flabby to my liking. I had a little stoop in my shoulders, and my back was not as straight as it had been. Too many weeks and months I had spent crouching over books in dingy cells and dusty yards, too many months squatting low on toilet seats and at desks, hunched over an ancient typewriter I had bought by foregoing a year's ration of sugar and tobacco. But I had mastered navigation, higher mathematics and astronomy. I had gained fluency in the English language in writing and speech, though my manner of expression still was immature and clumsy. I had learnt enough French and Spanish to read and to make myself understood in those tongues. I had studied the making of maps and meteorology, a little Russian, shipbuilding some sociology, theories of education, and I had made sallies into philosophies which were not those of Marx and Lenin. All this I could not have done if I had not gone to prison; life would simply have offered me no other chance to do it. I was grateful to San Quentin."[72]

As Rankins, who was by no means of the same opinion, noted, Krebs was still convinced of the necessity of 'violent revolution.'

The possibilities of existence within bourgeois society also became clear to him inside San Quentin. It is impossible that in the loneliness of his prisoner's life the son of a captain didn't recall his youthful dream of attending marine training college, which, given the success of his studies at the correspondence college in California, would have been relatively easy for him. His success in writing will also have shown him that there was a life for him outside of the Party. It appears that after returning to Germany Krebs really did try to square this very circle, to combine both facets: the intellectual motherland of his comrades with the fulfillment of personal aspirations.

The last lines that *The Bulletin* published by him appeared in February 1930, three months after his release. The piece *The Return* seems in retrospect an ominous prophecy of the horrors that awaited him in the years to come:

"A man stamped into the teeth of the tempest, stamped along the rim of the sidewalk where the wind chased a multitude of ripples and dark patches beneath his feet... Familiar spots he had known in years that swung away leered upon squelching shoes; fingers blue with cold, burning face, and eyes aimless in the chaos of the night...

The man shouldered away in the night, past a gnarled tree with sinuous skeleton arms and a network of ugly roots, roots upon which he saw crumpled a bleeding corpse after a day of death and battle between soldiers and rebellious workers behind guns. And suddenly the storm beat into his face, straight and true, with a primordial force vastly different from its vicious whine amongst the squalid houses."[73]

PART II Rise in the Comintern

Stalin's Shadow

On the fifth of December, 1929, the gates of San Quentin shut behind Richard Krebs, yet still he was not free. A prison train carried him across the United States to Galveston in Texas, and from there he was deported by ship to Europe.

In early January 1930, the ship arrived in Le Havre in Brittany. Those prisoners who had not yet reached the country of their destination were temporarily incarcerated in the town prison there until a decision had been reached as to their final destination. Richard Krebs landed by chance in a cell with a certain Chisholm, the very adventurer and gambler that he had met as a stowaway on his journey from China to North America. With his help, Krebs managed to escape from prison on his first night there.

He continued on his way to Bremen.

Out of the Night tells a very different story of Krebs' alter ego. This has him embarking on an odyssey through the Comintern underground and finally arriving in Moscow, where he takes part in a conference of seafarers. During this trajectory the reader is made familiar with the changes that took place within the Comintern in Valtin's absence. These changes, the background before which the drama of his life are unfolding, were born of Soviet domestic policy.

The revolution had turned down a blind alleyway. Wartime Communism, so called, the attempt made during the throes of the Civil War to abolish private enterprise, to collectivize agriculture and to introduce total planned-economy had failed in the early 'twenties due to economic chaos and resistance by the farmers. Since the civil war could not be won without the farmers, Lenin had had to turn tail and go over to the NEP, the New Economic Policy. The farmers kept the land that had been appropriated during the revolution, and a certain amount of private enterprise was tolerated in the city. In the course of the 'twenties it became apparent that state-run business, despite all the advantages that it was accorded, could not keep pace with private competition.

Worse still, in the eyes of the leadership, was the fact that many farmers contentedly went over to subsistence farming; there being no incentive by way of manufactured good, the farmers saw no need to produce a surplus. Without this surplus, however, there was no capital with which to import capital expenditure items, nor food to support industrialization. The war that at the time was generally anticipated due to the enmity of the capitalist powers to the Soviet system could not be won under such conditions.

The Party leadership had to make a decision; either to leave things as they stood, to let great stretches of land remain in private hands —and thereby risk the future of planned economy and with it that of Socialism itself — or to implement complete control of all economic resources now that they were free of internal war. The first of these options, the bloodless one that depended on the persuasive power of the correct *Weltanschauung*, had already proven unsuccessful in the 'twenties. The second variant would inevitably provoke a violent reaction from the farmers and could be implemented by brute force alone.

Among the representatives of the second school of thought was Joseph Stalin, who, having succeeded Lenin after a power struggle during the 'twenties in which he had vanquished Trotsky, was in the process of taking unilateral control of the Party. The representatives of the first school were the men of the old revolutionary leadership, at their head the brilliant intellectual and chief editor of *Pravda*, Bukarin. The fabulously educated "favourite of the Party," as Lenin had called him, like all the other essentially West-oriented intellectuals high in Party ranks, was no match for the unscrupulous cunning of Stalin, whose formal education amounted to only a short stay at seminary school.

The dispute was not only evident within the Party; at the VIth World Congress in autumn a quarrel arose as to the future of the German Party which turned into a struggle by proxy between Stalin and his opponents. The conspicuous cause of trouble was a corruption affair which implicated Party leader Ernst Thälmann and which his opponents were trying to exploit to depose him. Both sides sought cover from Moscow, Thälmann turning to Stalin, the losers of the struggle to Stalin's opponents. The background to this was the question of the strategy to be taken in Germany. Thälmann and his followers were proponents of the so-called 'radical left' option, the unconditional attack on the mainstay of the Weimar Republic, Social Democracy, in the hope of seizing power after the fall of the old order. Thälmann's enemies, later to be condemned as 'right wingers,' were aware of the danger that German fascists posed to this plan and called for cooperation with the Social Democrats to avoid a right wing dictatorship. The latter would have meant the revolution's adjournment, whilst the former was an audacious risk, the outcome of which is now only too familiar.

Once Stalin had asserted the position of his follower Thälmann, the 'right wingers' left the Party to found another. Not only the followers of Thälmann remained, however. Another group, later vilified as 'conciliators,' remained to submit like

Bukharin to Party discipline and to thereafter hold their tongues; they could imagine for themselves no future outside of the movement.

Stalin and his entourage, correctly interpreting the teeth grinding silence of their opponents, soon reacted after the VIth congress with a wave of repressions that also comprehended the Comintern.

The historian Fredrich Firsov, one of the first to have access to Comintern archives after Perestroika, offered a blueprint for the repressions that were to be repeated thousand-fold throughout the parties of the world in detailing the purges that took place after the Comintern Congress. During the 1930s their intensity increased, culminating in the mass slaughter of 1937. The trigger for the original 'cleansing' was a report from the Comintern machine to the local Moscow committee of the Bolschevik Soviet Union's Communist Party. This stated that there were some thirty Bukarin sympathizers among the three hundred members of the Comintern's Party organization.

"It was proclaimed in all departments and sectors that Party members and non-members alike could denounce comrades against whom they held incriminating material.

This offer brought about a wave of denunciations that greatly facilitated the work of the 'purges commission'. The people caught up in these witch trials recounted their biographies and confessed to individual instances of deviation from Party line and to offences, real or imaginary. They then answered questions before it was the turn of other attendees to speak. The process was in general both interrogation and accusation.

Those subjugated to this process were not only accused of real offences, but also of having had contact — sometimes of merely having conversed — with suspected subversives. The refusal to denounce another was considered a particularly serious offence…

Of the 239 people in question, 201 were categorized as 'verified,' seven were ejected from the Party, and the rest were given some form of Party-enforced punishment. The minutes of the meeting contained judgments and conclusions about many colleagues. None of these were to be without consequence."[74]

Bukarin was quick to surmise the inevitable end of this development.

On June 11, 1928, during a brief pause in the power struggle he wrote the following to his comrade-in-arms, Kamenev: "Stalin is interested in nothing except power. He is beating a retreat at present, but he holds the keys of power in his hands, and with them he will one day slaughter us."[75]

Why communists like Bukarin remained in the Party despite this is indicated in a letter that the emancipator and *grande dame* of the German Party Clara Zetkin sent from Moscow in 1929. Her farewell to the Swiss Communist and Stalin opponent Humbert-Droz, who had been sent "far from sin and Stalinistic frenzy" to South America, read as follows: " I shall feel entirely lost and alone in an organization that has transformed itself from a living political organism to a dead automaton which ingests orders given in Russian in one place and spits them back out in a different language somewhere else, an automaton which has taken the vast significance and content of the Russian Revolution and transmuted them into a rule book for the

Pickwick Club. One would grow mad without unshakeable faith in the path of history and the power of revolution, so in this dark hour of midnight, I look into the future with hope, yes, even with optimism."[76]

'Bourgeois' Dreams

Although that "dead automaton" absorbed his fictional hero immediately after his return, before Richard Krebs himself became one of its important components he was to lead another phase of his life. This was one of a quite private nature, and, as with all such affairs, Krebs was prone to either say nothing on the matter, or else report in only the most elusive terms.

In the year of his return, Krebs tried not only to revive his dream of training as a helmsman and to fulfill his new ambition of proving himself as a writer, but also to reconcile these ambitions with the duties of a faithful member of the Communist worldwide movement.

For the first time since his parting as ships boy in 1921, Krebs spent a lengthy period at home. He lived with his mother in an apartment on the *Seefahrtshof*, a complex of twenty-five apartments belonging to a foundation that supported sailors' widows.

He returned home in other respects too. The son of the deceased nautical-department manager of Norddeutsche Lloyd matriculated on February 1 at the Bremen Merchant Marine Training College that one of his father's friends administered.[77] The Bremen Merchant Marine Training College was at the time the *de facto* training center of the Norddeutsche Lloyd which was still the most powerful of Bremen's shipping companies and of considerable international significance. During economically good times it employed the majority of the college's graduates. The course only admitted fifteen students, and Krebs, after his three-year stint in San Quentin, almost certainly owed his place to the esteem that his father had enjoyed. It is unimaginable that the letter sent to the Californian state parole board in 1927 — which described the boy who had jumped ship in Autofagasta during his first voyage in less than glowing terms — had slipped the attention of the Lloyd administration.

Krebs did however submit to school discipline. The testimony that had claimed he was able to give a good account of himself was confirmed by the good leaving certificate he received from the establishment one year later.

Krebs had been given orders to organize a Communist cell among his fellow students during his studies. Presumably only the fact that this proved impossible from the outset prevented him from falling foul of the school administration. Almost all of his fellows were either of German nationalist leaning or even Hitler supporters. It is easy to imagine that Albert Walters must have been filled with enthusiasm at the prospect of breaching the ranks of ship officers if only to such a small extent. This was not the last mission of its kind that Krebs was to be entrusted with. He would later be charged with the abortive attempt to distribute a Communist paper for ship's officers, *Die Brücke,* which was only rescinded due to the paper's unpopularity. Sailors of bourgeois origins and communist leanings like Krebs were, after all, a rarity.

The distrust that such origins were liable to provoke among the comrades is testified to in Jorge Semprun's memoirs of the Buchenwald concentration camp, where he was incarcerated for Communist partisan activities. Semprun reports that on his arrival the German Communist Seifert, one of the bosses of the shadow organization within the camp, let it be known "what a kindness it was to accept me on the work gang despite my background"[78]- a privilege that indeed ensured his survival.

"A philosophy student of bourgeois origin – my God, Seifert had never seen anything of the kind in his office! That he made all too clear to me. I had the impression that I was only provisionally accepted, and that the slightest slip would have me burning in hell, stewing in the pot of my class origins.

These very class origins were in the shadowy background for the entire duration of my political activities,* incessantly threatening to undo me at the slightest deviant thought. I spoke to them as to a pet dog: 'down boy, down! Don't offend our visitors!'"[79]

The step of openly confessing his origins, later taken by Semprun, was one that Krebs avoided throughout his life. In *Out of the Night* he only hinted at the fact that admission to the training college was largely thanks to family connections.

Parallel to his studies —greatly facilitated by the correspondence courses he had taken in astronomy and map reading — Krebs attempted to realize his second dream. He wrote stories in English and sent them everywhere. In March 1930 a story he had written about his stowaway trip from Hong Kong to Vancouver was published in New York, and in July and September two further short stories were published in London. The *Lloydzeitung,* the bimonthly, bilingual organ of *Norddeutsche Lloyd* also published four of his short stories. This was no mean performance for an unknown writer, yet it was insufficient for both his unbridled ambition and his financial needs.

Besides the material published in the English language, the dates of which are known as he later listed them in exile, Krebs also wrote for the Party press. This is not only confirmed in his memoirs, but also attested to by an anonymous Communist from Bremen who was later to review *Out of the Night* after its publication in German translation.[80]

---

* Jorge Semprun, a member of the Politburo of the exiled Spanish Communist Party in Paris, was excluded from the Party in 1964 because of political differences.

As he was to tell the American CIC shortly before his death, after his return to Bremen Krebs met a man called Gehrke, Bremen's representative of the *International Arbeiterhilfe* (IAH or International Workers' Aid) organization.

The IAH was the brainchild of the talented organizer Willi Münzenberg, who created a Communist press trust from an organization originally designed to help Civil War-devastated Russia. This trust not only published the *Arbeiter illustrierte Zeitung*, one of the most popular papers of the Weimar Republic, but also ran a number of publishing houses and newspaper presses and even owned a film distribution company. As Krebs was later to inform the Americans, he was convinced that the bald and elegant Gehrke, dressed always in a gray suit that made him conspicuous in the port where his offices were housed, had quite a different agenda to the publishing of the *Bremer Bürgerzeitung* (or "cursed rag "as Gehrke himself was wont to call it).[81] Two factors in particular had convinced Krebs of this. One was the appearance of Gehrke's office, which, decorated with a couple of posters and collection boxes, gave the impression of a sham, the second was the course of a conference led by an instructor from Berlin to the agitation and propaganda (Agitprop) men of the Party district Weser-Ems. Its purpose was to instruct those present on the political situation and applied propaganda techniques.

As an IAH man, Gehrke should have been competent in Agitprop, but he sat in silence for the duration of the seminar. Only at the end did he contribute, and then he made the unoriginal proposal to introduce Münzenberg at a speech he was giving as 'the red Hugenberg,' an allusion to the German nationalist press baron of the day.

The IAH's *raison d'être* was agitation. If this had really been the main field of Gehrke's activities, then why should the instructor have reproached him in private after the seminar for having meddled in propaganda affairs?

We know since the declassification of the relevant archives that the humanitarian and informative nature of the IAH was nothing but a façade for the machinations of the secret services.[82] It is characteristic of the cloak and dagger atmosphere of the day that this front was maintained even to KPD members. It remained a matter of chance —or in Krebs' case intuition — whether such information became more common knowledge or not.

Krebs wrote stories for Gehrke, or, in his words, dashed them off in the evenings.

Either in late 1930 or early 1931, towards the end of the period in which Krebs attempted to live from writing, he fell foul of the German Communist concept of 'socially valuable' literature. This concept involved painting Communist protagonists in glorious colors and their opponents as black as possible. The latter were to be the inevitable losers in any kind of struggle. Psychological representation, subtleties of characterization, or any kind of experiment in form were frowned upon. Any conflict represented was always to be resolved in a manner delivering the reader an exemplary socialistic moral. *Scum's Wake*, a longer text or perhaps even a novel, that for Krebs represented the culmination of his work up to then, obviously did not fulfill this brief. As Krebs later wrote in America, the work was published in heavily bowdlerized form and under a different title by one of the Münzenberg concern's many subsidiaries. Although an unabridged version of the copy seems never to have been published in German, Krebs' later (and vain) attempts to recover a copy of the English original from America, an empty folder with the title *Scum's Wake* in his estate, and a letter to mentor Arthur L. Price in California in which the novel's publication in German is mentioned, all seem to show that the book was published. Obviously the version bore so little resemblance to the one he intended that he never included the title in lists of his publications and never communicated to anyone under which title and pseudonym or where it had been published. What was actually done to the text we shall presumably never know, as neither the original of *Scum's Wake* nor any corresponding translation has been seen since. Perhaps Sholokov's *Virgin Soil Upturned,* which described in execrable fashion the idyll of collectivization, gives a hint of the manner in which Krebs' work had been bastardized for Party purposes.

From Krebs' time as laureate of the workers only one poem has been found. It was published on April 16, 1933 in the *Bremer Arbeiterzeitung* under the title "And should the tanks roll on Russia." It exemplifies socialist realist poetry and describes the attack on the socialist motherland that was considered imminent:

War on the Soviet Union!
Declaims the tabloid press.
War on Bolshevism!
Scream Hitler and all the rest.
Trains steam to the harbor
Loaded with ammunition
Poison gas and soldiers
To suppress the Revolution.
Ships' holds full of weaponry
Ships' holds full of mercenaries
Canons, bayonets, murderous bands
To land upon the Russian coasts
To cut down all the Bolsheviks
To murder all the Communists…
Proletarian of this land!
Would you bury your brothers while they drink toasts?
General strike!
Stoker, extinguish now your fires!
Sailor, stay your hand and stop to slave!
Stevedore, let wind blow ships unloaded!
Your strike will thwart their bellicose desires
No munitions boat may sail!
Cry strike!
And leave the patriots to vainly threaten
And helplessly brandish their wicked weapons.

Three months later, on July 5, 1931, Krebs wrote to his mentor Arthur L. Price Bremen, July 1930: "So I dance my little dance. The dominant note in the monstrous squirming about me is Brutality, Hunger and Greed. Beauty and kindliness have very little place in it. But so much more pretty conceit, meaningless morality and obscure altruism. I would rather cut my throat than write about things I do not believe in — I would consider such writing success a miserable defeat... I feel like a little child groping through an immensity of fog. I read Conrad, and I am happy, and I mutter dismally: You can never write like that..."[83]

Firelei

Richard Krebs met Hermine Stöver, the love of his life, soon after his return to Bremen. Firelei, the name that he gave her in *Out of the Night*, like the pseudonym Valtin that he himself took in his book, indicate that that in 1930 there must have been a phase in Krebs' life during which he was little more than a young bourgeois. This is a side of his character that he was later to suppress and even deny wholesale. In 1941 it was a tough guy who would tell the press that he had chosen the name 'Valtin' during long, sleepless nights in the concentration camp to be used if and when he should ever escape Nazi Germany. It was a name, he maintained, that offered no hint as to the origin of its bearer.

It seems much more likely, however, that the name came from a very successful novel typical of the few happy Weimar years written by Vicki Baum. The protagonists of *Stud. Chem. Helene Willfüer*, a pair of lovers, have the names Firelei and Valentin. Presumably both Krebs and Stöver read this work and named each other after its heroes. It is even possible that the name Fitsch later taken by his wife in her letters is nothing but a variant on Firelei. Certainly it is no North German term of endearment, as Krebs tried to persuade the American authorities after they had confiscated the letters. This he maintained many years after her death, as if to shield her memory one last time from the prying eyes of the investigating authorities.

The image that Krebs evoked of the beginning of their relationship was a part of that legend which he spun around the name Valtin. It involves the Comintern agent and arms smuggler who, sent on a mission to Antwerp, meets a girl of Flemish-German origin in the port who is making drawings in her sketchbook of the picturesque sailors on the harbor.

In reality Richard Krebs met Hermine Stöver via his sister Cilly, who attended the Art and Design College in Bremen with her, Hermine Stöver, tall and with dark blonde hair was a well brought-up girl from a politically conservative Bremen merchant family. At the time she met Krebs, she had been working for four years as an advertising designer for the North German Wool-Carding Company. To the seaman and former inmate who had never been long enough in one place to form anything but a passing relationship, her respectable, professional character and the good family that she belonged to must have made her seem a part of a distant idyll. She was sociable and adventurous enough to follow him into the radical milieu of seamen and political conspirators. If the Gestapo file pertaining to her case is to be believed, at the time of their meeting she was without political affiliation or tendency. She was talented at drawing and, like artists of her generation, she probably had vague leanings towards the progressive ideas of the 'twenties.

According to court files, her parents were against the relationship from the beginning. In the eyes of her wealthy merchant family, the young man of shabby bourgeois origin, with his radical political ideas and his lack of professional ambition, was anything but a good match for their daughter. This feeling was exacerbated by her increased involvement in his political work, which due to the failure of his writing plans and the worsening worldwide crisis, was taking an ever-growing hold upon him.

Black Friday on Wall Street marked the beginning of the worst economic crisis of the 'twenties. In the already unstable Germany this was to have devastating results.

The crisis was exacerbated there by governmental policies which deepened the slump by cutting the state budget. State employees and the unemployed masses were the hardest hit.

In the largest cities such as Berlin, Hamburg and Bremen, where there was no immediate access to food, large sections of the population suffered from malnutrition and concomitant illness. The harbor quarters of Hamburg and Bremen, as in the crisis after World War I, were no-go-areas that the police force would only visit in double patrols.

In August 1930 Richard Krebs replied to a letter from Arthur L. Price in which he described his impressions on a journey to Italy and Greece: "Dirty and ignorant — that´s just what their capitalist masters want them to be — a lot of cheap workbeasts — what they need is not religion, but leaders who point out to them the way to bread and fair clothing and sanitation. Those things cost money. It also costs money to give these people shorter working hours and schools and libraries.— They are caught in a great cauldron, and they must boil until they scale the sheer walls of class difference and string up the satanic cook that stirs the fire to the highest possible point."

In October he wrote to him again, returning in the letter to the subject of that voyage: "But when You tell others about the wonders of the world, don´t forget also the hungry beggar hordes and the consumptive women in reeking alleys — and the circumstances that hold them there. That insight is only to be attained by painful and unhappy pondering I think."[84]

The committed engagement in social affairs that these lines reflect indicate a reason more powerful than Party doctrine for why Hermine Stöver might have followed her lover into political work beyond that of her love for him. She was only to join the KPD one year later, when Krebs was already deeply involved in its machinations and then, as was later to be revealed, not so much out of inner conviction as due to a direct order given to Richard Krebs as an agent privy to secret information.

Many years later, in 1957, as the German translation of *Out of the Night* appeared, an anonymous reviewer and comrade from Krebs' time in Bremen recalled the couple and the period with these words:

"Is the book true? Did Jan Valtin really live? Yes. He lived. His name was Richard Krebs, he grew up in the Hansa League city of Bremen. Back in those days he was already expressing his wrath and his dreams in novels and short stories. The times were hard though. The art student laid down her pastels, because the times demanded that youth should create the conditions of a blossoming future... Youth wants to know and comprehend truth. Richard Krebs... was among them, one who struggled to know the right path. The words 'better to die in the flames of the revolution than to rot on the dung heap of democracy' were those by which he lived. Were those not the times — Krebs described it himself — when truncheons were employed to maintain elementary democratic rights?

As the bargers' strike had begun, Krebs and his accomplices hindered the way of the strikebreaker boats. These were no dull theories and definitions; these were poor fellows who had to be helped to win a battle for bread. With a swollen head from police beatings but a smile on his lips the exuberant young man stood in the *Café Flora* and said: 'The police may have beaten us, but you can't use a truncheons to repair a sunk boat!'

His girl, Firelei, spent almost every evening with an agitprop theatre group, *The Red Reporter*, drumming the truth into the people, as the saying went. The rest of the time she was drawing political caricatures on placards. She embodied a certain purity — as some girls always have. At the annual Red Aid meeting in the artist's village of Worpswede near Bremen a whole bunch of resolute nudists bathed in the local lake before a thousand visitors. Many were outraged, not least the tenderly disposed Firelei: 'Don't you come me with the rubbish about having disposed of the last vestiges of bourgeois morality. Your behavior is absolutely inappropriate and I find it disgraceful.'"[85]

On November 20, 1930, *The Red Reporter* came to the attention of the secret police for the first time on their appearance in the *Café Flora*. From then until the end of the summer of the following year, reports were regularly filed on the appearances of the agitprop troupe. These performances were often accompanied by readings from the worker's writer Richard Krebs, who also appeared as a sort of compère. One of the most detailed of these reports covered the inauguration of the Union of Seamen and Harbor Worker's Club on 4.18. 1931 at Köhler's in the Gröpelinger Deich 30.

At the beginning of the event the song '*Brüder zur Sonne, zur Freiheit*' (Brother, to the sun, to freedom) was sung by all present... After another piece of music, Dr. Gross, Romanian, spoke on his work as a natural health therapist in the Holzminden sanatorium. The talk was poorly received. Krebs let the curtain fall halfway through.

The Red Reporter took the stage. The play, written by Krebs and Woile, was as follows: on the stage stood three characters, a ship owner, a brothel owner and a representative of the Salvation Army. The ship owner cursed the strikers at the shipping company's employment office, calling them *Schweinehunde* for not wanting to work. The brothel owner retorted that he would be glad if a ship came in, that he could grow rich from Schnapps and beer that his women sold to the seamen. When the seamen had no more money, he said, he would throw them out into the street. The Salvation Army representative complained that there were no sheep to lead to the Kingdom of God. As two seamen appeared on stage, the brothel owner said that they must all leave, as the seamen were not to know that all three were in cahoots. Only the Salvation Army man remained on the stage to hail the seamen with a halleluiah. Suddenly a distributor of the *Scheinwerfer**appeared on the stage, and tried to drum up membership for the *Einheitsverband*[+]. The two sailors also ignored him and left with two of the harbor girls.

After the curtain fell, Krebs appeared on the stage and said that this was typical of seamen today, but that it didn't have to be that way. Next to the stage stood a placard on which was written: 'The thinking worker doesn't drink and the drinking worker doesn't think.' On leaving the stage Krebs pointed to it… After a musical interlude, Krebs' girl 'Fräulein Herma' appeared on stage as a quick caricaturist, making her drawings to an appropriate variety of musical accompaniment:

A caricature of Hitler, music: *Morgenrot*
A caricature of Minister Frick, music: *Morgenrot*
A caricature of Dr. Goebbels, music: *Little Hans went alone 'cross the land*
Two swine from behind, music: *Hail to you, laurel bearer…*

The function ended at 11pm with a rendition of *The Internationale*. Dancing began."[86]

'Adolf'

In autumn 1930 Richard Krebs was being mentioned on a weekly basis in Bremen's secret police reports. From February on he was already known as the manager of the Bremen International Seamen's Club or 'Interclub.'

The International Seamen's clubs were originally a creation of the Comintern, intended as an alternative to the usual Christian Seamen's Homes. The first Interclub was founded in Leningrad in the early 'twenties, the second in Hamburg, and was

---

* The *Scheinwerfer* (searchlight) was the paper of the *Einheitsverband*

[+] The *Einheitsverband* was the German section of the Communist ISH, The International of Seamen and Harbor workers.

initially known as the *Internationales Hafen Büro* or International Port bureau. By the early 'thirties a whole row of such clubs had joined ranks with these first two establishments, including the one founded in Bremen in 1928.

The Interclubs were partly conventional seamen's bars, partly multilingual Communist lending libraries, and partly venues not solely for Communist meetings, but also for so-called agitprop theatre evenings, lectures of all kinds and for dances where, regardless of nationality, a seaman on shore leave might meet a girl.

A peculiarity of the clubs was their direct, secret financing from the Comintern. For this reason they were subject to international authorities but not to the local Party hierarchy. It is therefor unsurprising that Richard Krebs, almost unknown within the German Party but a conspicuously good organizer, was soon after his return running the International Seamen's Club. Secret police agents registered his ensuing swift rise within the *Einheitsverband* of seamen and harbor workers.

On February 14 he hosted a Seamen's conference, and in April he was appointed one of the four delegates from Bremen at the Einheitverband's national conference in Hamburg. On May 1, local police headquarters sent a communication marked 'secret' to the *Bremische Amt*, the senate bureau of the Hansa league town. It concerned Richard Krebs: "By means of secret investigation we have learnt that the leader of the local *Einheitsverband*, Richard Krebs, has announced that in the near future the *Einheitsverband* will send four to five men to Bremerhaven. They are being sent on a mission to disseminate Communist propaganda, etc. among the crews of the big ships there.

Krebs is politically very active, plays a leading role in the Communist movement of seamen and works for the *Scheinwerfer*. Since having been given control of the Communist Seamen's movement in Bremen he has expanded it considerably. Krebs, who recently passed his helmsman exam with flying colors, is an intelligent and talented man.

We request that attention be paid to all forms of subversive Communist activity on board, and that any useful information garnered be reported back to us."[87]

Another communiqué was sent to the Bremen Ship Owners' Association on May 19, 1931: "With regard to the above memorandum, we humbly submit that information secretly acquired on the meetings of the Communist *Einheitsverband* does not lend itself to the criminal prosecution of Richard Krebs or other key organization members. Information sources are not to be named as witnesses; if Krebs becomes aware that outsiders have infiltrated his meetings, he will do his utmost to dispose of them so as to avoid future information leaks. It is therefore desirable that Krebs is denied this information. No important success can be reported, since Krebs will certainly deny the veracity of reports and call his comrades to maintain his statements...

According to the information given in the meeting, Krebs' organization comprises a total of 781 seamen and harbor workers."[88]

Krebs' success in the *Einheitsverband* was not only due to his organizational and rhetorical prowess, but also to the fact that the body was only a few months old at the time of his admission. Its foundation was a late consequence of the 1928 Comintern Congress at which Stalin had asserted himself to the detriment of Bukarin and the 'right wingers.' It had originally been Communist Party practice to infiltrate extant unions and to take over their leadership from within. The so-called Propaganda Committees, IPC-Transport among them, had been created to centrally coordinate infiltration. This policy assumed that the Communists in most countries represented a minority — an accurate ascertainment of the state of affairs — and that there was therefore no point in founding their own independent unions. This was by no means the case in the sea transport branch. As German consular reports of the day attest, German seamen after the war were almost all revolutionaries or sympathizers; a good number of them had taken part in the sailors' uprising in 1917/18.

What was true of the sailors also went for the harbor workers. Even if orthodox Communists were a minority among them, these could always appeal to the latent rebelliousness of the majority. Nothing shows more accurately how disparate this milieu was to the rest of German society as clearly as the Gestapo reports on the mood among harbor and shipyard workers at the time.

Even in June 1939, shortly before the beginning of World War II, after countless arrests and six years of uninterrupted propaganda, the Gestapo officer for the district could report to his superiors in Berlin: "the masses, particularly the negative part of the workforce... are not ashamed to reflect on foreign affairs in the light of their Communist-Marxist attitudes...[and, further,] The clearest expression of the 'cooperativeness' of longshoremen and shipyard workers was given as they went to attend the annual obligatory march on the first of May. This they did, as they expected their attendance to be checked, and also because they presumed that they would receive a subvention of 2.50 or 3.50 Reichsmarks a head. As they discovered that the latter was not the case, a large proportion of them fell away from the ranks marching on the meeting place. Before the Führer's speech had began, another large group left. Before the end of the speech the rest had vanished..."[89]

In the Germany of the 'twenties, the radical, largely Communist union had many more members than the Social Democrat union.

Nonetheless, Communist Headquarters in Moscow insisted on applying Comintern policy on unions, which finally gave rise to a grotesque and ludicrous performance; the leadership of the radical union, contrary to the wishes of many members, were obliged to request acceptance to the smaller Social Democrat union. After much prevarication, and under humiliating conditions, they were finally accepted.

After the VIth Comintern Congress in 1928 the situation was inverted. Now the imperative was to leave the traditional unions and form independent ones, so-called revolutionary unions. In Germany the brief period of the *RGO*, the *Revolutionären Gewerkschafts-opposition* (or Revolutionary Union Opposition) began. All along the coastline Communists left the Social Democrat union and founded the *Einheitsverband* of seamen and harbor workers. This association held a special position among the RGO unions of Germany; not only was it the only union branch that achieved some measure of greatness, but, as opposed to all Communist unions in other branches, it was not under the supervision of any local or lesser Party authority. The *Einheitsverband* was the German section of the ISH, the International of Seamen and Harbor workers. It was founded shortly after the VIth Comintern Congress as successor to IPC-Transport, was not, however, dedicated to infiltration and subversion as was its predecessor, but to founding its own united associations throughout the world.

Officially, and to its lowliest members, the *Einheitsverband* was an independent organization with its own hierarchy. In reality, it was entirely under the orders of the ISH, which in turn was a Janus operation. Nominally, the ISH was an independent organization with an HQ in Hamburg. Its general secretary and public face was Albert Walter, the man that Krebs had met in Hamburg in 1923. In reality, all important decisions were taken by Moscow, and Moscow's man in Hamburg, the actual commander of the ISH, was a Pole who went by the name of Adolf Schelley. His very existence was a secret known only to the higher echelons of the Party. Even Richard Krebs, who was later his friend and subordinate, was only to discover his real name long after their last meeting.

Alfred Bem,[90] Schelley's real name, was born in Łódź, 1900, the son of a teacher. He joined the Polish Communist Party as a 19-year old law student. Only three years later he was organizing the election campaign for the elections to the Polish parliament or Sejm in the regions of Poznan and Thorun and was arrested for the first time in late 1922. Poland, as the traditional enemy of Russia, that, with the help of the western powers, had even successfully waged war against the Soviet Union, was one of the most dangerous places for a Communist agitator. Alfred Bem, who quickly became one of the most important figures in the Polish Communist Party and who, in 1926, was made general secretary of the Shipping Workers' Union, was made aware of this in no uncertain terms; in 1926, at this early culmination of his career, he was expelled from university, forbidden admission to any other Polish college and once again arrested.

As the Polish Communist Party had been banned in the interim, Bem, aka Adolf, was subsequently no more than a representative of a left wing socialist organization, a fact that did not avert further arrests. By the year 1928 he had been taken into custody eleven times, had spent several months in prison, and had almost certainly been tortured, a common practice in the semi-fascistic Poland of the day. By 1929 his health had been so gravely attacked that he was set free on bail. He fled for the Soviet Union, where he was immediately sent to a Caucasian sanatorium to convalesce.

Since 'Adolf Schelley' was not only the name by which he was known to Richard Krebs and other ISH workers, but also the one with which he signed secret reports to Moscow, it is for simplicity's sake the one he will retain here. The Gestapo, incidentally knew him under the further aliases of 'Fred' and 'Oberle,'[91] whilst Krebs, having become his second-in-command, asserted that he habitually traveled under the name of 'Adolf Siegvert.'

In the extremely detailed report that Krebs made years later to the American CIC, Krebs described the man that he had known as 'Adolf Schelley' in the following terms: "Medium height, slender but well built, fair complexion, light hair, gray eyes, always excellently dressed in a conservative way; had a slight and almost not noticeable limp on one foot; spoke excellent German with no more accent than a Jew would have (Hermann SCHUBERT,* who hated him, often referred to him as the 'Polish Jew'... Adolf never had any official connection with the KPD but always got what he wanted from the KPD regional management."[92]

Adolf, an excellent speaker and organizer, whose numerous reports to Moscow witness his clear speech and succinct formulations, had two weaknesses that would later bring about his downfall. One was the women, with whom he apparently had considerable success, and the other was a tendency, marked in his letters to headquarters, to take the revolutionary politics of the ISH all too seriously. In conflict situations between the Soviet Union's state interest and the revolutionary activities of the ISH he criticized his superiors, and although he did this softly, it was nonetheless evident for that. Normal relations between the 'first workers' state of the world' and its capitalist environment, including the supporting subversive groups located there, were simply hard to foster, That all controversial matters were decided to the advantage of the Soviet Union obviously played on Schelley's conscience, a state of affairs that a more career-oriented functionary would have simply overlooked.

The pertinent part of Krebs' statement to the CIC, transcribed in the third person, reads as follows: "Richard Krebs first met Adolf at an ISH conference...in 1931. At this time the Party was emphasizing youth work in trade unions and, since BREMEN was the only waterfront organization with a strong youth group functioning on the whole waterfront, KREBS was asked to give a report. Afterwards he was called aside by a complete stranger who said 'I am interested in you'. From that time on KREBS was something of a protégé of ADOLF's..."[93]

Among the ISH files at the Comintern archives in Moscow there is a report on one conference which can only have been the one where Krebs met the real leader of the ISH. This report, dated 13 June, 1931, states "Had on the 8th of the Mth a very thorough conversation with the Bremen representative (Comrade Krebs, a very active and politically enlightened individual)."[94] The report is not signed, which was common practice for security reasons, but, like the majority of unsigned reports, its content betrays it as almost certainly the work of the man known in the Comintern as 'Adolf'.

---

* Hermann Schubert was political leader on the waterfront from 1931 and appointed to the KPD's Politbüro in 1932.

Soviet Interlude

Kreb's meeting with Adolf Schelley was not only to lead to a fast rise in the ISH for Krebs; it was also to provide him with his first voyage as a captain.

Schelley was only too familiar with one of the major weaknesses of the *Einheitsverband*, its lack of support among the officers. In Krebs he had found a qualified helmsman who was not only a Communist but also a talented agitator. The only problem was that, although he had passed helmsman examinations, he had not yet captained his own vessel. How might he then command the attention of older and more experienced officers?

The ISH decided to get Krebs a ship. The *Pioner* was duly found. This was a fishing steamer waiting at the Vulkan shipyard, under Soviet orders to sail for Murmansk, the only ice-free port of the Soviet Union. Richard Krebs received several hundred dollars from the Soviet trade mission to cover traveling expenses and set about gathering a crew. He had, however, failed to reckon with the Bremen Party leadership. When they heard that a mission was planned to the Communist Mecca, as KPD propaganda had it, and that the trip was to be well paid to boot, they decided to change the trip into a pleasure cruise for worthy comrades. Despite the dangerous rounding of the northern tip of Scandinavia that stood before him, Richard Krebs reluctantly agreed to the Party's plan. As the friends of the leading local Communists proved entirely un-seaworthy, however, he found himself obliged to return down the Weser channel, so as to get rid of them and to hire another crew.

The local Party boss, Egon Nickel, was furious and had Krebs excommunicated. This decision was to prove premature; Schelley, who gave Krebs cover, had a direct line to Moscow's executive powers. Krebs was re-admitted to the KPD on his return.

After unemployed Communist seamen had been recruited, the *Pioner* sailed for Kiel. There a second fishing steamer was taken in tow, and thence they sailed along the Norwegian coast. By mid-July they had reached Murmansk.

The Communist members of the crew must have held high hopes. They had presumably all read the glowing reports of the Soviet Union that the Münzenberg trust's *Arbeiter-Illustrierte* published incessantly. For the leadership of the *Einheitsverband* the comparison of conditions in Germany and the Soviet Union was also a daily matter. The inevitable police informant could therefore report the main lecture at the International *Einheitsverband* Congress of 1931 in the following terms: "It was proclaimed that now is Capitalism's winter of discontent, but that it will stop at nothing to assert itself... that there is only one solitary country without unemployment, and that this is the Soviet Union. Advance in Russia is allegedly enormous. Production levels are three times greater than they were before the war, and within one year, all sectors will have fulfilled the five-year plan. In Russia, they allegedly have a 28-hour week, and instead of wage cuts they are given rises of between 30 and 35%. It was rhetorically asked why this was not the case in Germany and stated that this was for want of a man of Stalin's ilk. It was ventured that he was perhaps there among the audience, waiting only to be discovered. Wages for seamen were 'the best in the world'; there is 'a 30% bonus for tropical voyages' and a '60% percent bonus for polar voyages,' whilst 'in other countries seamen's wages are being cut.'"[95]

Even a dyed-in-the-wool Stalinist unfortunate enough to live in the Soviet Union of the day would have either laughed under his cape to hear such fun or else silently shaken his head.

The reality of those years, in which famine swept the land, was so horrific that it could only be publicly discussed after the introduction of *glasnost* sixty years later.

After Joseph Stalin had silenced the internal Party opposition, the NEP, won by the farmers as a compromise, was discarded, and a course was steered for the forcible state appropriation of all resources, which also entailed the forced collectivization of all rural workers. Now that there was no effective civil army opposition to fear, resistance by the farmers was brutally beaten down. Hundreds of thousands of farmers were sent with their families to Siberia. Those remaining responded by subsistence farming, harvesting only enough for their own requirements. The leadership, obliged to find food for city dwellers, sent requisitioners to collect every last grain. The ensuing famine cost millions their lives. The situation differed from the critical scenario of the early 'twenties in that this time the Soviet Union did not apply to the outside world for aid, but instead closed its borders and suppressed all information about the famine. To prevent the starving farmers from entering the cities *en masse*, the state had rural areas cordoned off, and forbade rail transport of all people without express secret police permission. Cynicism in the Party leadership was so extreme that at the culmination of the famine, in 1932, it had grain exported. That forcible collectivization was represented as a success was, at least from the standpoint of the Kremlin, not an entirely falsification; the transformation of the farmers into a mass of serfs slaving on state land without material advantage was the prerequisite required to win resources for industrialization. In the 'thirties there really was rapid progress in industrial production which put the production crisis in the West in a very poor light. World-class intellectuals, such as Romain Rolland and Lion Feuchtwanger, reported ecstatically on the new factories they visited on trips to the Soviet Union.

It was, however, not so easy to conceal the truth from simple seamen, who were neither given accommodation in luxury hotels nor courted day and night. This was the source of some trouble to the ISH.

One of the last reports sent by the Hamburg ISH leadership before Hitler's accession to power mentions such problems: "Of late we have heard many complaints from club activists who have come into contact with seamen that have weighed anchor off the Soviet Union, particularly German seafarers who have returned from the Black Sea coast. They claim it is very hard to reason with them because the sailors recount stories of how various people came on board and offered twenty rubles or more for a pair of torn trousers, etc.

The sailors also told that the Interclubs show them new factories and homes for children, that they organized amusements for them and such, but that they conceal the difficulties that Soviet proletarians are confronted with. We are of the opinion that class traitors secretly board ships and conduct business with foreign seamen, and request that the responsible bodies prevent the continuation of these practices. Also we request that the Sovietclubs inform foreign sailors about the difficulties encountered by comrades there."[96]

As chance would have it, Krebs and his crew were bound for Murmansk on the Kola Peninsula beyond the Arctic Circle. The wealth of raw materials there, and the fact that this was the sole ice-free harbor of the Soviet Union, had made the region into a common destinations for farmers sentenced to forced labor.

The unwitting Bremen Communists were deeply shocked. Although they were hospitably received, and, inasmuch as this was possible in this town under construction, well lodged, they could not avoid encountering scenes such as Krebs was later to recall in *Out of the Night*: "The only modern stone buildings in the town were the bank and the house of the GPU. In most of the log houses, every room was occupied by a family, often by two. Single workers were quartered at the rate of five to eight men and women in a room. The constant arrival of new hordes of toilers resulted in the overcrowding of the newly constructed log houses before plumbing, lights or even partitions could be installed. I saw families of five housed in rooms which contained no furniture beyond a huge pile of rags, a packing case and a few nails in the wall, - and the inevitable colour print of Stalin…

The whole population worked in three shifts, and under the gloomy midnight sun work progressed as in broad daylight… We stopped to watch a group of elderly women doing this labour. Their coats and skirts were old and ragged, their boots were cracked open at the seams, and the mud ran out of them. Their faces looked emaciated. Each time they struck their picks into the stubborn earth, they emitted long-drawn grunts."

Jan Valtin claimed that only his fanatical belief that the industrialization of the Soviet Union was essential to our victory in the whole world sustained him.

A manner of dealing with such circumstance prevalent among German Communists of the day was to resolve to do things differently and, needless to say, better themselves. In *Out of the Night*, Krebs had his ship engineer, who was complaining about the terrible lack of maintenance work on Russian ships, exclaim: "'Wait till we have a Soviet Germany, — then we'll show the Muscovites what efficiency in Socialism is.'"

Krebs was not prey to doubt, or, at least, he showed none. After a train journey through Karelia he remained several weeks in Leningrad. There, according to his confession to the CIC, he attended an ISH course for "general union work." During this time he also worked at the Interclub.

On August 11 the manager of the German Interclub division wrote to Hamburg, saying that she was in urgent need of a German worker:

"I already explained in my last letter why this is so urgent, and Comrade Richard Krebs will be able to furnish you with more details. I tried to keep Comrade Krebs here with me, but the Profintern decided that only the Hamburg administration can determine whether he should return."[97]

Comrade Krebs' report to Hamburg on the Leningrad Interclub can still be found among the files of the Leningrad Interclub. Of the many that he must have written whilst working for the Comintern, it is the only one still available.

"The organization of Club work is subdivided among the different sections. Each section makes a monthly work schedule. The lack of cooperation between the sections is conspicuous, as is the lack of interplay between the sections and Club management. There is no trace of communal work, no trace of executive instructions, no trace of supervision of the work as a whole...

Some examples: the sailors of the steamship Ida Blumenthal report that the captain has applied to have them prosecuted... because they took part one Sunday in an Interclub excursion without his permission. The sailors' names are to be entered in the ship's log and they are to be dismissed on arrival in Hollentau. What is to be done? – Great discussion. I proposed that a telegram be sent to the Bremen harbor employment office protesting against the dismissal of the Blumenthal sailors, that the Bremen stevedores be informed, so that the harbor workers boycott the ship. The answer... that I received was a passive 'the secretary won't do anything.'

And, again; there is a meeting of seamen. Simultaneously the band downstairs are playing dance music. Result? The seamen go dancing and the meeting is a failure... Another example: a drunken sailor sways through the Club, barging into other visitors as he goes. Instead of simply being put outside, he is wrestled to the entrance and held until the police, attracted by the janitor's whistle, come and arrest him. Foreign sailors come, see the scene, and leave quickly.

Young Russian activists who specialise in languages do the best Club work. In reply to my questions I repeatedly received the reply 'The work is alright, but it is not organized.' I also heard the words 'We are the opposition to the Club management.' I asked if this was an official position was told 'No, secret.' The whole Club management seems weak to me. Strict and coherent organization is missing, as are rigid checks. The German section must absolutely be manned by better staff, who can assert themselves without yielding, or humbly accepting whatever they find on arrival."[98]

The Strike

In spite of the wishes of the overworked comrade in Leningrad, Krebs did not return to manage the German section of the Club. He was not, however, sent back to

Bremen but instead appointed manager of the Hamburg Interclub, part of the worldwide ISH network and, with its Leningrad counterpart, the most important of all Clubs. A man of his capabilities was urgently needed as an agitator in the largest German harbor, because the ISH was preparing a worldwide strike of German seamen. This was due to take place at the end of September 1931, to coincide with the end of the tariff agreement.

The origins of the planned strike lay in the disastrous state of German shipping. More than a third of the German merchant fleet was at anchor. In Hamburg alone, there were more than eight thousand unemployed seamen. The shipping companies had decided to make radical cuts to the pay of those still in employment. On September 12 they made their demands known: wage cuts of thirty to sixty percent, abolition of the three watchmen system, increase of shift duration to ten, twelve and even fourteen hours, overtime to be unpaid and holiday abolished.

Arbitration was in the offing, but it was clear to all concerned that any compromise reached would still include wage cuts, as the Social Democrat union, official partner in the tariff agreement with the shipping companies, considered a strike a hopeless proposition in the light of such unemployment. The situation was further aggravated by the enmity between the two seamen's unions. To the *Einheitsverband* the Social Democrats' representatives were 'lackeys to capital,' whilst the Social Democrat union dubbed their Communist opponents 'Moscow's mercenaries.' It was therefore unsurprising that the Social Democrat union offered the *Einheitsverband* no information on negotiations, and thereby seriously incapacitated their plan making.

The Communist *Einheitsverband* had firmly decided to strike. Preparations had commenced in May. The man behind the scenes, Bem aka Adolf, kept Moscow informed every step of the way. Before it had started, he wrote: "This strike is to be conducted with the most radical means. It is not just a matter of wages, but of creating a general revolutionary consciousness among the workers and mobilizing them for the KPD."[99]

What a successful strike might have led to was expressed many years later by a veteran of the movement, Erich Krewet, who had played a leading role at the time in the Communist harbor organization: "If the street car drivers strike, people go to work on foot. If train drivers strike, things get a little more complicated. Other transport systems can't cover the distances and take care of the freight so easily. A strike by seamen in a land dependent on import and export, now that can bring a government to its knees, destroy a state even."[100]

From September 10-12 there was a final conference of delegates from all German harbors in the Hamburg Interclub. Adolf reported its decisions to Moscow:

"The matter of strike tactics: unlike past struggles of sea workers we (Comrade Walter and I) do not propose the slogan *Seamen, leave your ships!* but instead *Onboard strike!* This is a sharp turn-about in practice. We will use this slogan … to ensure that all the crew participates in the strike, and to avoid that a few Communists or Einheitverband members leave the ships at some harbor or other and thus rid the ships of Communist elements…

This solution is preferable to that of *leave your ships* in that it not only takes the matter of strikebreaking into account, but also immediately places the strike in a very serious light. It was clear to us from the onset that the police would be employed in its entirety to take the strikers from the ships. This would demonstrate to the masses that the police is no neutral authority but rather the henchman of the bourgeois ruling class.

The second innovation of this strike was the slogan *Strike on all German ships in capitalist harbors*. We wanted the strike to be held on all German ships and for the ships in foreign harbors no other slogan but O*nboard strike* would do. Leaving the ship can be construed as desertion."

At this juncture Adolf touches on a very sensitive matter for the Soviet government:

"In this context we earnestly considered the matter of whether German seamen at anchor in a Soviet port should also participate in the strike. All parties approved of the ISH's proposition that the slogan should read *Strike in all capitalist harbors*. Our argument was justified by the fact... that the strike in Soviet ports, if well organized, could last for some considerable time, and lead to diplomatic complications. Furthermore, it was a political question, because it was repeatedly emphasized at the time that the progress of the five-year plan was not to be jeopardized."[101]

From Adolf's point of view, the conditions for a strike were fairly propitious despite the high level of unemployment. The *Einheitsverband* really did have at least one representative among the crew of almost every ship, and some crews consisted entirely of its members. Its chances were reinforced by the general outrage due to the loss of wages that was shared by unionized and non-unionized workers alike.

In spite of all of this the strike was a fiasco. On the one hand were the 'reformists' from the Social Democrat union. Although they were not keen to be revealed as 'capitalist stooges,' they tried to prevent a strike that they considered hopeless. Immediately after the conference of September 13, the International Seamen's Club was attacked by the *Reichsbanner* (or Imperial Banner), the Social Democrats paramilitary arm. Whether this was a revenge attack— according to the *Reichsbanner* five of its foreign members had been wounded by shots coming from inside the Hamburg Interclub whilst on their way to a regional meeting, — or whether the attack, as Adolf reported to Moscow, was a consequence of the ongoing conference, can no longer be ascertained. An SPD paper inevitably reported the matter with the headline 'Bestial Bloodlust of Inner City Communists.'

The other factor was the fact that the local KPD administration was not prepared to support the strike. There was a panoply of reasons for this, some personal; Hermann Schubert, the Hamburg Party boss and Adolf "couldn't stand the sight of one other."[102]

The main reason, though, was that the KPD were sick of having no executive power; they had no control over the Interclub, no power over the *Einheitsverband* and no influence on the ISH. Any decision made by Adolf may have been given all due consideration, since he had Moscow backing, but, if his reports to HQ are to be given any credence, they were then to be sabotaged with all due haste.

All these factors were to run their course. The decisive one proved different. On October 1 the well-organized Danzig harbor workers union' initiated the strike by downing tools. Here Adolf's Polish contacts played a role. On the same day a ship's crew in Bremen went on strike. The next day, the day that arbitrators announced a wage cut of 13.6 percent, the strike proper began. By October 3 there were already eight inactive ships in the port of Hamburg. The strikebreaker counter force was, however, not always successful, and, worse still, it proved impossible to mobilize all harbor workers — indeed, some worked on picketed ships. A mass meeting on the next day revealed the reason why.

At the beginning all went well. Some two thousand seamen and harbor workers were present. The actual strike puppeteer, apparently dissatisfied with the speeches of Albert Walter and Hemann Schubert, "felt obliged to make a speech disguised as a Polish seaman" so as to clarify a few points, to wit: "Violence must be countered with violence." At the end of the meeting the attendees "decided unanimously to down tools and lay low the harbor." However, after the meeting had ended the "matter of the Stevedore Brigade was raised, as it had been at numerous meetings prior to the strike… The next day it proved impossible to suppress all activity in any one harbor workforce."[103]

Worse still, harbor workers continued to load and stoke picketed ships. On the afternoon of the same day events took place that caused Adolf "great consternation": as the harbor workers were leaving their workplaces and meetings were about to be held, six hundred women and harbor workers, incited by the reformists and the Nazis, gathered on the piers from which the skiffs were supposed to ferry Stevedore Brigade workers to work. From this position they then forcibly prevented the latter from departing for work."[104]

The Stevedore Brigade, one of the largest harbor workforces, was under Soviet control. It was responsible for the embarking and disembarking of Soviet and Soviet-chartered ships. For this reason, or, rather, because of the five-year plan, the Brigade had been exempted from the mandatory strike.

"The decisive factor though, the one that really made the Stevedore Brigade hated, was the fact that the Soviet's hiring methods were as bad, if not worse, than those of the capitalists."[105]

Harbor work was a spasmodic affair. If a ship came, dozens of workers were required. These then worked round the clock in several shifts. In bad times though, there were by no means enough ships to employ all the workers. This was exacerbated by a selection system that employed the best, strongest workers on a semi-permanent basis whilst leaving the rest without any form of employment. The abolition of this unfair system, and its replacement with a numbers system, was an age-old trade union demand that the very stevedore employer in Party hands refused to meet. Finally, and this was the straw too many, the greater share of work was given to Party members. To a certain extent, Stevedore Brigade practice was justifiable, since the other workforce employers excluded those employed by the Brigade. And, presumably, this was taken in part by the Brigade's management, since Soviet ships had a tendency to contain cargo better left unmentioned in public.

"The forgoing shows that stevedore brigade workers are entirely isolated from the rest of the workforce... and that there is a general resentment, among harbor workers in capitalist employ, of the Party, the *Einheitsverband* and, consequentially, of the Soviet Union... This hatred of the Stevedore Brigade led to a group of incited worker saying straight out: 'You wanted this strike. Now let's see you strike.' This challenge needs some explanation. All leading comrades of the *Einheitsverband* work for the Stevedore Brigade, and at least ninety-five percent of all harbor workers employed as stevedores are members of the *Einheitsverband*."[106]

On October 6, that is to say nearly a week after the beginning of the strike, Adolf traveled to Berlin to participate in a meeting of the West European Bureau (WEB), the highest Comintern policymaker outside the Soviet Union.

On his return the strike was almost broken. Hermann Schubert was sick of this foolishness and had pressurized Albert Walter to such an extent that Walter was composing a flyer announcing the strike's end. According to Adolf's letter to Moscow, Schubert had received a message from the cell meeting of Hamburg's central bar owners "expressing the opinion that the harbor workers' strike is only viable if Soviet ships are also included in the strike, (this is, in my opinion, the crucial factor according to bar owners)... [also,] bar owners complained that they can no longer pay for the heating, lighting, etc. of their premises without recompense, that the unemployed (and of course the strikers) do not consume anything, and that their ability to make sacrifices has its limits."[107]

The already fraught situation was then exacerbated by a piece of news that would have tied Adolf's hands even if he had wanted to end the strike: German ships were being picketed in the USSR. Why and how this came about in contravention of all previous decisions and even despite official ISH tactics is unclear. Perhaps it had been decided at the West European Bureau's meeting and agreed by Moscow's elite, perhaps it related to some solitary decision that had been taken by HQ. Whether Adolf had been given prior information on the strike cannot be ascertained from his extensive report. The relevant section of the report reads: "I was very surprised [that the strike in Hamburg was to be stopped] as the mainstream press carried the story on the 9th and in the morning editions of the 10th that German seamen in Soviet harbors had joined in"[108]. It seems as if Adolf had been obliged to simply grin and bear it.

The words 'joined in' were in fact little more than a euphemism for the way that the 'strike' was conducted in Soviet harbors. Even if the horror stories of the press are not to be taken at face value, internal ISH documents confirm that the strike order was carried out in characteristic style by the Soviet state. The minority that did not want to strike were forced, and captains who tried to sail without their crews were held at anchor. For the majority, the willing strikers, the stay in the Soviet Union was, at least initially, a very enjoyable time. They were well provided for, and the very linguists that Richard Krebs has met in August as activists and 'secret opposition to Club management' kept them in ideological company and good spirits.

The German strikers, having a good time in the Interclub, must have presented an astonishing spectacle to Leningrad's harbor workers. The consequences of 'sabotaging the five-year plan' was well known since the mid-twenties, when stevedores responsible for stowing wood had dared to strike and found themselves and their families banished to the far ends of the Soviet Union within twenty-four hours.[109]

Once the news of the strike had spread through Soviet harbors, it inevitably reached Germany. Adolf and Schubert argued bitterly (Adolf reported to Moscow: "He spoke to me in a tone in which no one had ever spoken to me before," [110]) but finally Schubert had to relent.

Although Krebs was already Interclub manager at the time and a member of the *Einheitsverband*'s national management, he was not yet so close to ISH inner circles that he would have been aware of all the background circumstances of the strike. He was entirely occupied with visiting ships new to the harbor and, as one of his men, Ede Nikolajczik,[111] later recalled, coordinating the daily work of Einheitverband activists. Of all those involved in directing the strike, according to Adolf's report, Krebs was the one who spent the longest on the ships and best understood the atmosphere on board. In his report to Adolf, Krebs maintained that the atmosphere was very good and that the majority of the seamen were in favor Fof the strike. The final ruling of the arbitrators had been draconian. Not only was seamen's pay cut by more than ten percent, watch duration was increased and holiday was abolished.

On 12 October the strike was broken at the top. Eighty men were arrested at an Interclub meeting including Richard Krebs and the entire leadership of the *Einheitsverband*. Adolf himself barely escaped.

He was obliged to concede that the strike could not be continued, dictated three resolutions, and, because he could not appear in public himself, had them read at a striker's meeting. This same public had applauded a decision to escalate to terror activities because of police brutality. "Comrade Deter succeeded in concluding his speech and asserting himself in the face of the prevalent mood and the catcalls by making indirect accusations of provocation... In my opinion all present understood perfectly why they were being read this resolution on the acceptance of negotiations. It was my duty to give German sailors in the Soviet Union the opportunity to break off the strike in the midst of the bourgeois press' hate campaign against the Soviet Union."[112]

The Soviet authorities interpreted this resolution several days later according to their own agenda. The edict for the strikers was to now return to their ships immediately and without further negotiations. This was regardless of the fact that after their pleasant stay at the Interclub, the seamen would face charges of mutiny at the other end — strike in a foreign port being thus considered under German naval code — and it also ignored the matter of prosecution for desertion, a charge which the seamen had opened themselves to by having left their ships. Due to the fear of incarceration, a number of seamen — in ISH documents the total is given as thirty — refused to return to Germany. To avoid an even greater scandal, these were granted permission to stay in the Soviet Union. Given the riotous temperament of these men it is unsurprising that a good proportion of them later ended in one or other of the Soviet camps. Of those who survived forced labor, some were sent back to Germany and into the arms of the Gestapo under the Hitler-Stalin Pact.[113]

The strike, insignificant in terms of success and quickly abandoned, developed into a spectacle due to the events in the Soviet Union that finally led to a diplomatic crisis.

According to the Commercial Treaty of 1923, the Soviet Union was not only debarred from supporting strikers at Soviet anchor, but should even have protected strikebreakers in their work. Captains were of course aware of this. When reproached by them, the Soviet authorities disingenuously recommended that queries be addressed to strike management.[114]

To the uninitiated, like the German General Consul in Leningrad, the whole matter was an enigma. It was particularly confusing that after all its leaders had been arrested, and the strike had been all but broken, strikers persisted in striking.

In retrospect, it is astonishing that the role of Adolf in all of this remained concealed from his contemporaries. On the face of it, the strike's organizers and leaders were ISH general secretary Albert Walter and those comrades in charge of the *Einheitsverband*. Soviet authorities exploited this fact to contain diplomatic damage. A German Communist, presumably Hermann Knüfken, was sent to the German Consul in Leningrad to persuade him that those responsible for the strike were among the leadership of the *Einheitsverband*, "intent on justifying their very existence as wage-drawing functionaries and proving their revolutionary courage — albeit at the expense of others... The Profintern consented to the strike in the belief that on German ships a large strike movement was in the offing."[115]

In fact, no German Communist had had anything to do with the decision. Clearly no one in Germany was even abreast of developments, otherwise no decision would have been taken to break off the strike in Hamburg when industrial action was taking place in Leningrad.

It is possible that Adolf Schelley was at least indirectly responsible, possible that he gave false information on the course of the strike at the meeting of the West European Bureau. Even if this was the case, however, he was certainly not aware, as he arrived in Hamburg, of a decision that could only have been made in Moscow.

Probably the decision to strike came from Soviet authorities, for whom the possibility of a German Revolution and ensuing self-assertive socialist Germany represented the only hope of externally counteracting Stalin's growing power.

The analysis of the German General Consul in Leningrad hints as much; on October 27 he wrote the following to Berlin: "One wonders why the strike directorate let the strike continue after the 11th and 12th of October although, after its end in Germany,* it was entirely pointless. There is only one plausible explanation; the leadership was desperately hoping for a positive outcome from the then-current political crisis in Germany. Apparently, a successful end to the strike was dependent on the fall of the cabinet deepening the political and economic crisis in Germany. The announcement that the Brüning cabinet had survived was reported to the General Consul by a Communist journalist on the evening of the 16th of October simultaneously with the news that the strike was to end on the 17th at noon. Under the circumstances, it is reasonable to suppose that this was no coincidence, but that the survival of the cabinet represented the end of all hopes for the strike's pupeteers."[116]

---

* Officially the strike was not over, but in real terms it had been discontinued.

It was clear to Adolf that the strike had been a disaster, not only because of its failure but, moreover, because draconian Soviet intervention in Leningrad had caused the Communists great loss of face.

He refrained from criticizing the way in which sailors had 'gone on strike' in Leningrad, and only mentioned that in the Hamburg Interclub he had heard that a crew had been forced to strike although only two of its members were in favor. However, he criticized much more severely the fact that the strikers had been forced back on board without even having been given the chance to negotiate for prosecution immunity.

A hardboiled functionary, cynical from long practice, might have been able to resign himself to the strike in the USSR as an 'error of judgment' because of the public relations damage involved. For Richard Krebs, however, still quite 'green' and having sincerely engaged in the strike, the Soviet episode must have been a severe test of faith. *Out of the Night* only depicted the events in Leningrad. Here Krebs made Valtin a strike leader who personally experienced all of that which was later recounted in the Hamburg Interclub. Krebs, in reality, was by no means so far advanced; neither was he a top functionary who suffered such disillusionment, nor was he privy to what happened behind the scenes. With his beloved, who had followed him from Bremen, he was earnestly going about work for the Hamburg Interclub.

The Hamburg Interclub

According to the address register, Hermine Stöver and Richard Krebs lived as subtenants of a certain Wieke in Jacobstraße 32b until they found their own apartment.

Both worked for the Hamburg Interclub. Richard Krebs, responsible for propaganda, was also charged with managing events, coordinating the various language sections and such mundane activities as ensuring that the bar was shipshape. Hermine Stöver designed placards and took charge of the cultural side of Club work. They were presumably under as intensive scrutiny as they had been in Bremen. The pertinent files, however, were incinerated in World War II, so that no detailed description of events is available. All that remains are several placards and flyers, drawn in Hermine Stöver's characteristic style.

The International Seamen's Club was situated in the lower floors of a four storey building on Roothesoodstraße in the Hamburg harbor quarter. Albert Walter had bought it in 1924 and located the predecessor of the Interclub, the International Port Bureau in it. In 1928 a large loan had been taken in the name of the Stevedore Brigade for renovation of the building. These renovations had included the construction of a back door entrance that led directly to the official (or nominal) head quarters of the ISH, the International of seamen and harbor workers.[117]

These premises contained not only the offices of general secretary Albert Walter, but also the office of the International Negro Bureau representative, who found it convenient to maintain worldwide communications from Hamburg, the offices of the Japanese and Chinese ISH sections, who operated from there for similar reasons, and a 'Scandinavian Bureau' with two departments. Richard Krebs worked in close cooperation with one of these departments, the one responsible for union work. The second department was cordoned off and, according to Krebs' statement to the CIC, was charged with secret coordination work involving the Far East. In total, eight to ten people worked in the ISH office complex. Adolf, who composed all reports to Moscow and, as was the way during the strike, was responsible for all final decision making in conjunction with Moscow, was accommodated in a secret office located elsewhere. Communication between this office and Rothesoodstraße was maintained by courier.

For the ISH, as for its predecessor IPC-Transport, the Hamburg harbor was of enormous importance. For the OMS, the communication and information services of the Comintern, the Hamburg harbor was a node of communication that was of a significance comparable to Leningrad. The crucial role that Hamburg played in the worldwide Communist movement was a result of international seafaring conditions.

In 1932 a third of all shipping tonnage was British and a fifth American. Neither of these maintained diplomatic relations with the Soviet Union. With the exception of certain splinter groups, there was no trade union in either of these countries under Communist influence. The three largest merchant marine fleets after these Anglo-Saxons were Germany, Norway and Japan, each of which had some six percent of world shipping tonage.[118] The Soviet Union did not at the time have a sufficiently large fleet to cater for its own import and export needs. The majority of cargo destined for Russia's most important harbor, Leningrad, was therefore transported to Hamburg, loaded by the stevedore brigade on to chartered ships, and thence shipped to the Soviet Union by Baltic vessels via the Kaiser Wilhelm Canal.

The Comintern's communications service were reluctant to use Soviet ships because of the potential diplomatic implications should OMS freight be discovered onboard. Japanese ships were excluded, as their nationalistic government was hostile to the Soviet Union. The only large fleets that came into question for such purposes were the German and the Norwegian ones. Both of these were of great importance to the communications service from its very beginning, as can be seen in the memoirs of the German revolutionary Hermann Knüfken. Knüfken, working from Leningrad after having been expelled from Germany in 1923, had been instrumental in the construction of their network system. The Norwegian fleet was perhaps even more significant in it than the German one, as the crews could scarcely be kept under the control of their homeports. Norway, with a population only slightly greater than Hamburg, had by no means sufficient freight to guarantee its sailors a frequent return home. It is likely that in an average month more Norwegian ships anchored in Hamburg in one month than in all of Norway's harbors put together. This is why both parts of the Scandinavian Bureau were not located in a Norwegian port but in Hamburg. Hermann Knüfken belonged to the management of that "special" Scandinavian bureau mentioned by Krebs. He had returned from Leningrad with his Russian wife in late 1931. His function in the special bureau presumably resembled the one assigned to him in Rotterdam during 1934. There he was familiar with all ships "on which illegals came from Leningrad. These were not exclusively Party members, but also people in high positions in the USSR's information service (military espionage)."[119] From this, the conclusion can be drawn that he was personally responsible for the reception and further transport of such people.

Knüfken, the "Comrade Pirate," was still to play an important role in Krebs' life. His arrival in Hamburg probably astonished not only the manager of the Interclub but all middle functionaries, as he was widely presumed dead. In 1929 he had been arrested on charges of embezzling the foreign trade union membership contributions which he had been collecting at the Leningrad Interclub. Among the Comintern's archives there are indeed letters from Scandinavia inquiring as to the whereabouts of the funds that Knüfken had collected.[120] In fact, although such matters were unknown to a lowly functionary like Krebs, the GPU, or Soviet intelligence agency, had prevented Knüfken from transferring the funds to discredit the man who was a legend on the waterfront. The involvement of the secret police makes it all the more astonishing that he was released after only nine months and allowed to leave the country in the company of his wife after another six.

After the Hamburg senate had freed him — following his seventh hunger strike — on condition that he forever leave the country, Hermann Knüfken had sailed for the Soviet Union. There he had received a hero's welcome, settled in Leningrad, been employed by IPC-Transport and established the local Interclub. With the backing of the communication and intelligence services, he had succeeded in turning the Club into his own personal lair, and one which he kept free of malicious propaganda and agitation (or "blood-stirring" as he calls it in his memoirs). Beside this work he was employed by the Comintern in a capacity which he only hints at in his memoirs. Franz Jung, the novelist and delegate who had traveled to the Second Comintern Congress with Knüfken aboard the hijacked fishing trawler, mentions in his memoirs that Knüfken had set up shop in Berlin during the late 'twenties. At the time he was a Comintern courier to Indonesia. We also know from his own memoirs that for a shorter time in Holland during 1926 he worked for the Rotterdam Interclub.[121]

His relations to various representatives of foreign powers were a much more sensitive affair, leading finally to the pretext for his arrest, as he was later to write in his memoirs. He avoids precisely explaining what his role was in these matters, only stating that these were always at the instigation of the 'right' authorities and always beknown to the GPU. We can only presume that Knüfken renewed the contacts to the British Naval Intelligence Service that he had formed during World War I. This is partially corroborated by the fact that, after breaking with the Comintern in the mid-thirties, he resumed work for the British.

From 1927 onwards Knüfken's position grew harder to maintain. The wild 'twenties were ebbing away, and the GPU were ever more reluctant to suffer Knüfken's autonomy. The man who, without further ado, had thrown Soviet secret policemen from the Interclub was now unable to prevent an informant follow his movements. He was nonetheless incapable of missing the opportunity to provoke the GPU, particularly its border guard and so, commandeering a boat that the Kaiser had once given to the Czar, he collected foreign sailors from their ships, brought them directly to the Interclub without passing through customs, and thus helped them smuggle valuable goods. For Knüfken, at heart still a sailor, this was nothing other than an act of solidarity, since the ruble was still extremely high, and the seamen had no other way of paying for women.

It was by quite different means that he garnered the hatred of the secret police. Comintern agents were repeatedly sent to him so that he might have them stowed away on board foreign freight vessels. These were predominantly Danish, Norwegian or Dutch ships. Only the men in Knüfken's confidence knew of the agent's preserve aboard, and the agents themselves were so well concealed that the secret police did not find them during border controls.

Knüfken was issued with special visas for these men, which he received via the GPU's courier service from secret police headquarters in Moscow. Once the Comintern agent had departed the waters under Soviet sovereignty, Knüfken would give the visas to whoever was running the border checkpoint.

The latter body, proud that no one ever departed from the port without its knowledge, always took the papers resentfully and forwarded them to Moscow, whence a punishment would ensue for this want of vigilance. Knüfken writes that in Moscow they laughed about this turn of events, but in Leningrad checkpoint command was naturally less than pleased. Officially they were not in a position to do anything about the matter, as the travel documents had been issued by a higher authority, but unofficially they were on the look-out for something that they could pin on Knüfken.

The story is enlightening in various ways: it illustrates to what extent the OMS was a secret operation, shows also the "Comrade Pirate" in a characteristic light as a man who rejoiced in the perpetual embarrassment of his opponents at the checkpoint — something that he might easily have prevented had he addressed the matter.

By 1929, the Leningrad GPU had collected enough material to put an end to the autonomy of the Interclub, whose 'extraterritorial' aspect was by then being availed of by Party-internal opposition. Knüfken was arrested.

The arrest was officially justified with charges of embezzlement. Internally the GPU claimed that Knüfken had entered into contact with foreign powers, and so forestalled the intervention of the Comintern. Its leadership was incapable of any action in the face of such charges, having no counter intelligence apparatus, and was entirely reliant on the GPU in such matters. Any one intervening on his behalf would automatically open themselves to a charge of spying. After several months imprisonment in Leningrad he was sent to Lubjanka's Vnutrenaya Tyurma, a special internal prison within the GPU's headquarters that held only prisoners on treason charges. The section of his memoirs that deals with this period is perhaps the only report on the dealings of this part of Lubjanka, and Knüfken one of the very few to have left it alive.

After ten months he was again at liberty. In late 1931 the General Consulate in Leningrad issued him a passport, and from 1932 he was in Hamburg again. How his fate came to take such an extraordinary turn is not recounted in the memoirs. The section on this period is formulated with the utmost care. Although they were written during the same period they differ from the sections prior to them by being written in English rather than German.[122] Knüfken claimed that he had to be very cautious to not furnish the Soviet secret police any information about himself. Anything that might betray his identity might have had consequences for people in Russia with whom he had had been in contact and who were still dear to him. He can scarcely have been referring to members of the Party-internal opposition with this comment, of whom in any case precious few had survived the purges, but was possibly alluding to the relatives of his wife. The hand written corrections of some Russsian expressions included in his manuscript were probably hers. This is likely to have also been the reason for why the manuscript was given to the Swedish director Staffan Lamm in 1987 under the condition that nothing was to be published without the express permission of Sonia Knüfken.

Knüfken describes the circumstances of his arrest in the German part of the manuscript in the following terms. The GPU had been trying to implicate him in a currency affair. He had traveled to Moscow in an attempt to try to gain the support of senior Comintern authorities and had spoken with everyone in an influential position. The leaders of the Red Union International were obviously terrified of the potential consequences. The situation in the Comintern was better: Abramov, leader of the OMS, talked to Bukharin and arranged a meeting with representatives of the secret police. Here the text stops abruptly. A few days later Knüfken was arrested. The events after his arrest belong to the section written in German.

Knüfken's arrest triggered severe protest among foreign seamen and ended in demonstrations in Leningrad that probably contributed to his release, but this hardly explains how a man initiated in highly secret matters was subsequently permitted to leave the country.

In this matter, the autobiographical description of the 'Captain Kidd of the Comintern' is of service. It is also confirmed in its essence by contemporaries such as Richard Krebs and Franz Jung. Knüfken was a man whose thinking was beyond that of any secret policeman. These were trained to spot ideological deviance, keen to urge their victims to think of Party allegiance, to freely confess to failings and waysidefallings and thereby furnish the rope with which they would be hanged. Knüfken was a man of action, an adventurer who had no time for ideological subtleties. His whole being was that of a rebel who never forgot his roots.

This is all too clear in his reaction to the strike of the Leningrad wood-stowing stevedores. According to his memoirs, he heard about the affair whilst in Holland, and, thanks to the fact that he had never had anything to do with Dutch Communists, he was in a position to pass a resolution demanding that the Russian authorities respect the rights of these workers. Such behavior speaks of an absolute fearlessness and a profound insight into the living and working conditions of the Russian population. Most other foreign Communists imperiously disregarded this issue, as if conditions that would have revolted them in their own land were fitting and appropriate in Russia and the Russian proletariat of negligible significance compared to its western counterpart.

It was precisely because Knüfken was entirely free of illusion with regard to the Soviet Union that he took no part in the incessant internal Party disputes that blighted the 'twenties. As a supporter of democracy within the Party, the representatives of the internal opposition — all of whom he knew personally — were no better to him than was Stalin himself. He wrote that this remained a mystery to his interrogators in Lubjanka. Probably it was this 'unpolitical' stance that saved him, convinced the secret police that they should release a man who had helped create the OMS and facilitate his employment in western Europe. If the assumptions of the historian Dieter Nelles are correct, and it really was Knüfken who tried to persuade the Leningrad General Consul that the leaders of the *Einheitsverband* were responsible for the seamen's strike, then he must have resumed contact with the representatives of foreign powers that he had been accused of colluding with whilst still in Lubjanka. These contacts, which the GPU must have been aware of, would also explain why German authorities permitted his return to Germany after the piratical act of hijacking the *Senator Schröder*.

The communications apparatus of the Hamburg Comintern was carefully concealed. So carefully that, at least to Richard Krebs' knowledge, the Gestapo had still not got wind of it in 1937.[123] Krebs himself had grown familiar with its most important participants during the strike. Whilst the strike was still ongoing, it was indicated to him which ships were not to be incapacitated so as to prevent the authorities ascertaining that there were Communists onboard. The communication network was more important than the strike. This was shown in the case of the *Partia*, a ship that was entirely manned by Communists and which Krebs and his men involved in the strike. Krebs was later to be severely reprimanded for the affair.

To avoid such communication breakdowns, Krebs was informed on the arrival of a new freighter whether it was to get the treatment or not. All seamen that worked in the communication branch were to be left well alone. Hugo Marx was responsible for the communication apparatus, and it was he that advised Krebs on how ships were to be handled. In Krebs' statement to the CIC many years later, he described Marx as a very calm and cold man who never gave a speech or spoke in a normal tone. All his utterances were made one on one and in a conspiratory whisper. In Marx's apparatus the seamen were always well dressed and seemed prosperous.

There is one point of contact between Krebs and the Comintern's communication apparatus as yet unmentioned. As manager of the Interclub and coordinator for propaganda work, he had dealings with dozens of seamen agitators of all nationalities on a daily basis. For this reason he was repeatedly asked to propose the names of dependable seamen at large. Should such seamen no longer attend the Communist meetings of the Interclub, but instead only came to the 'unpolitical' events, then it was clear to him that they were now in the employ of the apparatus.

Enter Wollweber

The longer that Richard Krebs remained manager of the Interclub, the greater the tasks he was entrusted with. Alongside the supervision of propaganda work and the organization of events, he was also expected to look after funds. He had hit upon a particularly cynical idea for improving the financial situation. Every time a Soviet ship arrived at port, Krebs invited the crew to visit the Interclub and gave a short speech to them about Communist victory and how Soviet seamen led much better lives than their western counterparts. The leader of the Party cell on board would already have agreed to publicly make a large donation — which was to be secretly reimbursed. His subordinates would find that they had no option but to follow suit. Given the high value of the ruble this process generated a considerable sum, and over the course of time attracted the attention of the *Einheitsverband*'s treasurer. Under the pretext of checking accounts, he attempted to 'privatize' these funds. With the backing of Albert Walters, Krebs easily managed to have the man ejected from the Interclub.[124]

This incident was part of a broader conflict between the leadership of the *Einheitsverband* and the ISH. Just as the *Einheitsverband* was founded under the supervision of a man in Soviet confidence, Adolf, without any reference to the German Party leadership, so after the strike fiasco German Party leadership succeeded in removing Adolf's man, Comrade Koschnick, from the top *Einheitsverband* job and replacing him with a man of their choosing.

This man was Ernst Wollweber, later to run the Stasi, German Democratic Republic's secret police. Wollweber was born in Hanoversch-Münden in 1898, and first came to the attention of the police in 1917 at the age of nineteen, when he played a role in the organization of the ammunition workers' strike. He was later to be a contact man between the Liebknecht-Luxemburg group and revolutionary bargemen, and was a leading figure in the marine uprising in Wilhelmshaven that was a contributing cause to the 1918 November Revolution.

In the early 'twenties he took part in various attempted coups, and was political leader of the KPD in Breslau until his appointment to the leadership of the RGO, the Revolutionary Union Opposition. In this body, established after the VIth Comintern Congress by way of Communist competition to the ADGB*, he was responsible for the bargemen and the employees of local administration.

The memoirs of GRU[+] worker Soya Voscresenskaya, published in Moscow in 1997, cast a new light on the Party career of Wollweber. Voscresenskaya writes the following on Wollweber, who at the time worked under the code name 'Anton': "I was in contact with Anton even before the war. He was of strong build, somewhat unkempt, a very good and extremely fastidious organizer. He had been in contact with the Soviet reconnaissance from its earliest days. During the Weimar Republic he was appointed member of the German ZK (Central Committee), and then all contact was broken with him."[125]

Wollweber was of modest character and refused wages for his position as Secretary of the *Einheitsverband*, since his material needs were covered by his Central Committee pay. Twenty years later, Richard Krebs could still remember a great deal about Wollweber's person and habits. These bore an almost eerie resemblance to those of the ideal Party functionary. Wollweber is reported to have never gambled, never gone to the theatre, never had any kind of personal relationships, never deviated from the Party line and never have been accused of this or of any other form of Party-internal heresy. According to Krebs, Wollweber only liked people "that he could use."[126]

Wollweber, a man who knew no mercy even for himself, known by his juniors not scornfully but admiringly as 'Ernst the man-eater,' commanded the absolute loyalty of his inner circle of friends and colleagues, whilst in his enemies – later to include Krebs himself — he aroused fear and hatred.

The contrast between Wollweber and Adolf could hardly have been greater. Adolf, a cosmopolitan former law student, spoke German, English and Russian as well as his native Polish, whilst the autodidact Wollweber had almost certainly never left Germany before Hitler came to power. Adolf was always expensively dressed, apparently enjoyed good living and loved women above all, whilst his counterpart cared neither for elegance nor for the fair sex.

Wollweber's appointment as Secretary of the *Einheitsverband* led to a power struggle between these two men. The German functionary had the backing of the KPD elite, who was absolutely sick of ISH interference in affairs they considered their own prerogative — as had been the case during the seamen's strike. The Pole, however, had the support of Moscow — and this proved time and time again the more substantial. Krebs, protégé and friend of Adolf, was automatically drawn into a

---

* ADGB Allgemeiner Deutscher Gewerkschaftsbund, General German Trade Union
+ Gossudarstvenoye Razvedivatelnoye Upravleniye (Soviet Military Intelligence)

struggle that encompassed the question of who was to control the Hamburg Interclub.

An undercurrent of political conflict accompanied this Party-internal friction between the KPD and the *Einheitsverband* on the one hand, and the ISH and the Comintern on the other. To Richard Krebs, Wollweber was a dyed-in-the-wool German to whom the only country of importance beyond his own was the Soviet Union. Whilst Wollweber recognized that a coup in Germany could only be effected by the Red Army, Krebs and Adolf were still hoping for world revolution. Perhaps they secretly hoped that this would put a stop to the oppressive influence of the Soviet Union on the Comintern.

After the seamen's strike fiasco had earned Wollweber an unassailable position at the top of the *Einheitsverband*, he demanded as chairman of the largest constituent group to be made part of the ISH's directorate. Adolf was obliged to reluctantly yield to this proposal in May 1931. After this, Adolf introduced the system of the double conference. First the directorate would sit with Wollweber's participation, then without it, and then a decision would be made.[127]

This conflict between Adolf, Walter and Krebs on the one side and Wollweber and his men on the other, which culminated years later in a bloody settling of scores, provoked a wild hatred of Wollweber in Krebs that in turn made him paint the man in the darkest possible manner in *Out of the Night*: in the portrayal there, Wollweber, keen to rid himself of an unwanted lover, played her into the hands of the Gestapo. This is one example — though not the only one — of pure fiction within the work.

When asked by the Americans about his fateful relationship with Ernst Wollweber, Krebs answered that Wollweber was "A functionary who everyone respected, yet who was hated in the ISH since unpleasant surprises were always to be expected from him."[128]

Although the conflict at the top of the ISH was serious, in 1932, given the rise of the Nazi Party that was not being played out at the country's polling stations alone, it must have seemed little more than a distraction to Krebs. Before having seized power, the National Socialists were trying to cowe their enemies with such shows of strength as public marches of their civil war troops, the SA.

The KPD leadership ignored the danger that the National Socialists represented as far as possible. The VIth International Comintern Congress had dictated that the principal enemies were the 'social fascists,' the Social Democrats. The theory invoked was to undermine the mainstay of the Weimar Republic in attacking its central prop, the Social Democrats, and to come out as victors from the ensuing governmental collapse. The idea that a single impetus was enough to create such a crisis was a popular illusion among the KPD leadership. This successfully ignored the issue of whether such an uncompromising policy was not merely playing into the hands of a National Socialist putsch.

It was plain to low level functionaries like Richard Krebs on the streets during 1931 and 1932 who the real enemies were. Once the Nazis had taken control of the flat countryside around Hamburg, they set about establishing themselves in the Communist citadel, the city's Harbor quarter. Countless punch-ups were the result. These were only mentioned in the newspapers if the wounds inflicted were extremely severe or fatal. Both of the parties involved had a vested interest in not attracting the attention of the police.

Another, slightly tamer form of conflict during this period was allowing a representative of an opposing party to speak at political functions. Krebs, a good speaker and a man who did not need to shy physical attack was often employed in this chancy role.

Ede Nikolajczik, "a simple Communist and seaman" in his own words, and a fellow of Krebs' in those days, still admiringly remembered the public appearances of a man who was later to be demonized as a Gestapo agent. At one SA function in a Hamburg hotel, Krebs had asked leave to speak. More than a hundred men were there, many of them SA members in uniform. Krebs and his men numbered between fifteen and twenty, and each carried a truncheon under his jacket.

"Then Krebs climbed up on the stage and gave a speech. He was attacked from all sides, and we were there too, and broke some heads with our truncheons. He finished his speech too. The Nazis that were there — perhaps they weren't all members of the party at the time — they also cried out that he should be allowed to finish. We took advantage of that. In the end though they all attacked but we got him down from the stage and gave him cover. He had a voice like a lion, spoke as a Marxist but also as a seaman. Sharp as a knife. He was a good speaker too."[129]

In May 1932 the violence escalated as the SA opened a meeting hall at the *Schaarmarkt* market place near the harbor quarter. This was an unheard of piece of provocation in an area where an unaccompanied SA man would never normally show his face. It was also a direct challenge to the Red Marine, a subdivision of the Red Front Fighter Division that was the paramilitary wing of the KPD. The Red Marine, a band that was capable of attacking as mercilessly as its rightwing counterpart, was not uncontroversial within the KPD. Its practices of creating funds by locking money courriers in lifts and robbing them, robbing banks, etc. attracted a group of men who would have been equally happy to do such work for a different organization. To the Hamburg Communist Helmut Warnke, who knew some of them personally, they were "fisticuff comrades," "apolitical and criminal elements" that were later to "grass each other up to the Gestapo."[130] This contrasts strongly with the opinion of one of their surviving members who bitterly remembered how the Party denounced them as 'Chicago-style gangsters' after the Nazis seized power, although in his opinion they had been the best fighters that the Party had had.[131]

It is certain that the Red Marine was the terror of SA members, and that this was the desired effect as far as KPD leadership was concerned. What happened after the opening of the SA meeting hall on the *Schaarmarkt*, however, was considered an atrocity by even the most hard-boiled functionaries.

According to case reports from 1934 it began as the Red Marine were given the order to prove that they were "not just some fun and lottery syndicate who passed the time playing ballgames on Heiliggeistfeld."[132] An attack on a small group of SA men ensued, and several SA men were injured in the knife play. One was so badly wounded that after several months on a waterbed he died as a result. This was unremarkable in the days of the Weimar Republic's decline, as, at the time, death in street brawls was a daily occurrence. What was remarkable was the cause of death.

This revolted Krebs to such a degree that years later he punched one of the perpetrators in the face for it, for, as the newspaper reports read at the time, Red Marine members had intentionally severed the spine of their victim Heinzelmann. Krebs was later to also be held responsible for this misdeed.[133]

Krebs always denied any involvement in the issuing of orders to the Red Marine, and it is indeed unlikely that he was responsible for it in any form or means. After all, although he was the manager of the Interclub, he was still no more than a regular member of the KPD.

In the ISH, however, he had reached a status that predestined him for greater things. As he told the CIC, he was responsible for transferring large amounts of money to ISH divisions throughout the world. This he conducted by the same methods that Knüfken had applied whilst working in Leningrad.

As George Mink, leader of a radical seamen's trade union, was to be transported to the USA with a large sum of money to finance an American Interclub, Krebs chose the *Albert Ballin*, a ship that sailed from Hamburg to America which had a strong Communist cell on board. The leader of this cell was a Party member by the name of Wilhelm Sievert or Sievers. Krebs trusted him sufficiently to hand Mink over to him that the latter might be stowed away and safely transported on to his destination with all his funds intact.

Before being entrusted with an even more important function, Krebs met on a weekly basis with Max Bareck. This was the special Comintern courier who brought funds from the Western European Bureau in Berlin and settled the details of further sea transport with Krebs in person.[134]

Iron Rigor

1932 is a turning point in the life of Richard Krebs. Not only had he reached the highest point that he was to attain in the Comintern, but it was the first year since his childhood that he was to spend in some semblance of family life — and the last for many to come.

After Hermine Stöver had followed him to Hamburg in spite of her parent's wishes, they lived together,[135] first as subtenants, then from March in a bourgeois residential area, and then, from September onwards, around the corner from the Interclub at 14 Venusberg Street. They were to remain resident there until they emigrated. [136]

To the Communist Krebs, marriage was probably nothing more than a formality to legitimize the child that Hermine was expecting. The fact that one of the witnesses at the wedding was a fellow-tenant who neither before nor afterwards played any role in Krebs' life seems to confirm this, as does the fact that Krebs could neither remember the date nor even the month of the event when questioned on the matter years later.[137] What we know about the relationship between these two can only be surmised from the report of Jan Valtin and the meager evidence furnished by Nazi criminal reports. It seems clear that Krebs loved Hermine and the son Jan, who was born to them in late September. If the surname that he gave his alter ego was drawn from Vicki Baum's novel, then the first name was that of the son that he was to lose in subsequent events.

The portrait that *Out of the Night* furnishes of Firelei in the year 1932 is one of a well-brought-up girl that follows her husband into the KPD because of a certain idealism and sympathy for the poor and oppressed who is then increasingly repulsed by the empty words and iron discipline of a Party that both she and Richard are subject to. In the novel she maintains a distance to the Party throughout their relationship, a distance that Krebs himself had long before lost. "We are as loyal as phonograph records" says Firelei in the novel "An Eiffel tower of Phonograph plates, all playing the *Internationale*". Two years later, as Krebs was a prisoner of the Third Reich, it took only a few months before Stöver left the Party for good.

Whatever private doubts may have been buried deep inside him, Krebs must have still presented the image of a Communist fanatic who had preserved enough initiative and clarity of thought to be entrusted with the most delicate of operations. In American exile seven years later, he described the function that he filled from July 1932 onwards in a text that for reasons of personal security was only published in abridged version.

"The Political Instructors are the traveling officer corps of the Third International. Unlike the mass of ordinary Party officials, they are not subject to the authority of the Central Committee of any national section of the Comintern. They are, in fact, the whips which Moscow cracks over the heads of a too sluggish or dissenting Party bureaucracy.

Whenever the Comintern bosses decide upon swift and energetic action in some part of their vast sphere of influence, instructors are sent into the field. The instructors receive explicit orders. They study all correspondence and confidential reports pertaining to their mission. After the consummation – or frustration of their task in one land, they submit their reports and are promptly diverted to another. Both enthusiasm and ruthless cunning are the chief attributes of the seasoned instructor. Loaded with optimism, yet wary as old wolves and masters of intrigue — survivors who rapidly develop into specialists for every considerable variety of subversive endeavor.

Every insider knows that the bearers of big names in the central committee, wide open to public admiration in the attack, the Pollits, the Cachins, the Browders and the Dimitrovs are little more than figureheads of the legitimate part of the Party machine, but the underground force, unnamed by party publicity and unknown to the bulk of Party adherents are the political instructors

Young, and unfettered by bureaucratic routine, they are still able to speak the language of the masses — a quality which Moscow highly prizes. They appear, seemingly from nowhere at Party headquarters. They tear into existing shortcomings, dictate campaigns, make and break Party officials, and generally cause things to happen. Their job accomplished, they disappear as silently as they have come." [138]

After the partial opening of the Comintern Archives in Moscow and the publication of works that drew upon this source, a hypothesis which must have seemed a fantastical exaggeration contradicted by Party press, the impressions of contemporaries and the best part of subsequent historical writings must now be reviewed in a quite different light: instructors were the invisible threads by means of which the Moscow Comintern Headquarters directed the activities of its national divisions.

Such omnipotence dates back to the year 1928 and the VIth Comintern Congress. It was the results of this meeting that Clara Zetkin described as the transformation of the apparatus into a mechanism "which ingests orders given in Russian in one place and spits them back out in a different language somewhere else".

The Comintern statutes stipulated at that congress obliged Communist parties worldwide to unquestioningly submit to Comintern orders. Complaints were only admissible at the World Congress, the highest Comintern organ. Between congresses all decisions were taken by the EKKI, the Comintern's Executive Committee. The EKKI was itself, however, a massive committee that consisted of leading members from all Communist parties, which only met every two years. The real work was conducted by the presidium of the EKKI. This was a much more exclusive club that made decisions in the name of the Executive Committee and which had been allocated powers at the VIth Comintern Congress that reduced the EKKI to little more than a discussion forum for decisions that had already been taken. The most important of these arrogations of power was the article thirty. This stated that "each leading position in the Party does not belong to its holder but to the Communist International in its entirety. Elected members of central leadership organizations may only use their powers before reelection* with the consent of the EKKI."[139] Since after the VIth Comintern Congress the EKKI was only a rubber stamp of its presidium, which in turn was controlled by Stalin, this article effectively meant that the Comintern leadership itself decided on the representatives of its own control organization, and the decisions of the World Congress.

The extent to which the Comintern controlled the world's separate Communist parties had to remain concealed at all costs so as to prevent the assignation to the

---

* i.e. in World Congress elections

Soviet Union of all unfriendly action by a Communist country against a non-Communist country. It was also considered desirable to maintain the fiction to ordinary members that their Party was acting in the interests of the working populace of their country.

Neither the practice nor the concealment of control could be run from Moscow. To these ends an operative headquarters was established in Berlin towards the end of September 1928. Known as the Western European Bureau (WEB), this was a form of scaled-down Comintern headquarters that only sought advice from Moscow on matters of the highest import. The most important aspects of the OMS were assigned to it, and it in turn sent on the most important parts of its dubious freight via Hamburg.

It was at a sitting of this Bureau that Adolf learnt that the seamen strike was to end in disaster. A Russian history of this same Bureau, the highest level with which Krebs would communicate within the Comintern, collated by archivists from declassified material in 1997, reads as follows:

"On November 1, 1928, the presidium of the EKKI... sent a letter conveying the information that 'in the interest of easing the executive load of its brother parties,' and in accordance with Comintern statutes, it had transferred the following rights to the Bureau: to decide on matters of such urgency as permits no further discussion and to publish resolutions; to give Parties written orders in its name; to convene congresses with one or more Communist parties if need be; to invite members of the various Central Committees to justify their activities; to pay Central Committee members visits instead of accepting EKKI activity reports; to represent the EKKI at Party conferences and congresses; to verify the activities of representatives and instructors of the EKKI, the Youth International, the Farmers International and the Profintern inasmuch as these are Communist; and to organize the activities of non-affiliated international organizations by means of the Communist factions that they incorporate... WEB instructors were to keep close contact with Communist factions in affiliated organizations and to fulfill the various commands of the Bureau, and all Parties were obliged to support them in their activities... Later, in early F1930, the presidium of the EKKI reaffirmed and extended the WEB's powers."[71]

The precision and detail with which the Cominten interfered in the daily duties of its workers is apparent today in the example of the American Communist Party, the Moscow archives of which were thoroughly investigated in the decade subsequent to 1990 with the financial support of large American universities. The publications of this investigation showed that after 1930, at the latest, all significant appointments and all changes of political tact were brought about in consultation with Moscow.[140]

However, as Richard Krebs was to find out on his first mission, the theoretical powers of a Comintern delegate were one thing, but their realization was quite a different matter.

A Man from Headquarters

On July 11, 1932, Richard Krebs landed in Grimsby, England. He was traveling as Dutch businessman Gerhard Smett, and registered with the London police under that name. To prove his identity to his British comrades he carried a further passport, this one Norwegian, and issued to Alfons Petersen. Krebs' mission consisted of 'clearing up' the British section of the ISH, finally installing a radical seamen's union and removing the Comintern veteran George Hardy from ISH leadership. In addition, he was expected to reorganize the East Indian Seaman's Union in London.

England was a troublesome spot for the Comintern. After the famous Zinovyev telegram affair in 1924 — the leader of the Comintern is alleged to have demanded that the British Communist Party attempt a coup, although it is unclear to this day whether the telegraph was genuine or a forgery of the British secret service — London had banished all Soviet diplomats. After this abrupt end of diplomatic relations, the embassy was searched and a wealth of papers discovered that evidenced a huge spy network. From then on the Communists didn't stand a chance. The British Communist Party, although heavily subsidized by Moscow because of the country's significance, was one of the smallest in Western Europe, and attempts to support it were all a failure, not least because London had cracked the Comintern's secret code and quickly identified all its delegates.[141]

The British branch of the ISH, which theoretically had access to the world's greatest merchant marine, also distinguished itself by complete failure. This was all the more painful, as an attempt to cut wages in 1931 had provoked a revolt in the navy that had swiftly forced the admiralty and the British government to revoke these measures. That revolt had been the origin of the wild hope among the Comintern leadership that Britannia might be humbled. As the British comrades had no income due to poor membership, ISH headquarters repeatedly sent large sums of money to England. The net result of this was a suspicious lack of zeal among the British comrades. The frustrated conclusion drawn in Hamburg was that the British cared nothing for ISH directives. It is evident in internal reports sent by Adolf to Moscow that the consequence of all this was an intense fury towards the English representatives, in particular towards the seamen's representative George Hardy. George Hardy was a long-serving functionary whose name was already appearing in IPC-Transport files in 1919. During the 'twenties he managed IPC-transport work in all countries with a Pacific coastline except America. After the ISH was established, he became its first general secretary in Hamburg, and after May 1931, having been expelled from Germany, he was given the mission of creating a revolutionary seamen's union in England. One year later there was still no sign of it.

The leadership of the ISH interpreted the various reasons that Hardy offered for this delay as poorly concealed feet dragging. Adolf suspected that George Hardy was leading a pleasant life on Comintern funds which he did not want to jeopardize by creating a revolutionary seamen's union. In late 1931 Adolf reported to Moscow that at an ISH plenum the British comrades named a lack of cadres for their failure to found such a union. Furthermore, they demanded that the manager of any such union be paid. This was followed by a series of "opportunist maneuvering" on the part of the British comrades. The claimed, among other things, that there was "a complete lack of fighting spirit among the transport workers of England," and that it was quite impossible to lead an "anti-religious campaign and to organize meetings or events or to load ships with propaganda material on Sundays."

Adolf was also infuriated by the "complete underestimation of the importance of work among colonial seafarers (that was expressed by Comrade Hardy's reluctance to publish a special chapter on colonial work in the English version of the ISH brochure among other things)." [142]

After Comrade Hardy had countered the request for further information with the reply that it was all written in the *Daily Worker* and had failed to publish a revolutionary flyer, for which both text and funds had been sent to him, enough was enough. Adolf decided to send someone across the channel to take over Hardy's duties, employ new men and finally establish a revolutionary seamen's union. This was not a simple matter. All proven instructors were known to the British, and since all foreigners that were de-masked were subsequently deported, Adolf was obliged to sit back and watch the dithering of the English for a further six months before he came upon the novice Richard Krebs. Krebs was thus to receive a first mission in a new career that was as important as it was difficult.

Admittedly Krebs exaggerated the significance of this mission in *Out of the Night*; there Valtin not only sounded out the seamen's union but the whole of the British Communist Party. The essence of the story is, however, confirmed in Adolf's reports on the situation in England, in which Krebs is referred to as 'Kr.' 'Comrade Anderson' or 'our instructor.'

Let us recall Jan Valtin's report. Having traveled to England under the name of Gerhard Smett, representative of a Rotterdam fishery in possession of a bona fide company letter of recommendation, he rents a room near Euston Station in London, is accorded a number of subordinates (their names really do appear in ISH documents), and sets about finding out what Hardy has been up to. Hardy, "a stealthy and fox-like intriguer" has indeed been using Hamburg funds to feather his own nest and pamper his elegant wife, safe in the knowledge that Scotland Yard will swiftly trace any auditor sent by headquarters. The East Indian Seamen's Union, financed by Moscow via Hamburg, is shown to be — and Gestapo documents confirm this — nothing less than an opium smuggling ring.[143] Comrade Hardy had kept this secret as Moscow subsidies were being paid directly to him. Krebs' reports, like all material from instructors to headquarters in the Comintern archives, are, unfortunately, still classified. However, the letters of George Hardy, sent by that talented intriguer directly over the head of Adolf to his superiors in Moscow, are preserved in the Russian capital.

He by no means denied irregularities in bookkeeping, but instead blamed these on his rival Fred Thompson. Thompson, although not officially a member of the

Communist Party, was, in Adolf's words to Moscow, "one hundred percent our man"[144] and, furthermore, the man designated to take over the founding of the new trade union.

Hardy didn't pull his punches. He hinted that Thompson had willingly accepted informers into the cadre organization that formed the basis of the nascent trade union, and even stooped to citing a purported anonymous letter in which the author joked about Thompson's arrest and mockingly asked how much the latter was being paid for disorganizing harbor workers.[145]

In short, Hardy presented himself to his well-positioned friends in Moscow as the one true revolutionary in the English seamen's movement and depicted himself as victim of an intrigue which the ISH were taking part in for reasons best known themselves.

When Hardy went over the heads of the ISH and applied directly to Moscow, Adolf found that there remained nothing else for him to do but to also treat Moscow to his version of events.

Adolf believed that he was holding all the trumps; having referred to the highest authority west of Moscow, the Western European Bureau, the ISH took steps by informing the English branch of the Profintern on June 11, 1932, that Hardy was being recalled from his post. When this order was ignored, the ISH sent first Krebs and then its general secretary Albert Walter to England. The ISH's decision was finally reconfirmed at a meeting attended by Comrade Allen, the Comintern deputy for all union affairs in the British Empire.

Comrade Hardy refused to concede the issue. To be rid of him once and for all an 'offer' was made of a stay in the Soviet Union to 'recuperate.' The letter that Hardy sent Comrade Alexander by way of reply was a masterpiece of deceit and intrigue. He cunningly explained his reticence to leave for the Soviet Union by claiming that Harry Politt, the leader of the British Communist party had accused him of running away from the fight. As a matter of personal honor he had therefore no choice but to remain in Britain.

During the three months of this toing and froing, Krebs was obliged, as Adolf remarked to Moscow in a report on the affair, to put up with Hardy.

By October 1932, Krebs was back in Germany; the British police had located the ISH envoy and promptly deported him.

Richard Krebs was convinced that his discovery was due to his having been denounced by British colleagues. In his treatise on the Comintern agent he was to write that "many Comrades fear and hate the emissaries from Moscow. Especially in Great Britain, where the party is totally corrupt."

Despite its interruption, Krebs' mission was considered a success. Shortly afterwards, Adolf wrote to Moscow: "unheard of progress had been made in England... New Clubs have been founded which are self-financing; new local SMM (Seamen's Minority Movement) groups are beginning to transfer small contributions to SMM central management, and there is significant growth in membership numbers in spite of the redoubling of the terror. Also a number of partially successful Unified Front operations have been carried out, etc."[146]

On November 7 a further attempt was made to send Krebs to England. Contrary to Adolf's optimistic reports to Moscow not all seemed to be going well there. This time Krebs was arrested on arrival and deported. The very same day Adolf reported the disaster to headquarters, remarking resignedly that there was no possibility of "sending any one but an Englishman to England"[147] in the near future.

The required native, Richard Krebs' unfortunate successor, was Comrade Adams. He was taken out of training at the Lenin School in Moscow and sent to England despite the sentence of several months' imprisonment which awaited him there; Adolf reasoned that since Adams was a British citizen he would not be subject to deportation.

It seems, however, that Adams was also employed to no avail. On May 10, 1933 the report was much the same as ever: "New management engaged. *Differences of opinion in the Hardy affair.* The Liverpool branch is virtually the only good remaining SMM organization."[148]

Hardy, a master of intrigue, was to survive both Krebs and Adolf. Although the ISH later managed to send him to the USSR, he apparently passed his stay there unscathed. Asked in 1999 about the Hardy he had known in the 'sixties, the former leading Party member John Tarver recalled a loveable veteran, well advanced in years, who was much admired by the comrades on account of his role in the social struggle of the 'thirties.

Krebs was given his next mission a few weeks after his involuntary return from England. This was a matter of inspections in Norway. Lars Boegersrud, the Norwegian historian who unearthed Richard Krebs' police file in Greenland, writes on the course of Krebs' trip: "Krebs' every move was observed during his voyage from Fredrickstad to Trondheim. The foreign police first noticed him during a routine check of the guest book at Oslo's Östfold Hotel on December 8. By the time police officers arrived on the scene, however, he had flown the coop. This series of events was to be repeated in other hotels."[149]

A telegram sent to ISH leadership, intercepted by the Norwegian police, bears witness to the fact that Krebs was anything but satisfied by the state of affairs in the various harbors he visited. A part of the money meant to pay expenses for a delegation's trip to Copenhagen, for example, had simply been spent on drink by its recipients. Only the groups working in Oslo and in three further harbors could be described as satisfactory.

In Norway, as in England, there was also a problem with personnel; if to headquarters George Hardy was known as lazy and truculent, not to say corrupt, then his Norwegian counterpart, Arthur Samsing, was considered overzealous, particularly in his tendency to criticize his senior comrades. In 1950 the CIC recorded Krebs statement on the Norwegian as follows:

"SAMSING was an extremely able man, mentally very alert and physically very active, a veteran of the Norwegian communist movement in spite of his age. Before 1930 he had worked in HAMBURG in connection with the Interclub, had been arrested and requested to leave. Before that, he had also worked in other countries. He had been in Russian frequently, and had had some sort of good revolutionary training. His main trouble, as far as the leaders of the communist movement were concerned, was his independence of mind. He never accepted instructions or orders without questioning their reasons and/or justification. People like LEO* looked upon SAMSING as a bothersome type...

[Samsing] often went off on revolutionary tacks of his own and then, when called to order, he made a practice of trying to embarrass the instructor personally. In one such instance, when he has been chastised in a meeting, he walked up to LEO, felt his fine new woolen suit, and commented, 'That's a fine suit, Comrade LEO; suppose we trade?'"

Samsing's remark on Leo's coat was particularly impudent, it being a reference to the difference in living standards between Moscow's representatives and lesser activists.

Arthur Samsing was replaced as leader of Norwegian seamen and sent to the Soviet Union, where the Scandinavian section of the Leningrad interclub employed him. Leif O. Foss, the man who replaced him, was accustomed to iron discipline having just completed training for 'professional revolutionaries' in the Soviet Union.

Krebs was certainly involved in the Samsing case on both his first trip to Norway and on a second during April 1933. Adolf reported to Moscow on May 6, 1933 "Norway: Samsing discharged and Comrade Leif O. Foss employed. Significant progress in organizational consolidation of the RGO."[150] As to whether Krebs was directly charged with removing Samsing can neither be ascertained from his statement to the CIC nor from *Out of the Night*. It is conceivable that he kept his counsel due to the shame of having ousted a man who dared to remain independent.

End-game

---

* Leo was an instructor very much senior to Krebs. Krebs, who met him repeatedly during 1932-1933 believed he was a WEB delegate. Leo's real identity remains a mystery.

On January 30, 1933 Richard Krebs received a telegram from Germany. His mother had died of cancer in Bremen. He interrupted his Norwegian mission and returned to Germany. Krebs was not to be accorded much time for grieving. That very day was also the date of a political earthquake, for it was the day on which Adolf Hitler became Chancellor of Germany. Krebs' comrades in Hamburg found themselves in immediate need of his assistance.

Krebs spent the six weeks prior to his next foreign mission in preparing for being outlawed and participating in the preparations for what was to be the last KPD electoral campaign — the campaign prior to the *Reichstag* elections due to be held on March 5.

Little is known about Krebs' activities during this period except what he was later to leave Jan Valtin report. The KPD's files contain a good number of indications as to the predominant mood that followed the initial shock of January 30. The leadership's first reaction was to call a general strike, but this fell flat due to high unemployment and the *laissez-faire* tactics of the SPD. The next stage was a wave of directives demanding the impossible from Party members. On February 28, 1933, one day after the *Reichstag* fire the following instructions were issued to the North Sea Coast/Hamburg regional management: "In the fight against fascist terror/ disarm the fascist bandits / place weapons in the hands of workers and farmers / chase the brownshirts from unemployment offices and working class quarters / antifascist policemen side with the workers / strike in protest against murderous fascist attacks / breach the fascist demo ban.

To effectuate such a solution, SA men are to be disarmed *en masse* in all workplaces and meeting points, etc. Such activities are to be broadly popularized and encouraged..."[151]

Presumably written on February 27, this call-to-arms, nigh-burlesque in the face of the nation's passivity, was made a mockery of on the very same day; the *Reichstag* went up in flames.

The new government, who had experienced how a general strike could sabotage all their hopes during the failed Kapp Putsch, and who had hitherto had little influence among politicized workers, used the pretext of the allegedly Communist terrorist act to attack their opponents with unrestrained brutality. An unbridled wave of repressions began. Following plans and using lists made in 1932 by Hitler's predecessors, thousands of Communist functionaries were arrested and the Communist press was outlawed.

The NSDAP's private army, the SA, was now turned loose and avenged themselves on the opponents of yesteryear in wild street battles. Compared with the Gestapo era that was to follow, this was a period of wild and disorganized terror during which hundreds or perhaps thousands were murdered in the rapidly improvised SA concentration camps.

KPD leadership was absolutely unprepared for all of this. They had been preaching for so long that the Weimar Republic was a fascist institution that they had even come to believe their own propaganda. Scarcely a week after the *Reichstag* fire their leader Ernst Thälmann had been incarcerated.

It was only after many years that those of the Politburo's leadership who had escaped the onslaught would acknowledge this defeat. At the time, affairs were continued as if nothing had happened, and even among itself Party leadership maintained that the terror would only exacerbate the crisis in the bourgeois system. It was much in this spirit that the KPD issued a resolution on April 1 proclaiming that every preparation must now be taken for the proletarian revolution. Even in December, Moscow was still announcing that the German revolution was nigh, and such KPD functionaries as Fritz Heckert were still publicly of the opinion that the fight against the fascists was not to be undertaken "in league with the Social Democrats but against them."[152]

Richard Krebs, as manager of the Hamburg Interclub, was well known and, like most other Party functionaries, found himself obliged to disappear. During this time he slept each night in a different apartment. When due at a secret meeting, he could never be sure whether his partner was still at liberty or whether, having cracked under torture, he had revealed the secret appointment to Nazis who would then be expecting Krebs at the appointed hour and place. One single 'broken' functionary could take down dozens more with him. A method applied by the newly invested Nazi men involved taking a 'turned' Communist to cruise the streets in search of his former fellows. Anyone pointed out would be dragged into the patrol wagon.

An episode that elucidates the degree of terror with which the nascent Gestapo proceeded against the Communists in their Hamburg stronghold took place during this era. During one of the many police raids of the day, Hermine Krebs succeeded in escaping from her apartment but circumstances forced her to leave her son behind. Her would-be capturers placed the child on the windowsill in the hope that his mother would not be able to bear its screams and would surrender. The desperate mother sent one acquaintance after the other to her apartment to collect the child. Although all of these people were not among those subject to Gestapo repressions, they were all held captive until finally the Gestapo gave up hope of thus ensnaring her. The scarcely six-month-old infant was finally picked up by its grandparents and taken to Bremen. Hermine Krebs had been made to recognize the fact that a newborn was irreconcilable with life as an illegal. She was not to see her child again for over a year.[153]

Hermine Krebs' treatment by the Gestapo was by no means atypical. An internal *Einheitsverband* report from October 1933 states: "In such cases where it... proves impossible to find the wanted functionary, their womenfolk are taken hostage. In some cases their children have also been taken to so-called Christian Reformatories, so as to capture the desired functionary by hostage-taking methods. The women and children of several E.V. [*Einheitsverband*] members were simply dragged off to such ends."[154]

The obstinacy with which the Communists resisted, despite such methods, is astonishing. After Hitler's appointment as German Chancellor, and even after the *Reichstag* fire, there were still attacks on SA men in Hamburg and foolhardy groups — newly founded after their predecessors had been destroyed — were still distributing illegal flyers. So-called mass raids were the official response to such activities. Streets, and even whole quarters of the city were cordoned off so that material and wanted functionaries might be captured. Not until late 1933, when the majority of Communist Party rank and file members had been arrested, did such blatant resistance activities begin to dwindle. Nonetheless, the Hamburg Gestapo had to remain vigilant throughout the 'thirties. As Gestapo archives attest, the fact that freedom of speech had been silenced had changed little in the harbor quarter's atmosphere.

Repression was not the only method employed by the regime to prevent a new wave of protest activities. In July one of the oldest union demands was heeded and a numbers system was introduced in the harbor. This guaranteed a fair distribution of work among workers; now each and every longshoreman was employed, even if at times for only four shifts a week. Linked to the right to work were both the obligation to work on demand and a system of monitoring and checking all those involved in the new system.[155]

Before he left in mid-March of that year, Richard Krebs set up an illegal printing press to be operated by his wife and colleagues from the Interclub. He himself departed for Denmark. In Copenhagen, where ISH headquarters had been relocated, he received funds and instructions; he was to travel to Sweden under the Comintern order to up the ante in an ongoing shipping strike, called by the Swedish seamen's union, who, principally Social Democrats, were the deadly rivals of the ISH.

Under Swedish law, seamen had to wait seven days after arriving on shore before they could legally strike. Should this condition not be met, shipping companies could apply for compensation. Richard Krebs had been charged with discrediting the seamen's union — who were obliged to keep this condition or risk its fortune — by calling them lackeys of the shipping companies, and persuading the seamen to leave their ships before the designated period had elapsed. He was, furthermore, to gather troops to do battle with strikebreakers and, if possible, to cause civil war-style disturbances. These were much the same tactics as those which Adolf had vainly employed in autumn 1931.

In Sweden everything ran as planned. With the help of his fighters, and the use of slick rhetoric, the ISH delegate managed to persuade the seamen to leave their ships and to transform what was originally an 'apolitical strike' into a violently confrontational affair. The attack on the *Kjell*, a vessel manned by strikebreakers anchored off Gothenburg, caused something of a sensation. A band of Communists boarded the ship, kidnapped some of the crewmembers, and took them to the Gothenburg Interclub. There they were beaten before all present before being swiftly transported onwards. By the time the men turned up inland some few days later, the occurrence had already led to the closing of the club and a raid on the offices of the ISH's Swedish section.

Although the police did not succeed in arresting Richard Krebs, handwritten notes left by him in the office, and the interrogation of the Swedish section's chairman, Gunnar Persson, put the police on his trail. Krebs was obliged to flee the country.

In the Swedish police report on the case it is noted: "Persson conceded that the above-mentioned Krebs is an international ISH representative chiefly charged with aiding and abetting the activities of the Profintern's Scandinavian section. Krebs helped Persson with the writing of circulars, strike notices and flyers, giving precise instructions during their drafting. He also helped finance their printing... Among documents seized during the raid were some pieces in Krebs' handwriting. These contain such expressions as 'form storm troops' and 'get the strikebreakers ashore,' etc. It can be inferred from these documents that Krebs transmitted information on the ongoing strike to the ISH office in Copenhagen."[156]

The descriptions of an instructor's activities are among the most precise, detailed and authentic of all passages in *Out of the Night*. Sentences such as "I was flushed with triumph" or "For the first time in my career I became the virtual dictator of a violent mass movement" show to what extent the power that he exerted behind the scenes went to his head. He describes the attacking of the *Kjell*, which caused a sensation because of its sheer brutality, as if he was by no means implicated. Presumably he feared the reaction of American public opinion; any involvement in the kidnapping of the strikebreakers would have exposed Valtin to a very negative reaction from the public.

In the depiction of these events in *Out of the Night*, the real goal of publicly mishandling the strikebreakers in the workers' club was not to incite the masses by means of example, but to have the Club closed by police force. The desired effect was to hamper the growing insubordination of the ISH's Swedish section, which depended on its well-run canteen for its finances, and to force it into submission by foisting dependence on ISH subsidies upon it. According to Valtin, the ISH had already succeeded in closing Club canteens despite Swedish resistance. In Gothenburg, however, all prior attempts at persuasion had been in vain. A laconic note from Adolf to his superiors hints that this might have been the ensuing and genuine cause of the strikebreakers' treatment: "Instruction trips before, during, and after the strike. Severe differences between ISH and Swedish officials in the question of strike tactics."[157]

That the strike should end in police deployment and failure was not a cause of concern to the Comintern. The goal, in their terms, was not a small improvement in living conditions for seamen but, as the Comintern motto of the day went, the "exposure of reformists as capitalist lackeys" and the radicalization of the masses in the face of the worldwide economic crisis. And this goal had been served.

Krebs traveled on from Sweden to Norway. This was no longer in aid of the ISH's Norwegian section, as there the most important decisions had already been reached: Arthur Samsing was already in the Soviet Union and Leif O. Foss was the new man in charge. Krebs' new mission was to take him to Narvik in the north of Norway and to the rail line from Sweden which ended there. This was the port where the iron ore from one of the world's largest mines, Swedish Kiruna, was embarked and, due to its proximity to Germany, a point of strategic interest to all European powers in war planning.

Although this time Richard Krebs did not come to the attention of the Norwegian police on arrival, they succeeded in arresting him in Oslo on April 26 when he was already on the return leg of his journey.

A dossier compiled on him at this juncture describes him as "6" 1' tall, heavily built, with brown eyes, brown curly hair, a high forehead, slightly pointed nose and thick, brown eyebrows."

The Norwegian police also noted: "He is in Norway to organize the Revolutionary Union Opposition with particular regard to the seamen and harbor workers.

"His trip to Norway also had a military background. It is a matter of the extent to which transport workers and seamen in Norway can be won for revolutionary purposes. This is an issue of great significance to the Soviet Union and for the general staff of the Red Army, particularly in connection with the rail line from Sweden. For these reasons Narvik is of great interest not only to the ISH but also to the organizations of revolutionary rail workers in Norway and Sweden.

Not only the Profintern but also the Comintern has given oral instructions to these organizations in this matter. The same goes for the extension of the line via Haparanda to Finland. The ISH has also issued a special circular stressing the significance of the line from Narvik."[158]

Like the description of the role played by Valtin during the strike, the description of the journey through Norway that followed corresponds closely to the descriptions given in accessible archives. The Norwegian historian Lars Borgersrud, who meticulously traced Krebs' journey through his country, reports that the investigative department of the Norwegian general staff was informed that Krebs' second visit to Norway was not only in aid of agitation of transport workers in order to bring the loading of iron ore to a standstill. "The purpose of his second visit was to reconnoiter means of destroying the Ofot line in the case of military necessity."[159]

When the Norwegian police captured Krebs on April 26 they were already in possession of a great deal of information about him. This was also supplemented by details furnished by a Swedish policeman, requested by telephone to attend the questioning of the Comintern delegate. The Swede had no difficulty in explaining the source of the many receipts found on Krebs' person; these were all proofs of expenditure for printing and travel costs from the Swedish seamen's strike.

Neither the Norwegian officers nor their Swedish counterpart succeeded in squeezing useful information out of Krebs. In the Swede's report on the interrogation, it is noted: "Krebs refused to offer any details about his dealings in Gothenburg for the period in which the *Kjell* strikebreakers were attacked and mistreated. He did, however, admit that he had been the ISH representative in Gothenburg during the time. He gave no answer to an indirect question as to whether he had been of aid to Swedish comrades in the attacking of the ship. Indeed, he stressed that the Communist Party is against all forms of terrorist activity and that, if such events had taken place, then this was off the bat of individual members and not under Party orders."[160]

Richard Krebs found himself in a dangerous position. The Norwegians had no intention of trying him, but were instead threatening to deport him to Germany. Nonetheless, two days later he was on a steamer bound for Antwerp rather than the fatal shores of Hamburg.

How had this come to pass? An act of civil courage was at least in part the reason.

On February 10, 1933, after Hitler had acceded to power, officials in the senate administration of the Social Democrat, Hansa League city of Hamburg dismissed the political police officer Peter Kraus for having links to the NSDAP intelligence service. Although he was reinstated on March 5, he found himself left to deal with the chaos that his Social Democrat colleagues had created before they themselves had been fired. When the Norwegians requested information from Hamburg about Richard Krebs, the man in Hamburg responsible for the Gestapo's Communist files was swamped with work and handicapped by the chaotic state of his archives.[161] It was thus that Hamburg replied that Richard Krebs had no criminal record and was not wanted.

Jan Valtin escapes by quite different methods; Arne Halvorsen, an Oslo doctor brings *Out of the Night's* hero a spiked meal that induces in him the symptoms of severe poisoning. Shortly afterwards he is released into the doctor's care. This man is in the employ of the Soviet secret police and under orders to observe the work of Norwegian Communists, in particular that of Communist seamen and harbor workers. This passage was later to cause the kind of controversy that typified the book's reception. The historian Lars Borgersrud was unable to find in the watchman's book or among police's records any note of Halvorsen's visit. Nonetheless, the story must have contained at least a grain of truth. In 1937, years before he was to start writing his novel, Richard Krebs was to report on Halvorsen to the Nazis. As his statements were liable to be checked and verified, his life depended on the veracity of his word: "A well-known doctor in Oslo… he harbored all international high-ranking functionaries, who stayed with him for free. His practice is at number 22, Aakebergvey street, his private apartment in a newly built complex, called the 'Sommer Früde Komplex,' in the Kampen district of the city. He lives together with a Norwegian girl called 'Karin.' Karin works as private secretary to the director of the largest Norwegian shipping line, Wilhelmsen, and through her the ISH received copies of all secret documents of the Norwegian shipping group. A brother of 'Karin' is criminal officer in Oslo and in conversation reveals much to the doctor during his weekly visits.

Dr. H's speciality is to visit prisoners arrested during the night and to declare them unsuitable for imprisonment so that they are immediately released."[162]

The CIC asked Krebs about Halvorsen in 1950. Krebs claimed that it was thanks to the doctor that he was deported to a land of his choice, and, although he did not mention the poisoned food, also claimed that the man paid for him to travel first class to Antwerp.

In early May Krebs arrived in Antwerp. He must have been greatly worried about his wife who had remained in Hitler's terror state to work the printing press that he had himself established before his departure.

Krebs, preempting the closure of the Interclubs subsequent to the *Reichstag* fire, had rented an attic apartment and installed there paper, propaganda material, typewriter and mimeograph equipment from the Interclub. A handful of trustworthy comrades, including Krebs' wife, had been charged with keeping this set-up operative. Hermine remained responsible for all drawings, plus all hand-drawn headers, sentences and slogans. These she created in that characteristic style with which the Nazis had become so familiar. The end came on April 19. As so often, it was not Nazi investigations that led to the discovery but an interfering neighbor who had reported suspicious activity to the secret police. When Gestapo men stormed the room they found no one present, although a 'make-shift bed and a supply of fresh food' indicated that the room had been occupied shortly beforehand. It took twenty minutes for one of the Gestapo men to discover that someone was sitting on a narrow window ledge on the other side of a blacked-out window."[163] Popovics, a Hungarian, was the first of the so-called Interclub group that fell into the Nazi's net. The search was intensified for Hermine Krebs and the others.

Krebs must have learnt of all this and the precarious position of his wife from German refugees or seamen from one of the German ships that regularly sailed from Hamburg to Antwerp. He succeeded in locating her and putting her in contact with one of the Comintern trans-border services that worked between Belgium and Germany.

"The route ran via BRUSSELS to LIEGE. There the traveler was picked up by another courier, who conducted him to VERVIERS, where another courier led over about 3 miles of backwood trails to AACHEN, where contact was established with a German courier at the railway station. All courier-runners were women; they appeared to have had considerable practice on this route, and it was used in both directions."[164]

The young woman, her infant child with her parents and she unsure when she would see it again, rallied with her husband to the cause. Together they wrote flyers that were smuggled from Antwerp to Germany. The Gestapo recorded these activities. A portrait of Hitler as an executioner that Hermine drew after the execution of Communists was also added to her dossier, as were the many other underground writings and flyers that bore her characteristic style.

Those two months that they spent in Antwerp might well have filled them with the hope that the German nightmare might yet vanish quicker than they had hitherto expected. In the harbors of countries surrounding Germany, seamen-refugees had formed themselves into foreign divisions of the *Einheitsverband*. The feeling of unity that persecution fostered upon these men gave a new lease of life to the utopian hopes that had been so characteristic among Communists in the latter days of the Weimar Republic. These men, having increased their prestige among German and foreign sailors by their uncompromising stance towards the new German regime, were reveling in a last melancholy victory over their Social Democrat opponents, who had capitulated to Hitler and fallen silent. The Hamburg section of the ADGB had even publicly declared its friendship with the regime and declared itself "prepared to participate in any enterprise that the Reich's leadership might deem necessary to the completion of the great work."[165]

When trade union premises in Germany were occupied and their finances confiscated, an ISH circular was published. This document cannot be read without a sense of bemusement: can the author or authors have sincerely believed what these slogans expounded, or did they merely hope to comfort themselves with such bombastic claims? The header reads: "Takeover of Reformist German Unions by The Fascists — New Significance of the Revolutionary Union Movement," as if this was the most propitious thing they might have hoped for.[166]

A report in the ISH Moscow archives is comparably grotesque given the situation in Germany at the time. In it, under the header 'successes,' the following entry can be read: "I might also add, from personal experience, that the transport of revolutionary literature to Germany is going very well, and that the Social Democrat transport network now belongs to us. This means that we are destroying [Social Democrat] literature and sending our pamphlets to their addresses."[167] It is unknown who the author of these Russian sentences was, but, since it revolved around ships that sailed the Rhine, and as Richard Krebs was organizing work in Antwerp at the mouth of that river, it is quite plausible that he was involved in the matter. To the CIC he only uttered a few laconic words on the issue whilst commenting on a certain Social Democrat who had fled to Antwerp: "The Communists did not trust him, and for a while they were opening each other's mail. Both sides were at odds and working to different ends, even in the matter of transporting propaganda to Germany."

The main thrust of the ISH's attack was not, however, against the few German Social-Democrats, who in any case mostly came off the worst against their much better organized and fanatical opponents. All real enmity was reserved for members of the ITF, the International Transport Workers' Federation. The ITF was a worldwide umbrella organization that incorporated a great number of unions, the majority of which were Social Democrat. Two and a quarter million transport workers were unionized within it, and the body as a whole was managed by the Dutchman Edo Fimmen, a social revolutionary who had shown great sympathy for the October Revolution in the early 'twenties.

This counted for little in the eyes of the ISH. The above-mentioned circular claimed that the ITF 'fascisized' the organizations that it incorporated, and that the same agenda was being followed that had "brought the German unions into the fascist camp... so as to prepare the way for more capitalist campaigns."

Small wonder then that the ITF wanted to counterattack at the first opportunity, and this they were afforded when German members of the ISH and the *Einheitsverband*, having fled abroad, started a campaign against the hoisting of the Swastika flag in foreign harbors.

In Antwerp, where the refugees who arrived daily were reporting on the brutal oppression of first the Communists and then also the Social Democrats, the call to boycott fell on receptive ears. Richard Krebs and his fellows were glad of the chance to finally take action against the hated Berlin regime. There were daily affrays between the emigrants, who were supported by the workers of Antwerp, and the Belgian police, who were under orders to hinder all activities that might jeopardize trade with the nation's powerful neighbor.

The campaign got off to a good start, as Adolf reported on July 15 to Moscow:

"In most large ports (and in some small ones) in all capitalist lands there have been dozens of cases where harbor workers have refused to work on German ships, have pulled down the swastika flag and torn it up or burnt it, etc. We stress that the first actions of this kind (in Belgium, Holland, the Scandinavian countries and later in Spain, France, Gdańsk, Gdynia the USA, etc) were prepared and carried out with careful planning.

These activities spread through different countries within a few weeks. We have registered ninety-seven cases up to now where tools have been downed."[168]

Unfortunately, 'ITF bigwigs' had no intention of leaving their Communist competitors to enjoy this propaganda victory. As Adolf complained in a letter, they instead cunningly took to exploiting the ISH's Achilles heel, its dependence on the 'Socialist motherland.'

"This movement has started to wane in the last few days. We received countless letters from our various sections and even from harbor workers and seamen, which all read in approximately the same way: 'Why do you want to strike against the swastika? The flag is being flown in Leningrad and Odessa and Russian harbor workers are doing nothing about it.'…

The arguments of the reformist bigwigs have caused a lot of harbor workers to distance themselves from the campaign against the swastika flag where initially it had been prosecuted with great enthusiasm. We have not entirely succeeded in revealing the perfidy of these reformist arguments to all workers, although we have repeatedly published bulletins and special articles on the matter.

We would be indebted if you could calculate the chances of carrying out a campaign against the swastika on your shores, although we are aware that the impudence of the Nazis is so great that they might take down our flag on Soviet ships in Hamburg or Bremen."[169]

Since the Soviet Union had rather more serious concerns to deal with, it seems unlikely that his diffident request was answered at all. The campaign that had started had quickly come to a halt. How Richard Krebs actually reacted to this further proof that Soviet interests were always primary is unclear, but seven years later he was to describe these events in *Out of the Night* as a further step towards disillusionment.

Richard Krebs and the Soviet 'Services'

Krebs and his wife traveled on from Antwerp to Paris, where, masked, he attended an anti-war and fascism congress as delegate to German seamen and harbor workers. He then took part in a strike of French bargemen in effectively the same role as he had played during the Swedish strike. His wife left in August or September 1933 for Copenhagen, where she offered her services to ISH headquarters. In a manner typical for ISH workers of the time, she did not travel legally but sailed as a stowaway to Gothenburg, where she was met by an ISH worker who smuggled her on to Copenhagen.[170]

The strike may have testified to the hardiness of workers in northern France, but it ended in failure much as the strike in Sweden. Krebs traveled on to Copenhagen in October. There he was to be involved in a dispute at the top of the ISH that was to bring his career to an end.

Let us first consider his time as one of the leading ISH functionaries that began in September 1931 with his appointment as manager of Hamburg's Interclub. Here the question as to whether Krebs was involved in operations for Soviet secret services is salient. The events during the Swedish strike and his following trip to Norway indicate as much. In the light of available documentation, it is reasonable to suppose that he was much more seriously involved in the kidnapping of the strikebreakers from the *Kjell* than he was later to admit.

If the GPU were only indirectly involved in the violence at Gothenburg, in that they brought Krebs into contact with suitable men for these activities, the investigation of the Norwegian general staff, as has already been detailed, indicate that Krebs' Norwegian trip was not only in aid of agitation among resident workers, but also had military objectives. If the general staff of the Norwegian army were right, then Krebs was probably acting under orders issued by the GRU, the military secret service of the Soviet Union, rather than for the GPU. Such a mission would have been nothing out of the ordinary in those days. At the time the findings of the VIth Comintern Congress were those close to the heart of any faithful Communist, and these included the presumption that the Soviet Union was in immediate danger of attack by the 'rapacious' capitalists, and that this danger was to be countered by all available means.

Not only investigative reports testify to Krebs' involvement with Soviet secret services. Some of Krebs' unpublished writings and the statement made to the CIC in 1950 also corroborate the presumption. These both bear on events involving the sinister figure of Michael Avatin alias Ernest Lambert, the man whom Krebs had met in 1924 as he had smuggled him aboard the *Montpellier*.

According to the presumably bowdlerized statement that Krebs made to the CIC, he was involved in secret service operations in Hamburg during 1932 in at least some peripheral capacity. At the time a Latvian by the name of Schmitt, whom Krebs had met in the Leningrad Interclub in 1931, had come to Hamburg. Avatin had taken Schmitt under his wing. Krebs had been charged with finding Schmitt accommodation and determining locations where meetings might be held between Schmitt and Avatin plus entourage. It was of primary importance that none of these places should be in the vicinity of the Interclub. Some time later Krebs learnt that Schmitt was in Hamburg on a mission to infiltrate a National Socialist seamen's association which was being subsumed at the time by the NSDAP's foreign division. There are indices that the new organization was also to be used for espionage purposes, and countless reports on crewmembers in Nazi employ photographing coastlines, harbor entrances and defense provisions.

All this is to be found in the CIC's report on Krebs. Since he had knowledge of Schmitt's mission and its purpose, probably his role as a helper was not restricted to mere logistics. He would have also been a good man for any such job, since only few Communists held an officer's commission, and he had already been entrusted with agitation among these ranks. Furthermore, because of his background he was particularly familiar with the milieu from which the National Socialist seamen's association recruited its members.[171]

A second secret operation in which he was probably involved can be reconstructed from his unpublished writings and from *Out of the Night*. This seems to have taken place during 1933 in Antwerp.

"We were in Strasbourg as the news reached me that the chief of the Gestapo espionage in Flanders, Ilia Raikoff — The Ox — had at last been executed by Michael Avatin and his aides. I learned the details of this execution later, partly from Avatin himself, partly from Cilly who had helped him, but mainly from Comrade Anton, the Antwerp liaison-man, who had collected the reports."

In the chapter "West of the Rhine" the story is told of how Avatin and his aides try in vain to discretely do away with 'The Ox.' Finally an attractive Soviet secret service worker, Cilly, is charged with the job of seducing him. After she has succeeded she gets cold feet and refuses to poison him. As he gets drunk and mistreats her, however, she takes him to a lonely spot near the Rhine.

"The Ox stood on the edge of the quay as if he were thinking, and abruptly he whirled and struck at the Greek's face. In the same instant Avatin plunged his dagger into the spy's groin and ripped it sideways. Then he kicked him. The Ox grunted. Then he pitched into the river, and the current carried him away."

That this murder actually took place and that Krebs was personally involved in the matter seems to be substantiated by his unpublished writings. Among them is a note consisting of a couple of sentences written in 1939, the address on the paper showing that it must have been written after he had fled Europe and before he started on *Out of the Night*. This reads: "Ilya Raikoff, chief of counterespionage in Belgium — Comrade Anton discovers him — Avatin seeks helper. A. in love with him, refuses to poison." The first sentence is more univocal, however. It reads: "We killed the Ox."

Finally there is one more piece of evidence of a more incontrovertible nature. In one of the unpublished versions of his treatise on Comintern agents and instructors, the examples he gives of a Moscow envoy's typical missions are almost exclusively ones that we know he himself was involved in. One of the few exceptions in this list relates to the 'liquidation of the boss of a spy ring in Belgian that was working against the Comintern.' As has already been stated, these are indices and not solid proof. Yet nonetheless there is much that points towards Krebs' involvement during his three years as an instructor in a second mission for the Soviet secret police subsequent to the failed assassination attempt of 1926.

A Fateful Affair

Hitler's accession to power was not only a serious political defeat for the Comintern; it was also a logistic catastrophe. All international organizations that had been based in Germany at the time, and the Western European Bureau in particular, had had to be moved to countries less easily accessible from the Soviet Union at break-neck pace. The port of Hamburg, which had been an essential node in the OMS' worldwide net, could no longer be used as a relay point. Its role was partially assumed by Copenhagen, where ISH headquarters were relocated. This city had not only been chosen for its proximity to the Soviet Union and the country's liberal constitution, but also because the Danish section of the ISH was among the strongest and most disciplined in the world. In 1933 the Danish section succeeded in something that its German counterpart could never have managed because of incompatibility with the Social Democrats; it had incorporated the official union of stokers and, by a brilliant piece of maneuvering — the fusing of the stokers' and sailor's associations — had brought the sailors back under their control, although that association had already parted company with the ISH in 1933. The man responsible for this wily move was Richard Jensen, the chairman of the stoker's union and subsequent leader of the new united association.[172]

Richard Jensen, 'a bear of a man,' was a former sailor, famous for being able to drink the most hard-boiled of Moscow delegates under the table. He was similarly popular among Danish seamen as former ISH general secretary, Albert Walter, had been among the Germans before the empowered Gestapo arrested him. Because of his position in Denmark, Richard Jensen was important to the point of being irreplaceable in the ISH, although, like Albert Walter, he was never to be invested with the kind of executive power that the ISH man from Moscow would exert behind the scenes. Further to being a union chairman, Jensen was also member of the Copenhagen city parliament and state employed nautical employment officer, an administrator responsible for all welfare payments made to unemployed seamen. The measure of his influence was visible at the Seamen's Conference in Paris. This he attended in the company of "a group of Polish sailors, illegal and without papers, whose entry to Denmark he had facilitated on the grounds that he needed them as crewmembers."[173]

Adolf's position in his conflict with Ernst Wollweber had been weakened by the imprisonment of Albert Walter and the rise of Richard Jensen, as Jensen, unlike Walter, got on well with Wollweber and was even something of a friend to him. This conflict came to a head at the time of Krebs' arrival in Copenhagen.

In the beginning the ISH and the *Einheitsverband* —and with it the KPD's envoy Wollweber —were employing all bureaucratic intrigues in the struggle for domination of the Hamburg Interclub. Now the increased stake in the power struggle was domination of the ISH. On the one side were Adolf and his men, Krebs among them, on the other Ernst Wollweber and his entourage. This struggle, in itself typical of the workings of any large organization, was exacerbated by political differences that had worsened since Hitler had come to power. Richard Krebs left his interpretation of these events to posterity in his statement to the CIC on Wollweber shortly before his death. Since in order to undo his old enemy, Krebs' personal agenda chiefly involved furnishing the Americans with material that incriminated Wollweber, it is likely that at least a grain of truth is contained among the loaded statements. According to Krebs, Wollweber wanted to bring the large ISH's large budget under his control so as to employ the brunt of it in Germany.

Krebs claimed that after Wollweber had investigated the French, Belgian and Dutch organizations in summer 1933, he probably felt vindicated in his belief that Germany had the only promising Communist movement outside the Soviet Union. Whilst Adolf and Krebs still had an *idée fixe* about the world revolution, Wollweber wanted to dedicate both ISH funds and its organizational capacities entirely to the German movement, as he was convinced that there could be no Communist Europe without the Germans acting as flagship.

That Wollweber was in any position to challenge the status quo, despite the fact that Adolf had undermined him entirely by operating the double conference system, was thanks to an unfortunate love affair that the Pole engaged in.

There are various accounts on the affair. Richard Krebs reported to the CIC that the ladies' man Adolf slept with Hildegard Thingstrup on a few occasions, and because he wanted to keep her as a mistress, was obliged to involve her in the movement to avoid trouble; a functionary of his ranking would never have been allowed to have any kind of relationship with a non-member, particularly not with a bourgeois like Thingstrup.

According to the Danish author Erik Nørgaard, who for years has been considering writing the story of this couple, Shelley was in love with Hildegard Thingstrup. Why else, he avers, would he have sent her love poems of his own composition? [174]

Certainly to Nørgaard, Adolf was the love of Hildegard Thingstrup's life.

Thingstrup was seventy-five by the time she committed to paper the story of how she had met a handsome and well-dressed man in the train on New Year's Day. This man introduced himself as Alfred Siegwert and claimed to be a Swiss national. The twenty-five-year old woman, who despite her Danish-sounding name had grown up in a residential area of Hamburg, realized by the way that the stranger spoke that this man was not Swiss, but her suspicions were allayed as the charming figure explained that he had lost his accent during a lengthy stay abroad.

Aboard the ferry from Puttgarden to Gedser the couple promenaded together on deck, and Thingstrup gave the stranger her address, who in turn promised to look her up. A few days later she received a huge bunch of flowers and an invitation to one of Copenhagen's most expensive restaurants. Soon the charming stranger had won her heart, and some few weeks later they started to cohabit. Slowly the man started to confide in her, and Thingstrup learned that neither was the man's name Alfred Siegwert, as she had originally surmised, nor was he a representative of a large firm, as he had initially maintained, but instead, as he was to inform her by degrees, the secret leader of an international revolutionary seaman's union. For this reason, he told her, she was not to be concerned should he frequently make trips abroad.

Adolf must have quickly decided that his girlfriend was trustworthy, because he introduced her to his superior, the Russian Leo and to Leo's wife, and even involved her in his work; in his office — officially that of "Selvo & Co." — she carried out translating and secretarial work for him.

Leo was probably that most senior ranking instructor whom Krebs had met in the affair of the overly assiduous Norwegian Communist Arthur Samsing. Hildegard Thingstrup, who could no longer talk openly with any of her old acquaintances, began to confide in Leo's wife Anja.

The crisis came around the time that Richard Krebs arrived in Copenhagen as Hildegard found perfumed letters, written in Polish, among her lover's papers. Furious and jealous, since Adolf frequently visited the French capital for meetings such as the Seamen's Conference, she brought the letters to a translator and told the whole story to Leo's wife. Anja immediately reported this breach of security to her husband, and he in turn called a meeting of the ISH's highest echelon. From one day to the next, Adolf was forbidden to maintain his relationship with Thingstrup, and Hildegard was informed that Adolf had gone abroad and that she should relinquish hope of ever seeing him again. Even in the latter half of the 'thirties, as she was secretary to the Danish Communist party chairman Axel Larsen, she neither saw Adolf again nor could she even find out what had become of him in spite of her repeated entreaties for information.

Hildegard Thingstrup's memoirs smack of bitterness; she obviously felt deeply betrayed by Adolf placing Party loyalty above her love. As to whether he really had had an affair in Paris she makes no comment.

Adolf himself was made to pay dearly for his time with her. He was summoned to Moscow to answer to the heads of the Profintern on his "relations with un-vetted persons" and "gross disregard of the elementary rules of conspiracy"[175] What he reported on Hildegard reveals a figure far from the spurned lover, a woman much stronger than she gave herself credit for at the end of her life, who was very much involved in her lover's concerns.

"She was working in a large firm as a secretary. Whilst so doing, she performed services for our firm, which was in contact with hers for business reasons, and was sacked as a consequence. H. became a Party member under my influence, working in cell H, and began to work for my firm, where she rewrote articles and translated various things from Scandinavian languages into German (— gratis, of course).

In June I met a Comrade in Paris at an international anti-fascist conference, a pole who works for a French comrade at the central apparat of our firm. I began to correspond with her, the nature of our correspondence being apparent from the letters I have with me. Because H was jealous, (believing I was in closer contact with that comrade than was actually the case,) and since she spoke no Polish, she brought the letters to an acquaintance and recounted the matter to my superior at the European Comintern office, to which is my firm is subordinate and for whom she had been working (against my advice). I must stress the point that my firm is involved in legal trading, and I am the only illegal thing about it… I must confess that in my relationship to H I acted in what was doubtlessly a foolish manner…" [176]

Adolf's statement to the purges commission in late 1933 was of course coded in accordance with Comintern secrecy regulations, as can be seen in the words about H. performing services for his firm, it being in contact with her own, etc. In his statement to the CIC, Krebs recalled how Hildegard Thingstrup had forwarded to Adolf internal memos from the Danish Consulate in Hamburg, where she was employed at the beginning of their relationship. Since according to Adolf's words to the purges commission she was working for his boss, it would be wrong to reduce her role to merely that of girlfriend and part-time secretary. If Krebs' CIC statement is to be believed, then she was more informed about internal events in the ISH than he was himself, and indeed involved in a breadth of ISH conspiracy activities.[177] She was, as shall yet be seen, an attractive woman with nerves of steel, and one who knew well how to exploit her looks.

After Adolf Shelley's forced departure, Richard Krebs was completely in the power of Ernst Wollweber. The relationship between these men had long-since turned sour, as in the struggle between Wollweber and Adolf, Krebs had unequivocally sided with his mentor. These political differences were joined by personal ones, which could in part be explained by their respective biographies.

The perfect functionary Ernst Wollweber, and the would-be author Richard Krebs were simply worlds apart; one was a resolute Party soldier without personal weaknesses, from a background where higher education was virtually unheard of and only action counted, the other a bourgeois intellectual despite his years on the high sea and in San Quentin. Because of his background, Krebs could not do other than to think in international terms, had taken Conrad as a role model and was the tender lover of Hermine. There is no evidence that Wollweber, who received no secondary education, had either any artistic tendencies or any relationship of anything more than the most temporary kind.

In *Out of the Night* Richard Krebs mocked his old enemy for his ignorance. In a conversation between Valtin, Firelei and Wollweber the name of the then popular author Henri Barbusse is mentioned, but means nothing to the object of Krebs' ridicule. Firelei explains that Barbusse was the author of the book *Under Fire*.

" 'He wouldn't last long under fire,' Wollweber commented sardonically 'He's too tall and thin. Any fool of a detective could pick him out among a million others.'

Firelei laughed. 'Comrade Ernst, how about this fellow Goethe?'

'Goethe is dead,' Wollweber said. 'Goethe wrote *Faust*.' "

The inferiority that Wollweber must have felt among the educated was probably one of the reasons for the enmity between him and Adolf.

"WOLLWEBER himself was shrewd rather than intelligent. He was, KREBS believed, a good judge of people within his scope. ADOLF, for example, was completely beyond his scope. When confronted with superior intelligence, as e.g. in the case ADOLF, he would draw back into his shell."[178]

This estimation of the relationship between Wollweber and Shelley that Krebs offered the CIC was equally applicable to his relationship with the former. As in the struggle between the Party theoretician Bukharin and the practitioner Stalin, the victors in the ISH power struggle were not of the intelligentsia. The jump that Adolf and Krebs had on the narrow-minded Wollweber was made up for in common sense by Ernst the man-eater. After all, the program for the 1930's did not so much involve worldwide revolution as the impending war.

After such humiliations as the double conference system, Wollweber had no particular reason to set store by Krebs' assistance in Copenhagen. The fact that Adolf might still overcome his difficulties in Moscow and return to promote his protégé — perhaps even onto the ISH headquarters, where he would then inevitably lend support to his mentor — this must have deeply unsettled Wollweber. It was presumably for such reasons that Ernst Wollweber sent Krebs on a suicide mission to Germany shortly after Adolf's departure for Moscow. Hildegard Thingstrup was selected to accompany him on it.

The two of them were under orders to re-forge links to *Einheitsverband* members in Hamburg and to reorganize them in to the sort of units that they had formed in the days of the Weimar Republic. The Weimar Republic, however, was history. Richard Krebs and Hildegard Thingstrup knew what was in store for them in Germany. In Denmark and the countries that bordered the Germany of the Third Reich, Communist refugees and stories of desperate comrades on the run were legion.

As *Einheitsverband* reports show, and these were available to the ISH elect, by October 1933 the *Blockwarts,* low-level local nazi stooges, had informers in almost every Hamburg house. These observed the comings and goings of all occupants, and kept an eye out for illegal meetings, Communists hideouts, transportation of packets and suspect communications. Stoolpigeons were everywhere, particularly in the harbor where, disguised as traders and beggars, they would visit restaurants and bars to spy on suspect individuals. This was supplemented by so-called 'mass raids,' during which whole streets were cordoned off that Communist functionaries might be flushed out. To read the report listing all the arrests at the end of the communiqué is to feel the terror that Krebs and Thingstrup themselves must have felt on receiving this order. "Almost four hundred functionaries have been arrested, among them the entire former office staff of the *Einheitsverband.* Of the twenty-seven strong *Einheitsverband* national management, twenty-four have been arrested. All regional, and river basin managers are under arrest. The wave of arrests has not been restricted to association functionaries, but has caught up with other important communication nodes such as employment office A. in Hamburg. Of the 110 or 120 members working in the association's work group, 55 have been arrested. The largest employment office for harbor workers on Hamburg's Sägerplatz Square has suffered a similar fate… The entire Clubactive* has twice been raided with ensuing arrests."[179]

The order to rebuild an association, most of whose members were already behind bars, was just as preposterous and inappropriate as countless other KPD drives under Hitler. In the attempt to reconstruct the Party, old methods were employed that even included such bureaucratic paraphernalia as membership cards, complete with contribution stamps, which alleviated any difficulty in proving Communist Party membership and enabled the Gestapo to clean up whole Party regions after having

---

* I.e. the Interclub management

arrested any single Communist. Until the Brussels Party Conference in April 1935, when the KPD changed their m.o. to one appropriate to the waging of war, regional management on the northern coast, in the Ruhrgebiet and in Hessen-Frankfurt was subject to repeated raids (each of the above were visited on seven occasions and the Baden region on eight). Mecklenburg alone survived relatively unscathed with only two raids.[180]

It is implausible that Adolf would have given a man who had repeatedly proven himself on difficult missions such a senseless task, particularly as arrest was little short of inevitable. It is even harder to believe that Adolf would have treated Hildegard Thingstrup in this manner. In her memoirs she states plainly that on this occasion she had been intentionally sent into a trap.

However, there is also no reason to believe that Krebs reacted to Wollweber's order with anything but the unconditional subservience to a superior's command. Both the "fervent energy of purpose" ascribed to him by a Nazi judge, and the tenacity that he showed after arrest, attest to the fact that his dedication to the cause was untroubled by his differences with Wollweber. It seems that his belief in the 'historical mission' of Communism was too great, his faith in the precedence of the Party too unshakeable, for doubt to be entertained.

In late October 1933 Krebs received his final orders and contact addresses in Hamburg. He was instructed to exercise extreme caution in making contact, as it was unclear who was already under arrest, who had escaped capture and who might have turned traitor, and to travel as the American journalist Robert Williams. And then he was issued by Richard Jensen with a passport made out to a certain Otto Melchior. That passport was the most damning evidence that Wollweber had decided to be rid of him, "since ISH headquarters at Vesterport produced plenty of passports,"[181] some of which would surely have been more suitable. Erik Nørgaard, who later investigated Hildegard Thingstrup's claims, was convinced of the fact, particularly since the Jewish sirname, Melchior, would have been so conspicuous to Nazi eyes. Melchior himself was a well-known Danish Communist, and the German Consulate had already reported to Berlin that not only was he traveling through Denmark in order to agitate against the new order in Germany, but, furthermore, that he was a member of a committee campaigning for the release of Ernst Thälmann.

Krebs was supposed to keep up communications with Hamburg by means of a seamen-courier called Martin Holstein. Hildegard Thingstrup, of whom the Gestapo were not, as yet, aware, was to follow him a few days later and help him make contacts.

Richard Krebs took leave of his wife, who in the interim had returned to working for the ISH, this time in Copenhagen, and traveled to Hamburg without being stopped on the border. It is possible that he was under observation from the first moment, since Martin Holstein had already been working for the Gestapo for some time.[182] The few days that he was to spend on the loose were occupied with contacting the ever cautious and mistrustful contact men whose addresses he had received in Copenhagen. This he did at first alone, later in Hildegard's company, and with varying success. He slept at least once at his sister Cilly's house. On November 7 the game was up; both he and Hildegard were arrested.[183]

A kind of postscript to Krebs' time as an instructor is to be found among Gestapo archives. This comes from an unknown informant who reported thus on an antifascist congress from 25-26 November, 1933 in Paris: "May it be noted that Krebs' arrest has caused great dismay, since his skilled organizational abilities were employed only three weeks ago, when he kindled the harbor workers strike in Rouen that is still ongoing. The most important assertion is that of Neumann: since Krebs' recent incarceration, the ISH's connection to Germany has been interrupted."[184]

PART III Double Game

The Arrest

From the moment of his capture on November 7 to his appearance in before the magistrates on January 18 Richard Krebs was held in 'preventative detention.' This left him entirely at the mercy of the new regime. If he was not being tortured by the Hamburg Gestapo in the Hamburg Townhouse, where Gestapo headquarters were located, then he was in the Fuhlsbüttel Concentration Camp, where fanatical SS-men gave free reign to their sadistic impulses. He experienced the first days of that shadow world which the new government created as counterpart to a justice system which, largely unaltered, had been adopted from the Weimar Republic. All the rights that were guaranteed in Germany were of no significance in Gestapo custody or in the newly founded concentration camps. There were no restrictions to the arbitrary violence among guards, and the only hope — one which, in general, proved vain — was that of pressure being brought to bear from abroad. On November 10, three days after Krebs' arrest, an anonymous Hamburg Communist sent a report on conditions to an émigré comrade with the request that the latter "publish the following authentic facts, since a number of the comrades involved are in mortal danger...

"The State Police officers Kraus and Deutschmann are directing the so-called interrogations. They are both taking part in the illtreatment of the prisoners, and are accompanied in it by other officers. Rubber truncheons, steel bars, whips and chains are being used to beat the prisoners... Prisoners are being taken to the so-called *Lenin Room* in the Townhouse, a room draped in red and decorated with Communist emblems and pictures. They are being pulled across a table covered by a red flag during interrogation. Whilst they are beaten with leather straps, rubber batons and ox whips, a gramophone plays revolutionary songs."

Between questionings the prisoners are taken to one of Hamburg's concentration camps. Conditions in Fühlsbuttel are the worst of all. There the SS do not attempt to beat new information out of their old enemies; they are, instead, to be humiliated until they are broken and can no more think of posing opposition to the new regime. Some of those who remain recalcitrant have been shot whilst 'attempting to escape.' Others have had themselves killed by provoking their captors rather than continue life in a concentration camp.

All SS men wear a steel helmet and carry a carbine, a pistol, a bayonet, and a long, leather strap some two inches broad. The order in the camp is strictly military. New arrivals have to stand to attention for up to four hours. At any sign of movement the prisoner is beaten with a rifle butt. If the cell door is opened, the prisoner must jump up and stand at his locker whatever the hour of day or night.

The beatings are arbitrary. At all times of day and night prisoners are pulled from their cells, taken into the corridors and beaten. The screaming and crying is incessant. The prisoners cannot sleep because of this, though they stop their ears and hide beneath their blankets. Everyone knows that they might be the next. Many are close to insanity because of the perpetual sleeplessness... A comrade, who lay there unconscious after hours of mistreatment, was stripped by SS-men, who then screamed at him: 'you swine, we know you're feigning. You'd like to be dead, huh? Your life is worth nothing to us, but we're going to put the screws on you more than once first, Bolshevist pig.' "[185]

Richard Krebs' interrogation was conducted by Peter Kraus, one of the two Gestapo men mentioned by name in the report on Gestapo officers at the Townhouse. Krebs was later to describe him as a "short, broad-shouldered man

[with] dark, deep-set eyes his face... strongly lined." Peter Kraus was already responsible for Communist affairs during the Weimar period, and, unlike many a policeman who was accepted into the Gestapo because of a dearth of trained men, had been a NSDAP member prior to 1933. He had, in addition, worked for the NSDAP's secret service, the SD. In short, he must have been a ruthless fanatic to whom a human life was worth nothing, as the Gestapo employed him in Lviv shortly after the attack on the Soviet Union, where, in 1941, one of the first mass-executions was carried out.[186]

The two months during which Krebs was in the power of Peter Kraus were to leave him with lasting health problems. He ended almost deaf in his right ear from the repeated beatings, and his kidneys were also badly damaged. Years later he would still suffer from pain so intense it prevented him sleeping.

The profit drawn by the Nazis from torturing him was meager. Krebs characterized his tactics to an American investigating officer in 1943: "Confess as much of the truth as possible and deny only what can't be proved"[187]

Incidentally, this officer was particularly disturbed by this "insidious form of perjury," and noted it down as a further proof of Krebs' untrustworthiness.

His role in the Hamburg Interclub and during the establishing of the secret press, complete with club material, was scarcely to be denied. He was arrested with some short, coded sentences on his person, and the meaning of these was beaten out of him. In this way the Gestapo got onto the trail of some of the contact men, that Richard Krebs and Hildegard Thingstrup were visiting. Fortunately for both of them, the Gestapo knew nothing of ISH structure and had no idea what luck they had had in capturing Adolf's secretary. The cover story that both of them kept to — the dumb, wayward and naïve blonde and the cynical agent, who exploited her love for him without a qualm — remained unbroken by the Nazis.

In the dossiers on interrogations and accusatory papers it can be seen how the two of them were playing together in order to explain Thingstrup's known activities for Krebs in Hamburg and her contacts to Danish Communists. "The accused claims, however, to have never been politically active. She allegedly never belonged to the Party, but only the organization for trade and office workers, which, according to her impression, was Social Democrat oriented.

It is, inevitably, impossible to investigate more closely Thingstrup's activities in Denmark. It is, however, a fact that she maintained contacts with several men who were known to the secret police as Communist functionaries. These include Otto Melchior and a man that she calls Alfred Siegwert*. She may well have been romantically involved with both of them.

On 10.25.33 the accused went to Hamburg, her explanation being that this was in order to make a visit. However, she claims that as she was preparing to leave Copenhagen, friends gave her the details of a friend who was leaving for Hamburg and whom she might meet. She left them with the telephone number of her parents. This was all done in light spirits, she claims but then she really was called and invited to a meeting in Café Vaterland. There she met with Krebs, who was known to her

---

* Siegwert was one of Adolf's cover names.

from her time in Copenhagen, where she had known her as Williams. This character had claimed to be an American journalist."[188] So it continues in the dossier; secret meetings, the sense of which remained a mystery to her and a series of people who she had never seen before. "The accused claims to have not known what the purpose of Krebs' secret activities... She confesses that she noticed Krebs' peculiar behavior and asked him what the meaning of it might be. He never gave her a proper answer, and she calmed herself repeatedly, as she had grown to like him well and he had also acted as if he also felt the same way towards her."

Krebs substantiated Thingstrup's statements;

"I first saw Hildegard, whom I was later to meet in Hamburg, in the Copenhagen Seamen's Club, shortly after my arrival around mid-October in the port... I saw her then sitting with a man in a café, but didn't speak to her. I noticed her because she was reading a German paper. I asked a seaman if she was German and he replied that she was Danish. I was trying to find out with this question if she had been sent by the German consulate, to see if Germans were frequenting the Interclub. We had been warned of such eavesdroppers, etc.

I didn't see her again in Copenhagen, but rather ran into her in Hamburg after my arrival... I introduced myself to her under the name of Williams."[189] By both sticking to their story, Krebs and Thingstrup stayed clear of the worst danger.

When Krebs appeared on February 1, 1930 before the examining magistrate he was able to make the following irrefutable statement: "the man I have called 'Adolf' looks very similar to the man... in both of these photographs. He wore a pair of spectacles, however, as I knew him. I do not know Adolf's surname. I only saw him once, and that was on the day I left Hamburg, in March 1933, after Walther was arrested. As to whether his real name was Alfred Siegwert — cf. Thingstrup's statement pages 108 and 109 — I can say nothing. I am not familiar with anyone of that name. I never saw those photos in the possession of Thingstrup. I cannot judge whether Thingstrup knew the Adolf I have in mind. I think that Adolf was English, because he spoke German with a strong English accent. I do not know whether he ever traveled for a steel wool company in Stockholm. I do not know if Thingstrup knew Adolf. We never talked with one another.

I wish now to tell the whole truth about what happened in Copenhagen since my arrival, because I am convinced that the German Communist movement is absolutely hopeless."[190]

The kind of truth that Krebs had decided to dish up to the Gestapo now becomes apparent: "I came to Copenhagen from Antwerp, a town I had never previously visited." This combination of indisputable facts and stealthy deceit continues for page after page. The statement on Wollweber again typifies the proceeding; "We met there a man called 'Ernst.' I suppose he is one and the same as Ernst Wollweber. I did not know him personally before then, but knew he was in the national section for water transport of the RGO. There then follows the story of how 'Ernst' forces the 'shirker' Krebs to accept the dangerous mission to Hamburg. "I considered, together with my wife, what would happen if I refused to accept Ernst's request. We thought that my wife might well lose her job."

His hero, Jan Valtin, recounts the following on Gestapo interrogations: "In the democratic countries the communist rule for arrested comrades is to say nothing. If you say nothing here, I thought, they'll bear you to death."

Ironically it was not his real activities for the ISH that were carrying maximum punishment. The accusations of having been one of those who commissioned the Red Marines attack in which one member severed the spine of the SA man Heinzelmann was much more dangerous. Due to his low position in KPD Krebs could hardly have been involved at such a level, but the fact that the Gestapo wanted to pin this charge upon him might well have had something to do with the fact that the 'rebuilding of the *Einheitsverband* carried a maximum sentence of three years imprisonment, since at the time it did not constitute High Treason. In the Third Reich prior to his arrest a series of laws had been altered to carry more severe punishment, but at the time attempted murder still carried a heavier sentence than a political crime.

The trial, known as the 'von Bargen trial' after one of the accused, was held in late April. It was, in reality, a show trial, there to reveal to the public at large the fate that Hitler had saved them from. The case not only dealt with the Heinzelmann murder but also a gun attack on SA men in front of the Hotel Adler, ascribed to the Red Marines, in which two civilians lost their lives. Hamburg's *Gauleiter*, the Nazi head of that administrative region, attended the trial in person, as did relatives and colleagues of victims, so that the tension really mounted. Fifty men were charged, and of them only one was acquitted whilst eight Communists were sentenced to death.

The ruling states "that Krebs attempted to defend himself with extraordinary skill, and would only concede his involvement as representative of another, but [that] the court is convinced of his having attended the pertinent meeting... The court could not find sufficient evidence that at that district sitting the order was given to not only attack but also to murder National Socialists that would justify a homicide conviction."[191] Once again Krebs got away lightly with a sentence of two years and three months imprisonment for affray.

Two months later the next trial was held. This time the proceedings were against him, Hildegard Thingstrup and five of the contact men that they had visited during early November. All seven were being charged with Conspiracy to commit High Treason). Three were acquitted, as the meeting between them and the two principals allegedly were of no import. According to what Krebs later told the CIA's predecessor organization, at least one of these, Karl Nettkau, was really member of the Harbor Supervisory Organization, a body charged with recording the cargos and destinations of anchored ships. Richard Krebs had intended to employ him as manager of the ISH harbor worker section.

"NETTKAU was an ideal man for conspirative work. He was always calm, never rushed matters, often waited for days in setting up a meeting, was very patient and security-conscious. His acquittal is testimony of his ability."[192]

Rudolf Obermüller and Carl Meinhart were found guilty. Meinhart's guilt was essentially that of having enabled Krebs to contact Nettkau. "The court finds a sentence of one year's imprisonment appropriate, recognizing that Meinhart may have been subjected to pressures from Thingstrup and Krebs."[193]

Obermüller, sub-tenant of Richard Krebs' last Hamburg apartment, was sentenced to eight months imprisonment, as he was severely ill. Krebs himself was given the maximum sentence.

"In fixing the penalty the court took into account the fact that Krebs is a grave threat to the state and that his treasonous activities date back to autumn 1933. The legally stipulated maximum punishment of three years incarceration is thus appropriate in his case. This punishment is to be combined with the two year and three month sentence he received from the Hansa League Special Court on May 2, 1934 to yield a total sentence of four years' incarceration.[194]

The climax of the trial must have been Hildegard Thingstrup's performance. She portrayed herself as the wronged innocent daughter of a German nationalist. Her furious father, entirely unaware of his child's real activities, almost assaulted Krebs in court. The Danish Consul called her a loyal Dane and a wonderful worker. The Gestapo men present must have been gnashing their teeth when they heard the verdict:

"The accused, by her manner, does not give the impression of being a Communist sympathizer. With regard to her circle of Communist acquaintances, the Senate can only presume that her life-style and vivacity led her inadvertently into a circle in which she remained to enjoy the pleasures available without herself becoming indoctrinated by the beliefs prevalent there."[195]

It was only in 1937 that the Gestapo really recognized with what aplomb Hildegard Thingstrup had carried the thing off; an apparently innocuous photo of a child that had been found in Richard Krebs' possession, that Thingstrup had had returned to her on departing, claiming that this was a picture of a relative that had been entrusted to her for enlargement, proved to be the image of none other than Adolf's daughter, given to Krebs for identification purposes.[196]

Hildegard Thingstrup was sentenced to seven months, with those served in custody before trial counting in her favor. She should have been released on August 29, but the Gestapo avenged themselves for a punishment they considered too mild. Hildegard Thingstrup spent the month before her deportation in a concentration camp.[197]

Richard Krebs was sent to Fuhlsbüttel penitentiary. He must have known that in the best case he would not be released before November 1937, and that even then he might be taken into preventative custody and languish in a concentration camp at the Gestapo's pleasure.

Hermine Reneges

After her husband's arrest, Hermine Krebs remained alone in Copenhagen. She was twenty-eight years old, could neither return to Germany nor practice her profession, and she had no prospects of ever seeing her child again. The talented graphic artist from the bourgeoisie found herself in an eerie environment, the oddity of which was all the more accentuated by her husband's absence. She had joined the Party and worked alongside him, had even created her a sphere of her own in which to work, but her projects had always been secondary to the idea of working together with him. After his departure it was soon evident that the girl from the well-off Bremen merchant family was incongruous in the Copenhagener masculine atmosphere of political conspirators and seamen. The code of conduct among them bore little comparison to those applied in the North German Wool-Carding Company where she had spent so many years. Furthermore, the refugee German Communists, under pressure from both local authorities and subject to permanent Gestapo informants, had increased their vigilance and treated all outsiders with redoubled suspicion.

Hermine Krebs had no one to turn to. She was dependent on the camaraderie of her husband's comrades, since as a foreigner she had slim chances of finding work in the Denmark of those crisis years.

Initially she worked at the Copenhagen Interclub. She painted murals and frescos, which could still be seen years later, and she composed précis of reports given by German seamen on the Third Reich, which she also illustrated. These reports were incorporated in underground magazines which were smuggled into Germany.

She was soon, however, to come into conflict with Wollweber and leave the Party. Like Firelei in *Out of the Night* she held the now-unbridled boss of the ISH responsible for the arrest of her husband.

Wollweber's retaliation was in character. Erik Nørgaard, having interviewed survivors on the period, came up with the following on this period of ISH history: "Wollweber gave the order that Hermine be vetted. Michael Avatin and the Danish seaman Rasmussen set about it." Rasmussen told Nørgaard: "We checked Herma's apartment on the Tordenskjoldgate on one occasion as she was out. There was nothing to substantiate any suspicions."[198]

This must have taken place three or four months after Krebs' arrest. In the court case held under the Third Reich against Hermine in autumn 1934 it was maintained that in February she was already working as a house keeper, having resigned from ISH work.

All this must be painstakingly pieced together from Nørgaard's publications, Krebs' CIC statements and the trial held against Hermine, as in *Out of the Night* the story of Firelei is not the real story of Hermine Krebs. In that rendition the stalwart and courageous comrade works in exile for the KPD until an informant tricks her into coming to Germany. There she is arrested and sentenced to six years imprisonment. The informant of that story, however, really did exist. His name was Hermann Beilich, and he played a somewhat different role in Hermine's life to the one he was accredited with by Jan Valtin.

The three or four months during which Hermine worked for the Interclub after her husband's capture must have been torturous. The latent distrust of her, a child of the bourgeoisie, must have been almost tangible, and Wollweber's activities can only have made it even more apparent. In those weeks Hermine Krebs probably took Hermann Beilich as a lover.

Krebs himself had known Beilich since 1933, when he had examined the man's work as German section manager of the Rotterdam Interclub charged also with sending propaganda material to Germany and maintaining Communist units aboard German merchant marine ships. Richard Krebs was entirely satisfied with the work of the man who he would later describe to the CIC as "slender, medium height, very well dressed, good looking, calm [,] narrow face, made a very pleasant and capable impression."[199]

The affair between Hermine and Beilich cannot have lasted long, as Wollweber sent him to Hamburg as Krebs' replacement in either late February or early March 1934. There the Gestapo arrested him quickly; he had the same courier as Krebs had had: the informant Martin Holstein. Two of the letters found on his person by the Gestapo had been written by Hermine Krebs. The letters themselves have disappeared, but the explanation given by Beilich to the Nazis remains: "They are from Herma Krebs to me, sent from Copenhagen. We were intimate, that is why the content of these letters relates to our relationship... Moreover... I include... the first letter... as it offers some insight into the unpleasant personal relations between German refugees there."[200]

It is presumably no coincidence that Hermine's break-up with her husband's comrade coincided with Beilich's departure. For the second time Wollweber had sent a man important to her to Germany.

She was unaware that judging by what can be reconstructed from Gestapo archives pertaining to Beilich's later career, the good-looking, pleasant man had abused her trust from the very outset and had informed Wollweber of all that she had confided in him.

To the Gestapo, who had no difficulty in breaking him, Beilich presented himself as a small-time harbor informant working in Hamburg, a milieu that he had known all his life. The son of an engineer, Beilich had interrupted an agricultural apprenticeship to go to sea in 1923. In 1930 he lived as typewriter repairman in Constantinople, then traveled six months later to Italy "There, in Genoa I worked until February 1933 for the Italian police in their criminal and political reconnaissance service. My work consisted of observing the movements of foreigners and seamen in Genoa with particular regard to their political activities."[201] To prove these credentials to the Nazis he named the names of his superior Italian officers in this branch. He furthermore reported to the Gestapo that he had had to leave the city as the German Consul had refused to extend his passport and that in May 1933 he had arrived in Copenhagen where "under the orders of the political police of Genoa [he] attempted… to find his way into Communist circles."

All of this seems to add up, but, as we shall yet see, not all is as it seems in the case Hermann Beilich. After having been obliged to enlist for the Gestapo as informant, or V-man,* Beilich returned to Copenhagen.

Did he resume relations with Hermine Krebs? Probably not, but if so, then it was clandestine, as the KPD leadership already had qualms about liaisons between their functionaries and non-Party members during the Weimar days, and this was all the more true of the exile era, when German Communists were under observation not only by the Gestapo but also by local authorities.

After his return, Beilich sent ISH-internal information on to Hamburg. He is alleged to have forwarded the Gestapo a list of seamen aboard German ships working as ISH contacts in this manner.[202]

It is impossible to ascertain now, after half a century, how much of the information he furnished was actually new. What Beilich reported on Hermine Krebs is contrary to all we know about her from other sources. He claimed that she had had a sparkling career and that by 1934, when she was replaced by a V-man, she was leader of the German section of the Interclub and then even "employed as a closer aide to Wollweber."

In August 1934 Beilich reappeared in Hamburg. He reported to the Gestapo that he had been unmasked whilst compiling a list enumerating all German contact points."[203]

In early 1937, as Richard Krebs was embarking on his audacious and precarious double game with the Gestapo, inspector Kraus spoke to him about Beilich. It appears, according to Krebs' CIC report, that the Gestapo were looking for Beilich and were prepared to kidnap him if need be. Krebs never discovered why the Gestapo were so desperate to get their hands on him.

The historian Dieter Nelles reports that Beilich disappeared from Hamburg in October 1935 and was thereafter to be seen on 'wanted' posters. "Investigations revealed that he had embezzled 1000 Deutschmark from the National Welfare Service where he was employed. There is much evidence that until his departure from Hamburg he was in contact with the Communist underground. According to his sister, who was arrested in 1937, he was also playing a double game in order to learn about the Gestapo's m.o.

On the occasion of his last meeting with his sister, Beilich claimed that he was leaving for Spain so as to again work as 'a double'; he intended to work as a Communist spy in Franco's army.[204]

This would explain Beilich's statements on Hermine Krebs: the double agent, obliged to deliver information to maintain the Gestapo's confidence, gave them an explosive story on a character who had long since left the organization.

Hermine's mother traveled to Copenhagen in August 1934 so as to bring her back to Germany. Before this, being the good bourgeois that they were, Mr and Mrs.

---

* *Verbindungsmann*, contact man

Stöver had established contact with the Gestapo, trusting no doubt in the integrity of that state body. On August 14 Inspector Kraus wrote to Berlin:

"Mrs Krebs had enquired recently, via her father, resident of Bremen, if the police have any charges that would prevent her safe return to Germany. I responded in the negative and intend to arrest her the moment of her return, as she has been wanted for High Treason since 1933 and had been involved in comparable activities abroad since."[205]

Beilich's statements may well have contributed to this decision.

After she had been observed for several weeks, the unwitting Hermine Krebs was brought in. This must have come as a terrible shock to the young woman that had ceased to work for the KPD several months before. She was to spend the first weeks of detention in a concentration camp. When interrogated, she cracked at once. According to the memoirs of camp survivors, those who did not know why they had been brought to this hell were those who suffered hardest. Having trusted the Gestapo and returned to Germany, the mental defense mechanisms that Christian and Communists applied to survive torture at the hands of the Nazis without revealing all apparently failed her.

She revealed everything, including all she knew about her husband, and, as was later seen at her trial, much that she need not have revealed, it being material that the Nazis could not otherwise have ascertained. This included information such as the fact, that she had been employed by the counter intelligence service, her mission being to observe people "who approached Communist and Interclub functionaries in a manner provoking suspicion."[206] She tried in vain to recant these accusations against her at her trial, as the public prosecutor evidently could not furnish any further proof of them. The fact that the prosecutor was in possession of all the flyers that she had illustrated after fleeing for Antwerp was, however, to prove fateful. A drawing in which "the Führer was depicted as an executioner" was given close consideration. Furthermore, some of the papers on which she worked contained information about armament measures. This, it was claimed, constituted Treason.

On October 10, 1935 the Hansa League High Court passed sentence upon her. The title page of the court ruling was marked with a stamp that read: Secret! Charge of Treason: "In fixing the penalty the court considered as mitigating the circumstance that the accused entered into the illegal work for the KPD whilst heavily under the influence of her husband, and that she finally turned from Communism of her own volition — this being an undisputable fact. However, given the education of the accused, the proven charge of Treason may not be treated too mildly. For this reason a sentence of two years is considered appropriate. The eleven months and three weeks that the accused had spent in custody prior to her trial are to be subtracted from that total in accordance with article 60 of criminal legislation.[207]

Three years after Hermine's arrest, in autumn 1937, when Richard Krebs succeeded in fleeing Germany, there was a dispute between him and Wollweber on Beilich's role in the affair. Krebs reported to Wollweber that he had seen Beilich in Gestapo headquarters, and that the Gestapo held in their keeping a detailed report on the special bureau that Beilich had established in Amsterdam. Krebs had concluded that Beilich was responsible for his wife's arrest. Wollweber countered that Krebs' wife had cooperated with the Gestapo, but that an alliance between Beilich and the Gestapo was out of the question.

Perhaps Krebs had found out about the relationship between his wife and Beilich. In *Out of the Night* there is a more than a hint to this effect. In the chapter on Valtin being tortured at the hands of the Gestapo, the prisoner thinks of his wife: "Somewhere Firelei was still alive. If she knew, I thought, she'd weep. Maybe she wept. Or maybe she was now sleeping with a comrade bound to go to Germany and his doom." Nonetheless, as shall yet be seen, she remained the great love of Krebs and Valtin's life.

Double Agents

Even if a secret service is aware that an agent in its employ is taking orders from another service, it remains convinced that in reality the agent is working for it alone. The archives that contain Hermann Beilich's letters from Copenhagen do not offer any hint that the informant was actually working for the other side. His statements to the Gestapo include no indication that, having agreed the plan with his comrades, he had intentionally deceived the Nazis on the matter of Hermine Krebs. Beilich was not alone in feigning to have himself recruited. A much more famous and significant case was that of Walter Trautzsch, who traveled repeatedly from France to maintain contact with the incarcerated Ernst Thälmann. To these ends he met regularly with Thälmann's wife Rosa. On one visit he was stopped during a border control in Aachen and brought to Berlin. Fortunately for him, the Gestapo had no idea about his connections with Rosa Thälmann. When the German Secret State Police showed interest in recruiting him, he cooperated "as prescribed" (as the authors of the standard work on the secret service of the KPD put it), returned at once to Paris and reported to Central Committee headquarters. After 1945 the case was reopened and

Trautzsch's statement on the matter confirmed. Nevertheless, he was disciplined by the SED*[208].

Anyone examining archives pertaining to cases such as that of Trautzsch or Beilich fifty years after the fact can only hope to come up with the truth when the Gestapo, in the case of Beilich, or their opponents, as in the case of Trautzsch, had themselves stumbled upon it, and the relevant archives have been declassified. If the counterpart to the Gestapo involved the Soviet secret police or another organization whose archives are unavailable, then the project becomes nigh impossible. For such reasons it is easy to falsely estimate men such as Beilich whilst investigating the Communist underground of Hitler's Germany. The Gestapo, however, were not the only ones to be deceived by double agents.

When the Hitler movement became the strongest among the right-wing movements, but also after it had taken power, suitable Communists were ordered to join the SA, the NSBO (The National Socialistic trade union) or the SS. This was in part because the KPD believed that, as in the case of the SA, it would be possible to infiltrate the ranks and exploit the well-known demands for a 'real revolution' to their own ends, and in part, as in the case of the NSBO, in order to stir up discontentment. If a Communist succeeded in infiltrating a Nazi mass organization, then his or her tasks were to include, among other things, denunciation of discontented Nazis to the leadership — in order to win their confidence — and also organization of hatred against this repressive apparatus.

How many such comrades really did continue in these tasks, how many changed their convictions, and how many survived the 'thousand year Reich' in unrecognized inactivity, having lost all connections when the Gestapo captured the others in the network around them, cannot be ascertained.

Such practices created confusion not only in Gestapo rows, but also among its own ranks, and this uncertainty was to remain long after the war's end. A prime example of this is that of Albert Walter and Paul Borowiak's. Borowiak, born into a Communist family, was still a child when Hitler came to power, and was little more than a boy when he first went to sea. Some time after 1935 he made contact with a group of German seamen who organized resistance to Hitler from Antwerp. He judged by the reaction of older crewmembers, whom he told of this group, that he was not the only one among them to have such contacts. The Antwerp group and those few crewmembers in contact with them were even known to the only man onboard of Nazi allegiances. The Hitler supporter chose not to denounce anyone, as he intended to continue to make his living as a sailor, and the Gestapo would not have been in a position to save him in the case of an accident on the high seas.

After the war had ended, Paul Borowiak joined the Party and started to work for the Seamen's Union. He met many Party members and began to write down their stories as part of a book on Nazi resistance among seamen. In 1968, after the suppression of the Prague Spring, he broke with the Party, but still continued work on his book.

---

* SED The Socialist Unity Party of Germany

In 1999 Paul Borowiak died before completing his project. The author is indebted to that committed unionist and Hamburg man for having taught him so much about the world in which Richard Krebs lived.

After 1945 Paul Borowiak attended a meeting for the victims of Nazi persecution. Albert Walter was among them, until those present ejected him from the hall in disgust. Borowiak himself shared the sentiment. In 1995 though, as he recounted the tale, he said something astonishing; perhaps Walter had at all times been following orders. Perhaps Walter had been another of the ostensible turncoat functionaries. To appreciate just how extraordinary Borowiak's pronouncement is, let us consider Walter's career in the Third Reich, for it was one that apparently admitted no doubt as to its proponent's intent.

Krebs himself, writing in 1941, described how in 1933 the Gestapo managed to break the former ISH general secretary within a short time of his arrest; the Gestapo brought in the bachelor's aged mother and threatened to torture her in front of him. Albert Walter prevented this passage being printed in its German translation. Perhaps Borowiak would otherwise have interpreted the case differently. It remains unclear how much Walter revealed to the Gestapo. Initially, at least, it appears that he held back information, for otherwise Richard Krebs and Hildegard Thingstrup would not have been able to pass off their respective accounts. Whilst Krebs was still in prison awaiting trial, Walter was released. He passed over the chance of escaping abroad, and even the repeated attempts of emissaries from Copenhagen to make him leave the Third Reich were in vain; Walter refused to go.

No later than 1937 the former ISH general secretary was consulted by the Gestapo on marine affairs, and he worked for the Nazi propaganda division during the 'forties. The statements of his contemporary, Richard Krebs, the Gestapo's archives, the mere fact that the Nazis set him free — all this incriminated him to such an extent that no reasonable doubt could remain. Richard Krebs, who met him again in 1937 after his release was later to describe him to the CIC as a broken and penuried man who lived in mortal fear of the Nazis.

Nonetheless, when American secret service men questioned him as to whether the man — who by then was a member of the West German parliament — had been a Communist plant, Krebs gave much the same reply as Paul Borowiak: "In the case of Albert Walter, anything is possible."[209]

As for Beilich, Richard Krebs had divined the truth of the matter. Krebs would tell the CIC seventeen years later that Beilich, whom he only knew as 'Hertig,' had been a much discussed theme in Fuhlsbüttel. There had been much dispute as "whether he had gone into underground work or was not to be trusted."[210]

Krebs himself had experienced how Beilich, dressed very well and appearing very sure of himself, had entered the room where he was being interrogated. As soon as Beilich saw Krebs he turned and left. When Krebs reported this and other comparable causes for suspicion to Wollweber in 1937, the latter rejected the thesis that Beilich was working for the Gestapo.

Krebs' own comment to the CIC reads "It is possible that WOLLWEBER had accepted Beilich in good faith and then would not admit his mistake to an underling. It is also possible that BEILICH was a communist agent in the Gestapo."[211]

Solitary

At the time that Hermine Krebs was imprisoned, Richard Krebs has already been in solitary confinement for two months. Valtin recounted that in Fuhlsbüttel penitentiary at the time there was a permanent dearth of food. Given his perpetual hunger and the absolute ban on speech during the daily twenty minutes exercise in the yard, it is unsurprising that he was often on the verge of despair. Valtin combated such moods with iron rigor. Sometimes he flung his bread from the window, and on occasions forced himself to sit in agonizing positions for hours on end. In order to forget the hatred cell that confined him, he would play himself at chess, listen in his imagination to symphonies he recollected, and hum folk and Communist war songs of the Comintern.

After his turbulent years, his almost continuous employment on Comintern missions, with their countless meetings, discussions and endless journeys, Krebs now found himself for the first time in enforced isolation and inertia.

He was suddenly presented with huge stretches of time in which to consider his life prior to imprisonment and the future after his release, which, should he be spared a stay in concentration camp, was due in late 1937.

The recollections of imprisonment in *Out of the Night*, are of some service in reconstructing his thoughts and their conclusions during this period, as is the autobiographical short story *The Execution of Bert Adrian*. This text, being of fairly poor quality and its characters little more than ciphers, was never published. Krebs presumably wrote it at a low point in his life, shortly after his arrival in America. Its principal characters are Bert Adrian himself, a weak and lowly functionary, and his wife Anne. Anne is a Communist stalwart who dearly loves the story's protagonist and who is also sentenced to imprisonment for Communist activity. It seems plain that Krebs is projecting his own mood subsequent to Hermine's imprisonment and his despair as she fails to write to Bert Adrian.

"Through the tiny window of his cell Bert Adrian had seen the winter pass. He had seen the green of spring break from the trees beyond the walls. Summer had come, and autumn and winter and another spring. The birds returned from the south... The square patch of sunlight moving lazily over the walls of his cage taught him to be patient.

No news had come to him from Anne. When a luckless butterfly meandered through the opened window into his cell, he would shield it with minute care. He would speak to it as if it was Anne. Where have you been? How has life treated you?

Oh, it was hard to be patient. "Our life doesn't belong to ourselves; our life belongs to the cause." That was what he had told her, he, the serf of an idea. He had thrown their happiness into the winds. He had harnessed her love to his fanatic endeavor and he had forced her to like it."[212]

Richard Krebs, who here finds himself guilty vis a vis his wife, was yet to project the qualities of the real Communist, Anne, who overcomes her repulsion towards empty phrases and unquestioning discipline, onto Firelei. Yet this proved to be the butterfly's demise:

"One day in June a butterfly meandered into my cell. I shielded it like a great treasure. 'Have you come from Firelei?' I asked. It fluttered through the clouds of dust and beat its wings to shreds against the walls."

Whilst Bert Adrian thinks in solitary about his wife, Jan Valtin is suffering from quite different problems. Among them are the shameful defeat of the KPD, and the share of guilt that resulted from Party leadership decisions. They also include his own role as instructor, and whether this had served seamen or Stalin was a source of worry to him. Perhaps he even thought back to his time in San Quentin, as he took the decision to renounce bourgeois ambition for the sake of the Party. The schism in Krebs' own thought was not peculiar to him alone; many other functionaries recognized that they were serving an organization whose original aims were only still present in the worn-out and empty words of its slogans.

The logical next step, leaving the Party, meant nothing less than "the loss of the sense of belonging in an international, world-encompassing, brotherhood... of the warming and consoling sense of solidarity which gave that massive, anonymous mass its coherence and family ambiance,"[213] as Arthur Koestler put it in his memoirs. Koestler broke with the Party whilst in one of Franco's prisons, but it was many months before he admitted the fact to himself and still longer before he confessed it publicly. Arthur Koestler was already an adult by the time he joined the Party and was a member for seven years in total — scarcely comparable with the trajectory of Richard Krebs, who undertook illegal activities under Party orders from an early age after having joined their ranks as a youth. Krebs also differed from Koestler by remaining a stalwart in prison. Later, in exile in America, he wrote about his doubts whilst in solitary confinement: "There were hours in which I saw my whole past life as one gigantic and miserable mistake, bur I shied away from such insight, and defeated it deliberately by intoxicating myself with the concepts of Bolshevist duty and pride."

In the summer of 1935 Richard Krebs was moved into a shared cell. That this was a cell shared by the top functionaries incarcerated at Fuhlbüttel was no coincidence. Communists inside had been manipulating internal affairs there for some time and to such an extent that the Gestapo were later to dub the prison in Fuhlsbüttel "the stronghold of Communism."[214] The doubts that Krebs had been harboring in solitary were ousted — although this proved to be conviction's last reprise.

Three years later he would describe this shift thus in *Out of the Night:* "Now… I was surrounded by communist militants whose minds were dominated by but one thought: 'The Party comes first!' It was unique. Such a thing, I felt, had never before existed in any prison at any time. I felt the power of the Party. It gave me a wild sense of pride. In me the old revolutionary enthusiasm awoke with might."

In the chapter 'Man-Cage Magic' Krebs describes the energy and wiliness with which the fantastically organized Communist prisoners first gained dominion over the criminal prisoners by establishing control in the distribution of smuggled chewing tobacco and cutting off the supply of anyone who tried to resist them. They then divided all domestic posts within the prison among their number, even housing a man in the prison directors' office. Once they had gained power over some of the warders by means of bribery and blackmail, the so-called elite prisoners, Krebs among them, were able to assert influence over all prison-internal affairs. Last of all, they founded an establishment—the Red Help—that kept those in solitary in chewing tobacco.

Even four years later, as Krebs had long been subject to the persecution of his former comrades, he still wrote with unfeigned enthusiasm about the events of those months:

"They belonged to the most crowded months in my life. They showed me that even in hopeless defeat men can retain their morale as long as the conviction that they are fighting for a worth cause is alive in their brains. The individual may give up the cause and sink away in despair, but banded together with other castaways for a common purpose he sees his place, feels his strength, and salvages his belief that life still has a meaning."

A Stronghold of Communism

"Dear O, old confederate, well how are you? You've really been making a lot of progress of late. What's new? … Did you hear that George has been sent (for four weeks) to Esterweg.[*] Wist and Maier tell me its retribution, as the Stapo[+] felt that he'd got off too lightly. They do keep themselves busy. Last time they had me know that,

---

[*] The concentration camp Esterweg near. Oldenberg
[+] Gestapo

given my behavior during interrogation, they'd be availing of retributive technique in my case too. That won't be in the near future in any case... Incidentally, whilst confronted during interrogation with some written statements I found out some pretty unpleasant things about my own case. What led certain people to tell them about conversations we had in 1933, I cannot possibly guess. Nonetheless there it was in black and white. Stiff upper lip though and we'll pull through. Keep yourself in good spirits and health. Send me word too from your side.

All the best.

W."[215]

This guarded missive from the worker Walther Schmedemann to a fellow prisoner was confiscated by the penitentiary administration in February 1936. As the Hamburg Gestapo came to deal with him in 1937 they were already aware that Fuhlsbüttel had become a semi-lawless zone. Even in 1934, as Krebs was still a prisoner, the Communist majority of its eight hundred prisoners had already begun to exercise that influence over the Fuhlsbüttel penitentiary's administration which effectively transformed the establishment into a Communist stronghold.

In the summer of 1936 a Communist who had made an extensive statement a year previously — which he then suddenly revoked — made a written request for an interview with the Gestapo. This man, a certain Dose, stated on 7.8.1936: "My initial statement was factually correct. I was under so much pressure from fellow-prisoners that I no longer dared to incriminate anyone... I am aware that the political prisoners in Fuhlsbüttel penitentiary and Oslebshausen are organized, that the "Red Help" exists, and that there is such solidarity among the political prisoners that no one dares say anything accusatory."[216] Since Dose had no further information — his fellow prisoners presumably gave him a wide berth — he advised the Gestapo to consult prisoner Willi Muss, as the latter was prepared to make a statement but did not dare come forth of his own accord.

When the denunciator was interrogated, it became apparent that the penitentiary administration had prevented him from appending a letter to the public prosecutor with one written to the Gestapo. "I was summoned by the Chief Inspector, who reproached me and stated that if I had a letter for the state attorney, then it was to him alone, and not to contain other material. If I wished to write to the Gestapo, then I was to inform him first. The Chief Inspector then demanded to know what I wanted to tell the Gestapo. As there were other prisoners in the room, I told him that I did not wish to talk about it there and then... when I continued to refuse his requests he dismissed me."[217] The Gestapo received no letter.

Investigations proved troublesome. One frustrated officer wrote: "nothing can be got out of a Communist once he is serving a sentence." As they continued their investigations the Gestapo then came across a 'middle class conman'— the criminal prisoners of lower origin mostly being pro-Communist. They soon learned from him that the majority of important functionaries were employed in the prison raffia-weaving workshop. This was no coincidence; from there the majority of other cells were supplied with necessary material for weaving work. The most significant workers in that hall were Richard Krebs and Anton Saefkov, *Out of the Night's* Tonio.

"He was a powerfully built man of thirty-two, light-haired and blue-eyed, and as dauntless as he was cheerful. Resourceful and just, he was a driving personality, but... never demanded any thing of other comrades which he would not do himself."

The security that prisoners there must have felt is reflected in the songs that were sung in the workshop; Richard Krebs taught the other prisoners the Comintern March and Saefkov doctored the Horst-Wessel Song, hymn to the Nazi Party, that it read as follows:

"We asked for bread, you gave us military marches.
Brownshirt broadcasting you favor us with too.
You play the good Lord, would have us play Moses,
That we might sing the praises of scum like you
And though the winter's coming, the coal is over
And backbreaking labor takes upon us its toll.
If in the celestial Reich all things are in clover,
Why then does my son's shoe not have a sole?
And while you sow shut the lips of us the folk, sir!
Enforced silence cannot hunger satiate.
And while we may be bound beneath your yolk, sir!
For speech and plenty we've the strength to wait.
Our men and women you don't stint to murder.
Half Germany you keep 'neath lock and key.
Brown brigades patrol our streets - and what's absurder
Than their watchword countersigned: 'Hail Victory!'
The day of reckoning is doubtless coming
Where no fear may thwart a rallying cry to sound.
In Germany the red flame kindled will start burning
And raze the whole Third Reich down to the ground."[218]

In mid-July, 1936, Richard Krebs, Anton Saefkov and other ringleaders were moved from Fuhlsbüttel to ensure that they did not interfere in investigations. Saefkov, whose prison sentence had come to an end, was transferred to Dachau concentration camp, and Krebs was moved on July 17, 1936, to Plötzensee penitentiary, the Third Reich's centralized location for executions.

By late November the Gestapo had intimidated the remaining prisoners to such an extent that they dared to then bring the ringleaders, Richard Krebs among them, back to Hamburg. To make sure that they were kept under pressure, they were not returned to prison but instead placed in the near-by concentration camp. In the months thereafter the Gestapo succeeded in gleaning a first insight into the working of the secret organization. They only really amassed details, however, when Paul Tastesen, a Communist with links to the elite, started to sing for them.

In Fuhlsbüttel there was an organization called the Red Help. This delivered the prisoners in solitary chewing tobacco. There was also an intelligence service, that, with the aid of the warders, maintained contact to the outside world, and there was even an administrative system that conveyed the orders of the elite to the lower ranks: all this information was won after countless interrogations and torture sessions, by a combination of threats and promises and the good cop/bad cop routine. Prisoners were transferred and returned to their original detention center, warders were fired and prosecuted, the prison pastoral care service, that had turned a blind eye to these goings-on was discharged.

Now the principal suspects could be confronted and pressurized with this new intelligence. The intention was to pressurize Anton Saefkov and Richard Krebs into revealing all they knew. Krebs later told the CIC that the Gestapo were not aware, for example, that behind Anton Saefkov there was another man among the prisoners who was higher in the secret hierarchy. Just as behind Albert Walther stood Adolf Shelley, so Saefkov referred to a man in solitary confinement called Karl Schaar on all contentious prison-internal affairs. The Gestapo never learned of his existence, and in part this was due to a change of tact by Krebs and Saefkov.[219]

Threadbare as Nazi philosophy now may seem, to its adherents in the Third Reich this was a state built upon ideological foundations. As opposed to a naked dictatorship, a military power, say, that merely exerts power and considers unconditional obedience ample proof of improvement, the Nazi regime entertained the possibility of improving the faithless by conversion to the cause. This, needless to say, was only available to Aryan prisoners, and became scarcer as the amount of those incarcerated swelled.

Even in 1943, as the Spanish writer Jorge Semprun entered Buchenwald, the slogan *Erziehung durch Arbeit**, was still current in the camp. This camp rationale, part of the ideological basis of the German dictatorship, was to Semprum "the betterment terror... the essence of which was to consider the inhabitants on the one hand as a workforce and on the other as a creatures in need of improvement."[220]

Among the Gestapo there were not few men to whom Nazi paroles were essentially pro forma. They served the Third Reich, as they had served the Weimar Republic before, and would later serve the GDR or the FRG. These were the classic policemen, characters like Napoleon's egregious Fouché, a man who first spied on and imprisoned the enemies of his master, and then helped Napoleon's successor in much the same way.

Inspector Kraus and his assistant, responsible for the investigation of Fuhlsbüttel, were not of that type. Indeed, they were so firmly convinced of the soundness of their philosophy that instruction in Nazi ideology was provided in Fuhlsbüttel. According to Valtin in *Out of the Night*, this was welcomed as an interruption to the monotony.

The instructors at these events had themselves been taught only to parrot off Nazi slogans. This meant that they were often no match for the prisoners, who in part had attended KPD Party school. One instructor is reported as having used the word 'imperialism' without being able to define it. A prisoner obliged him with Lenin's definition, and the next day the instructor proudly repeated it to other prisoners as his own.

The ruses played on these helpless instructors were not just sport to the prisoners. They were also instructive because they illustrated how easily deceived someone is who, by holding absolute power, had become oblivious to his victim's disdain. The

---

* Edification through labor

Gestapo torturers, aware that their victims were fellow Germans and being fanatical admirers of soldierly values, could not fail to tacitly admire the steadfastness of their opponents. These combined factors made them prone to gullibility.

The first to take advantage of them thus was Anton Saefkov. The 'conclusion and postscript' of the Gestapo report on investigations in Fuhlbüttel, written on 2.22.1937 – probably by Teerge, Kraus' underling — reads: "Saefkov avowed repeatedly that he had finally broken with Communism. He attempted, nonetheless, to depict all the activities in the penitentiary as essentially harmless and inconsequential."[221]

Teerge made his superiors the following, unorthodox suggestion: the prisoners were to be divided into three categories; those functionaries who have been recognized as "incorrigible, who are to be quarantined off from other prisoners," those who "whilst actually being functionaries, by their behavior give indication of improvement" and finally "the so-called fellow travelers," who were to be removed from the pernicious influence of their superiors.[222]

"To return to the matter of instruction within penitentiaries; there are a number of men among former elite functionaries who claim to have lost faith and have parted ways with Communism... Well, if they maintain that they have lost their faith, then they should prove it... men like Saefkov have a name among the Communists. If the rank and file should hear that a man like Saefkov has turned from Communism, it might have an enormous effect on morale. The attempt is without precedent but can do no harm and might prove profitable."[223]

The author of the report was also the one who conducted investigations. His prisoners probably knew his considerations. The ground was laid for a further conversion. This time it was Krebs' turn and the transformation took only a few weeks.

Even in the conclusion and postscript report, Krebs is noted as "a man whom we can get nothing out of."[224] When on March 12, 1937 he was interviewed outside of Fuhlsbüttel no three weeks after the report had been completed he gave a lengthy statement. The greater part of this consisted of Krebs playing dumb. He claimed that meetings between prisoners were merely to do with daily affairs and not political,"[225] He maintained also that tobacco distribution by no means constituted a Red Help, or that such a thing even existed. He concluded, however, with the words:

"In discussions I often maintained a point of view that diverged from that of Saefkov the leading figure of authority in the hall. Due to personal reflection and having read the works of Darwin, Schopenhauer, Günther, etc, on questions of decent, race, morality and works of political nature I decided to part from Communist dogma.

I decided, for example, that my children would join the Hitler Youth, that they should be in harmony with their environment and develop accordingly. These opinions provoked consternation among my fellow prisoners... Although, like the Communists, I believe that it is right for important sections of industry and commerce etc, particularly the armament industry, to be taken out of private hands and turned over to the state, I differ from Communists in that I do not consider the principal factor in the development of humanity to be economic, but instead find cultural, historical and the race question to be of at least comparable significance."[226]

The Game Commences

Of course the Gestapo knew that Richard Krebs was privy to the meaning of "Red Help" as well as to the fact that there had been regular ideological training sessions in Fuhlsbüttel. Nevertheless, they accepted his refusal to report more about the Communists' actions in Fuhlsbüttel, because he himself gave them the idea to use him on a completely different scale.

On March 12, 1937, Richard Krebs called the warden and told him he would make a statement to the Secret Police. "Through my experience as an active functionary of the KPD's international work and through my studies and reflections on ideological issues during the three years of my imprisonment, I have come to the following fundamental views:

1. that communism cannot be reconciled in theory with the facts of life and that in practice it even has a life alienating and hostile effect. That I have lost faith that humanity will ever be made happy through communist practice.

2. that I first found the opportunity in prison to intensively study national and racial issues. That it is my view that popular and racial ties have proved stronger in the history of all peoples than the class ties represented by communism.

3. that the development of world politics has led to communism no longer being a domestic issue but, through the division of the world into Bolshevism and National Socialism, to communism becoming a fundamental foreign policy issue. It follows from this that anyone who is still a consistent communist today must also commit himself to the Soviet Union in foreign policy and thus become a traitor to his own people. Faced with such a decision, I decided to openly admit that my connections with Germany are stronger than with Russia.

4. that I voluntarily make all the following statements with the purpose of thereby liquidating all the remnants of inner political and personal ties with Bolshevism and making any return to this worldview impossible for all time.

5. I agree to participate in the fight against communism when assigned duties and to publish or withhold the following information at the discretion of the leadership of the Gestapo."[227]

Saefkow's and Krebs's renunciation of communism became known to their fellow prisoners. Gert Conrad, an independent socialist, was released after the prisoners' organization was uncovered and escaped to Denmark, where he fell in love with

Hildegard Thingstrup, who had become secretary of the Danish KP leader Larsen after her return from Germany. Decades later, Conrad described the following scene to the Danish journalist Erik Nørgaard:

"I remember clearly that Krebs and some other communist prisoners, Anton Sae[f]kow and Paul Helms, were divided into groups of two and took on various political tasks. It's true we received smuggled communist material. One day during the march on the farm we were suddenly ordered to strip completely. We were to be be searched for illegal material. We all knew what that meant in terms of maltreatment. From that day on, Krebs and Sae[f]kow went into the service of the Gestapo."[228]

Several circumstances suggest that Conrad's recollection is essentially correct. On the one hand, he remembered both Krebs and Saefkow, which corresponds exactly to the Gestapo files. On the other hand, Conrad was not a communist, but an independent socialist and didn´t know that Saefkov's "conversion", who was executed in Berlin in 1944, was only a trick. The KPD's standard work on the intelligence service states that dismissals of Communists from concentration camps and prisons "at the direction of the head of the Gestapo Heydrich since July 1935 were only admissible if those concerned committed themselves to informing or otherwise indicated that they were prepared to abandon their political convictions"[229].

Although he had been the leader in Fuhlsbüttel Anton Saefkow was released in the summer of 1939. So he must have continued on the path he had taken at the end of 1936 or the beginning of 1937 and successfully deceived the Gestapo over the next few years of his imprisonment. Of course, this does not fit in with the later hero worship image of Saefkow in the GDR who became head of a large resistance group and was executed in 1944. Accordingly Saefkows long entry in the encyclopedia "Deutsche Widerstandskämpfer – German resistance fighters"[230], fails to mention his "renunciation of communism", which had made his deeds possible in the first place.

That Anton Saefkow's double play was connected with Richard Krebs's "conversion", which followed soon afterwards, is also apparent from other files. In 1950, Richard Krebs knew nothing about Saefkow's fate, the CIC recorded:

"In 1936, among the Communists serving a prison sentence, Saefkow initiated the trend of writing to the Gestapo to affirm their inner conversion. Saefkow himself wrote the first such letter, which one day was shown Krebs during an interrogation of Kraus. It said that Saefkow had broken with the Communist Party. (...) Saefkow's wife had
delivered the instruction to write the letter to Kraus from outside. She transferred it to him with her mouth, while she kissed him just before she left Germany."[231]

That Saefkow had messages slipped to him is also a fact recorded in the files of the secret police. The content of those messages though was not known to them. Whether Richard Krebs's double play was due to an instruction from outside cannot be verified. Had he followed Saefkow's example to escape imprisonment, or had he actually received a commission? Did the agreement with his comrades, which can be taken as given, refer only to a revocation, or had he gone one step too far with the offer made in his declaration? Were the doubts from solitary confinement revived, and did he now see the possibility of getting out of prison without major remorse?

After all, he had mainly worked abroad and was able to report to the Gestapo much more openly without endangering others than a KPD official.

Perhaps the answer comes by comparing his wife's portrayal in *Out of the Night* with her true story.

In the autobiographical novel there is not the slightest trace of her turning away from the Comintern. Firelei is sent to Germany with a secret order, arrested there by the Gestapo and sentenced to six years in prison. Moreover, Ernst Wollweber is indirectly blamed for her fate, as she travels to Germany at his behest, accompanied by the informer Beilich.

In the novel, the hero makes Firelei's release a condition for his collaboration with the Gestapo. In fact, he soon sees her again. She is portrayed as a steadfast comrade in whom "the soldierly spirit of the battle years had been preserved", "despite all hardship, despite madness, despite suffering and humiliation".

Hermine Krebs was released with an incurable disease in the fall of 1936 after serving her two years. Richard Krebs hinted at the true motives of his wife, the great love of his life, in a very personal letter after her death: "She degraded herself to get her child back."[232]

His love for her may have played a role in his decision to work with the Gestapo. This one might surmise from the aforementioned short story *The Execution of Bert Adrian*, which he wrote shortly after his escape from Europe. Although the hero's wife is again a steadfast communist, the course of events is in many other respects more consistent with real events than *Out of the Night*.

In the key scene the hero receives a letter from his wife telling him that she has been released from prison.

" Anne was free! Bert longed to shout it along the gloomy hallways and across the barren yards. She loved him. It was not true, that time dissolved the strongest bonds. The knowledge of it filled him with a mad desire to live. To live at any price!"[233]

There has also been this moment in the life of Richard Krebs. When Hermine Krebs was released, her husband was in Plötzensee. He knew that, once the prisoner organization had been uncovered, he would either be given a new sentence or - even worse - be sent to a concentration camp for an indefinite period.

In this situation Bert Adrian succumbs to the whispers of a criminal fellow prisoner, becomes a traitor and is released after a short time. He confesses to Anne, who is still a staunch Communist. She denounces him to her comrades, who execute him shortly afterwards.

In the autobiographical story of Bert Adrian, the true roles of the two are reversed. There is no doubt Hermine Krebs was nothing but a traitor in the eyes of her comrades. And not because of her statements to the Gestapo where she had mainly incriminated herself and her husband - she was shielded from the true bearers of secrets anyway - and this only after her arrest and for quite understandable reasons. What was decisive, however, was that she had already detached herself from the party in Copenhagen and had returned to Germany after consultation with the Gestapo. The last was unforgivable according to the rules of the illegal KPD.

Even in times of party legality a communist with security clearance was not allowed to marry a non-communist. It was so much the worse in 1937, when hundreds of thousands were executed in the Soviet Union for minoroffences.

In all probability, the main accusation against Richard Krebs later was that he disobeyed an order of his superiors because of a "traitor". It was an indictment which must have deeply affected him, because he could not deny the truth of it. Perhaps for this reason in *Out of the Night* the transformation of the desperate young mother, who had long since ceased to believe in the communist cause, into a downright exemplary communist heroine. Ultimately, this is an indication that Richard Krebs did not act out of personal calculation but in consultation with his comrades when he offered his services to the Gestapo.

His collaboration with the Gestapo was to haunt Richard Krebs for the rest of his life. He could never completely free himself from the suspicion of having been a "real" Gestapo spy, of having joined the Gestapo in a mixture of cowardice and pure self-interest. His former comrades, who by the way only began to hunt him after the end of his double play, which they were well informed about were to do everything they could to keep up this suspicion. Many of his later American fellow citizens, inhabitants of a country in which the horrors of Gestapo terror were unimaginable, regarded the fact of his double play alone as proof of his "immorality".

Of course Richard Krebs couldn't describe what really happened in *Out of the Night*. He would have handed Anton Saefkow over to the Gestapo. Instead, he invented the visit of a double agent in his cell. This Gestapo official named Heitmann, who actually worked for the GPU, supposedly gave him the order to sneak into the Gestapo. How Krebs was to testify to the CIC, this man never existed.

Nevertheless, the description of this fictitious encounter is highly informative. The sentences he puts in Heitmann's mouth describe the strategy he must have followed himself in order to overcome the mistrust of the secret police.

"The point is not to make an outright offer. Nothing that's clumsy or suspicious. The problem is to bring the competitors to a point where they'll come and invite you: 'Brother, how about it?' Understand?"

Valtin doubts that the Gestapo will trust him because he is known as one of the leaders of Fühlsbüttel. Heitman talks to him:

"A man in chains is likely to do anything to get rid of the shackles. You have rummaged for years. You have given up the old ideas. You are ready to capitulate. That'll be your line. It's not so hard to fool people who think they're all-powerful."

Gradually Jan Valtin familiarizes himself with the terminology and thoughts of his opponents. He reads *Mein Kampf*, begins to distance himself from his fellow inmates and starts to argue with them. After months of efforts, which of course have not remained hidden from the Gestapo, he has prepared the ground to such an extent that the Gestapo starts to believe in his "conversion".

Was that Richard Krebs's way, too? Only that it did not take months, but only a few weeks, until the same man who had been designated by the Gestapo as "a man whom we can get nothing out of" signed the declaration on March 12, 1937.

Duel in the dark

When Richard Krebs offered the Gestapo his cooperation in the fight against communism, he did not know whether they would be satisfied with the small propaganda coup they could achieve by publishing his revocation. They could also keep secret his "conversion" to National Socialism in order to reintroduce him into the communist movement. The latter would mean sending him to his former field of work, ISH, i.e. abroad.

The Gestapo opted for the second variant. Such a mission for Richard Krebs was - particularly interesting for the Hamburg Gestapo as he might be able to bring them back on the trail of Ernst Wollweber, whom they had completely lost sight of.

Before the Gestapo released him, they had to be absolutely sure of him. After all, the secret police had been fooled by allegedly "converted" Communists before. Only a few months later, the headquarters in Berlin was to issue a circular that categorically prohibited such practices.[234] How the Gestapo proceeded to make certain of their prospective Agent can be reconstructed from *Out of the Night* and the Gestapo files.

Many things in the novel, such as the course of Valtin's "Conversion", are pure fiction in order not to give the Gestapo any clues for new investigations. Why, however, should Richard Krebs have invented the hour-long conversations, partly small talk, partly interrogation, with his torturer Inspector Kraus? The passages in which Jan Valtin empathises with his opponents' way of thinking, explains his departure from communism and explains why he from now on wants to be of service to National Socialist Germany are among the most fascinating parts of the book.

He writes in the introduction: "I was fully aware that the slightest slip of my tongue, a single wrong word or gesture under the experienced ears and eyes of Inspector Kraus, would plunge me to ultimate destruction."

A cat-and-mouse game began between the two. Kraus could not check the credibility of his prisoner on the basis of his willingness to testify as his knowledge of the ISH apparatus was outdated, and the prisoner refused to talk about Fuhlsbüttel because he did not want to denounce simple comrades who had only been seduced. The only course that remained was for Kraus to put to the test the newly found belief in Adolf Hitler's Germany claimed by Valtin.

In contrast to his fictional character Jan Valtin, Richard Krebs's duel with Kraus was helped by several circumstances: on the one hand, his bourgeois origins, which would have predestined him, like his younger brother Julius, who was a Luftwaffe instructor, to become a follower of Hitler. Secondly, his wife's renunciation of communism and finally the fact that the Gestapo did not know the true background of the deed in Los Angeles. The secret police, who had only limited insight into the international structures of the communist world movement, not least because of their ideological blinkers, assumed that Richard Krebs had only become a communist in 1931 because of the crisis in his profession as a helmsman.

Yet Richard Krebs must have spent hard, painful hours with Inspector Kraus. His alter ego Jan Valtin would later describe how Kraus sometimes stared at him in silence for minutes. He then looked up at Adolf Hitler's picture or, if he could no longer bear it, finally broke the silence with a quote from the Führer.

While trying to convince Kraus, Valtin was overcome by the doubts that had plagued him in solitary confinement. All those forbidden thoughts which a communist who did not want to be expelled kept for himself or, if he made them known to his best friends, immediately qualified with sentences like "in Soviet Germany everything will be different" or "the revolution unfortunately won in the most backward country of Europe", he now spread before Kraus: He talked about the transformation of the Comintern into an agency of the Soviet state apparatus, the cynicism of the higher functionaries, the true conditions in the motherland of all labourers and much more.

The prisoner contrasted this with the set pieces of Nazi propaganda such as social improvements and the liberation of Germany from the Versailles dictates. He presented himself as a typical child of his time who had been radicalized by the conditions of the time. He had joined the KPD for the same reasons as others had joined Hitler´s movement. Now that Hitler had been in power for several years, it was clear to him that he had made a grave mistake.

Valtin's answer to the most difficult and dangerous question, why he remained so stubborn despite previous insights, is a very clever appeal to the mentality of the former free corps men from whom the majority of the Gestapo were recruited: " The Hitler movement is built on the soldier ideal... The Comintern is built up on military discipline. Hitlerism has an ideal. Communism rejected ideals—it recognized only historical materialism. What both had in common was the soldier attitude. I was a soldier. The soldier's highest virtue is loyalty."

He continued: "Allegiance to the Comintern was allegiance to the Kremlin, and equal to the crime of high treason. I had, at last, discovered that I was a German, that I belonged to Germany, that there was only one way in which I could atone for the crimes I had committed: to serve Germany by fighting its enemies, the communists, the overfed democracies, the emissaries of Judah! "

After the prisoner has succeeded in convincing Kraus, he has to overcome one last hurdle. He is introduced to the head of the Hamburg Gestapo, Bruno Streckenbach. Of all the Gestapo people Richard Krebs met, he was to have the greatest career. In mid-May 1940, he was one of the three high-ranking officials of the Reich Security Main Office who were commissioned by the Governor General of Poland, SS-Obergruppenführer Hans Frank, to carry out an "extraordinary pacification operation" involving Polish intellectuals, including the professors of the Krakow University. They "were liquidated by the Gestapo and the SS without due process of law and without any possibility of pardon". Frank said goodbye to him with the words: "What you, Brigadier Streckenbach, and your people in the Generalgouvernement have accomplished must not be forgotten, and you need not be ashamed of it."[235]

The hero of *Out of the Night* convinces the later mass murderer with a cynical variation of a soldier´s ethics with which he had already impressed Inspector Kraus: "I am German," he tells him. "I prefer to fight with the winning army."

The original Gestapo files of Richard Krebs, whose agent name was "Erka", are lost. The "Erka" file of the headquarters in Berlin though was preserved in which the summaries of the Hamburg Gestapo were filed.

Here one finds the information about his former field of activity, which finally led the Gestapo to send him as an agent abroad. For instance there is a meticulous description of the ISH, which had already been dissolved at that time, together with a hand-drawn scheme with the handwritten note: status of the organisation at the end of 1933.

In addition, there is information on important ISH officials assigned to the headings Eastern States (9 names), England (21 names), Northern States (23 names), Coloured States and America (6 names).

The Gestapo may not have been interested in facts about the organization for operational reasons, as they were clearly outdated; however, they provided information about the credibility of Richard Krebs and his state of knowledge. Krebs knew that the Gestapo had the opportunity to check his statements against the testimony of a much more competent man. The following sentence indicates this: "Albert Walter should be able to give information about the amount of subsidies in legal time."[236]

Whether Krebs informed the Gestapo about new persons or only confirmed what was already known through Albert Walter, who from the beginning played a leading role in the espablishment of IPK Transport and his successor, ISH, cannot be judged without knowledge of the relevant personal files.

How much he concealed from the Gestapo can be judged from the files of the American CIC, to whom Richard Krebs later revealed much more. An example of this is the information about Avatin. In the Gestapo file there is no indication that Richard Krebs considered him to be a representative of the GPU. Avatin's attempt to infiltrate a National Socialist officers' association in Hamburg, in which Krebs himself was involved, at least marginally, according to his own statements, was also reported only to the CIC. Of course, he now spoke to the Gestapo about things that he had concealed in 1933. So he made statements about Bem's real role. However, the Gestapo already knew more than he did. They knew his true name, while Bem for Richard Krebs was still called Adolf Schelley, and the Gestapo was also informed of Bem´s biographical background.

On April 1, 1937, Bruno Streckenbach wrote to Standardartenführer Müller (later the head of the Gestapo), that he had succeeded in "persuading Richard Krebs, a former active functionary of the international work of the ISH, to turn away from communism and to engage in the fight against it."

Streckenbach further wrote to Mueller, that Krebs had made the attached reports voluntarily and that his sentence was to be served in November.

"Here is the intention to free him now, so he can work internationally as our agent. He undoubtedly has the abilities for this and his work is therefore of extraordinary importance."[237]

A desperate plan

At the end of July Richard Krebs went to Copenhagen. From there he sent his first report at the beginning of August. The months up to his departure belong to those periods in his life about which there is almost nothing except what he would later write himself.

The account in *Out of the Night* differs greatly from what actually happened and the story of Firelei definitely has no resemblance to real events anymore. Whereas Richard Krebs must have arrived in Kopenhagen some time in July in *Out of the Night* Jan Valtin is travelling to Copenhagen at the end of May. Maybe he changed the timeline to protect somebody with whom he had contact in Germany. It is also conceivable that after the torture that probably preceded his "conversion" and the exhausting conversations and interrogations, he collapsed and concealed this weakness in *Out of the Night*, as it would not have fitted the heroic posture of his protagonist.

Some things in Jan Valtin's account are quite imaginable. For example, that his superiors in the Gestapo fabricated a "legend" for their agent that would conclusively explain why he suddenly appeared abroad before ending his prison sentence. In *Out of the Night* the Gestapo transfers Valtin to the barely used city prison in Hamburg, and fakes his escape from there so skillfully that even the guards are deceived. Then, having "escaped", he sends a coded telegram to Richard Jensen on behalf of Kraus with the request for help. Jensen sends 200 dollars to Valtin immediately. This reaction convinces Kraus that Krebs still has an excellent reputation in Copenhagen and that it will therefore be easy for the agent to reconnect to Wollweber.

Krebs's statements to the CIC confirm that the main features of this particular story are correct. Krebs also mentioned to the CIC that Inspector Kraus had put half of the dollars Jensen transferred to him into his own pocket.

Particularly interesting is a passage about Otto Kemnitz, his deputy, who had led the Interklub during his instruction trips, which the CIC, as always, recorded in the third person: "In 1937, shortly before he left Germany, Kraus asked Krebs whether he could stop by Kemnitz to see what he had in mind. At that time Kemnitz lived in a clean little apartment on the outskirts of Hamburg. The remarkable thing about the meeting was that Kemnitz, who seemed to be happy to see Krebs again, said, 'My

God, I wish I could go with you, but I have to stay here' after Krebs's remark that he would leave Germany.

Then he asked if he had Krebs's permission to tell Kraus that Krebs had escaped from Germany, and Krebs said yes.

Kemnitz passed this on to Kraus, which must have given him a better position in what he was doing. He was then involved in some kind of illegal activity that had nothing to do with the port. After his dismissal he had married a Hamburg girl and attended a special course dealing with submarine construction. It may be that the Gestapo had imposed certain conditions before he got the job, and he had therefore asked for permission to report Krebs's departure. He gave the impression that he was still completely faithful to the movement."[238]

The communist secret apparatus, which had so miserably failed in Hitler's seizure of power, had stabilized in some respects as a result of the persecutions. Comrades who were still free had become masters in concealing their true thoughts. This is the only way to understand the course of the meeting of the two former functionaries, who must have known of each other that they were still on the same side.

Apart from Valtin's report and his statements to the CIC, Richard Krebs was not to tell anything about those four months between Streckenbach's letter to Berlin and his arrival in Copenhagen. It certainly would have taken a few days or even weeks for the decision to be made in Berlin. At least that long Krebs must have remained in custody. It seems just as certain that the Gestapo trained their agent in all secret techniques.

During this time Krebs acquired a comprehensive knowledge of the Gestapo's foreign apparatus operating from Hamburg. Four years later he was to use this knowledge to make a lasting impression on a committee of inquiry of the US Congress.

How the last meetings between him and Hermine went remained Richard Krebs's secret. The corresponding passages in his autobiographical novel are in any case fiction. At the end of a joint stay of several days at the North Sea, the "steadfast comrade" discusses with her husband how to proceed. Firelei has only been released because of Valtin's collaboration with the Gestapo, and both are aware that they cannot flee without help as the borders of Germany are too well guarded. Unbroken and ready to resume the fight, Firelei finally says to him: "You have to go abroad first. ...you have a hard job ahead of you. I'm sure you'll find a way to get Jan and me out after you get back into the organization."

In reality Hermine Krebs had been released after her prison sentence expired in September 1936.

She wasn't the same anymore. In prison she had contracted a severe, painful nervous disorder that sometimes tied her to the bed for days. Hoping to recover and then to study at the art academy in Hamburg she lived with her son at her parents in Bremen. Whether Hermine and Richard - as in *Out of the Night* - spent some time together in a village on the North Sea is uncertain. Definately though Richard´s sister Cilly was there when they said goodbye to each other for the last time. It's in a letter she wrote to him after the war.

Probably in those spring days of 1937 all the children of Captain Hugo Krebs and his wife Pauline met again. The occasion was the death of their brother Julius. Julius, just like his older brother a helmsman by profession, had taken the opposite political path: he had joined the NSDAP and, after Hitler's seizure of power, had become one of the first officers of the newly established Luftwaffe. He died when he couldn't get out of a burning plane. As Richard Krebs indicated in a letter one year later and again in *Out of the Night, the* death of Julius was related to Communist sabotage.

While Julius appears cursorily in *Out of the Night* under the name Hermann, Richard's youngest brother Hugo, called Peps, does not appear at all. Neither does Richard ever mention anything about Hugo in any of the numerous interrogations that American authorities were to subject him to.

Hugo was the only one of his siblings whom he involved in his underground work. Hugo´s daughter Martina remembers that her father lived with Richard and Hermine in Hamburg and even helped set up an illegal print shop.

Peps, the Benjamin of the family, was in many ways the exact opposite of his seven years older brother Richard. He had a slight stutter and was a rather calm, thoughtful and down-to-earth person. After years as a sailor, he was about to apply to the Bremen Maritime School when Richard Krebs was unexpectedly released from prison and involved him again in his activities.

Peps was to cheat the Gestapo and smuggle Hermine Krebs and her son Jan out of Germany.

Here we have the reason why Hugo was never mentioned by Richard. If the Gestapo had ever heard of this plan, Peps would have followed his brother to a concentration camp. It is not known how far they had already advanced the preparations when Richard Krebs left for Copenhagen. Later letters at least show that Krebs promised to organize the necessary money for the purchase of a cutter with which the escape was to be accomplished. They must also have made appointments to keep in touch. For even after Richard Krebs's escape to America they wrote to each until the communist secret apparatus finally interrupted the contact.

The rescue of his wife and child, could only succeed if the Gestapo did not shadow Hermine and Jan too closely. And that in turn depended on the behavior of agent Richard Krebs.

Agent Erka

We can only speculate at Richard Krebs's thoughts when he arrived in Copenhagen at the end of July 1937. In any case, he had no intention of playing the Gestapo game "honestly". After all, he had given his brother the contract to smuggle his wife and child out of Germany. But what about his own comrades? He could hardly count on their help when it came to getting a renegade out of Germany.

He would have got into serious trouble had they found out about this plan. After all, Hermine had turned to the Gestapo, had voluntarily returned to Germany and thus had become a "traitor".

Like in 1930, the year he met Hermine, Richard Krebs was trying to square the circle. At that time he had tried to combine his "bourgeois" ambitions, his literary attempts and the acquisition of helmsman's patent with his communist convictions. Seven years later, it was a question of reconciling the woman he loved and the movement to which he belonged. At an earlier stage he might have succeeded, but in 1937 it had even become impossible to separate from his comrades by mutual agreement.

At first he was kindly received by Richard Jensen, as he later confirmed. Jensen must have been already informed about the events in Fuhlsbüttel as Gert Conrad, who had observed Saefkow's and Krebs's "transfer to Gestapo service", lived with Hildegard Thingstrup after his emigration, who was then secretary to the Danish CP chairman Larsen. Jensen's friendly reception of him is further evidence that Richard Krebs's collaboration with the Gestapo was carried out with the full knowledge and approval of his comrades.

On the outside, little had changed in Copenhagen. Richard Jensen's office was still in that modern office building at Toldbogade 10, and Richard Jensen himself was still a respected member of the Copenhagen City Council, an influential trade unionist and a prominent communist who didn't hide his convictions. But nothing else was the same.

In the communist world movement, changes had taken place which the prisoner isolated in a German prison could not have grasped in their entire scope. Although the news about the show trials in Moscow had also penetrated behind prison walls, the old solidarity and brotherhood that had characterized the beginnings of the communist movement were still unbroken in the German penitentiaries and concentration camps. If anything they had even intensified under the intense pressure of the Nazis.

At the headquarters of the world revolution, Moscow, the entire old Bolshevik guard was brought to justice and executed: Bukharin, the chief theorist whom Lenin had called the party's favourite, Zinoviev, the former leader of the Comintern, Antonov-Ovseenko, the leader of the storm of Winter Palace, Kamenev, Radek and many of the German party leaders who had fled to the Soviet Union. Most of the foreign employees in the central apparatus of the Comintern were liquidated or were worked to death in a camp, and no department had a higher percentage of victims than the OMS, the Comintern Liaison Service, whose secret character provided excellent material for the paranoid fantasies of the torturers.

Richard Krebs could not know – and was never to know - that at the time of his arrival his patron Alfred Bem alias Adolf was probably no longer alive either. He had survived the investigation at the end of 1933 and returned to Copenhagen in the spring of 1934. There he took up his old post again and moved to Paris in 1935, where the headquarters of ISH was relocated to. But he had not been forgotten in Moscow. An unknown inquisitor left these lines in his file in December 1935: "In our opinion an extremely dubious person. I believe that we must take him very seriously in order to expose him ... We must therefore bring about his recall."[239]

After his arrival in Moscow in February 1936, he was appointed temporary head of the Soviet office of ISH. Then months of interrogation began. Again and again he had to justify his relationship with Hildegard Thingstrup and having taken part in 1921 as a conscript in the fight of the Polish army against the Red Army. The Inquisitors took both together as justification for the suspicion that Bem alias Adolf was a "Polish spy". The last entry in his cadre file concerning him is dated 13 May 1936: "submit to the ECCI for decision".[240] From the fate of his then seven-year-old daughter Danuta, which was the subject of all later entries in his cadre file, it can be concluded that he was subsequently either executed or died in a labour camp.

After the arrest of her father, she was sent to an orphanage because her mother, from whom Adolf lived separately, was also arrested and like him disappeared without a trace. In 1955 the authorities contacted Danuta Alfredowna to tell the young actress the happy news that her father had been posthumously rehabilitated. The very last entry in Adolf's file dates from 1960. The Polish CP had invited Adolf's daughter to her native country for her first visit and asked in Moscow whether "Adolf" was really "clean". So he was and Danuta Alfredowna was allowed to go to Poland.

Anyone who wanted to survive in Soviet service in those years - and this of course also applied to Ernst Wollweber and Richard Jensen, - would do well to keep everyone who had come into contact with the Gestapo as far away as possible.

There are different versions of the events that led to Richard Krebs being declared outlawed by the Comintern just four months after his arrival in Copenhagen and slated for immediate liquidation. Both Wollweber and Jensen have put their point of view on record several times. In addition, there are countless messages from agent Richard Krebs, which were sent from Copenhagen to Hamburg, and finally the description in *Out of the Night*.

In the novel Jan Valtin arrives in Copenhagen, is taken back into the organisation and then used to mislead the Gestapo with a flood of half-true reports. From the very beginning he demands the "good comrade Firelei" to be smuggled out of Germany with the help of the communist secret apparatus, but Wollweber refuses to do so. The longer the double-cross lasts, the greater the danger that the Gestapo will notice the deception and turn on his wife. Finally, he withdraws on his own authority by informing the Gestapo that he is to be sent to the Soviet Union for training. After this breach of party discipline, Wollweber and Jensen put him on ice for the time being, reinstate him briefly in the Netherlands and finally bring him back to Copenhagen for the final trial of his case. There the decision is made to bring him to the Soviet Union. Until a suitable ship arrives, he is arrested in Jensen's country house, from where he can finally escape under adventurous circumstances. After an odyssey through Denmark and France, he reaches Antwerp, from where he finally flees Europe with the help of Edo Fimmen, the leader of the international seaman´s union ITF, the great rival of the ISH with which the Communists had fought fierce propaganda battles in 1933.

Like the story of Heitmann's visit to the concentration camp, who allegedly gave him the order to sneak into the Gestapo, the version of Valtin's break with the Comintern served on the one hand to refute the Gestapo accusation and on the other to protect himself, his wife's memory and his brother's life. In Copenhagen, Richard Krebs was nothing more than a small figure in a long-distance duel between the Soviet secret police and the Gestapo. That was something which he was never to fully understand and which he did not want to admit to himself. It also contradicted the picture he was to paint of his hero Jan Valtin. Thus the fictional parts of the autobiographical novel like the legend of "good comrade Firelei" help to gain an understanding of his inner life.

In *Out of the Night* Jan Valtin is held prisoner in Jensen's country house after refusing to pass on any further false information to the Gestapo. Richard Jensen, a prominent figure in public life in Denmark, disagreed with this version and set his - own against it after the war. After his arrival in Copenhagen, Richard Krebs by no means laid his Gestapo identity card on the table and thus immediately announced his commission, but secretly contacted Hamburg. Jensen reported to the Danish author Erik Nørgaard: "This summer I had rented a small summer house, outside in Jägerkron on Köge. I suggested Krebs should come and camp in the garden. So he could regain his strength in the fresh air with good Danish food after his stay in Fuhlsbüttel. To Krebs this seemed like a good idea". [241] Since they controlled Krebs's correspondence, the comrades soon knew: "Krebs was Gestapoagent No. 51. Through a secret post box he was in contact with Inspector Kraus, who was an expert in Scandinavian affairs. In his letters, Krebs informed Kraus of the worthless information I (Jensen) had given him. Every time he went into town, he had one of our people behind him and we noticed that he also visited the German embassy. The letters that Krebs received were previously photographed by us. Krebs put a hair of his into the letters, and we made sure that the hair was back in the letter after our inspection."[242]

Richard Krebs, Jensen says, even tried to lure him to the harbour to have him kidnapped by the Gestapo. His very detailed description of that alleged abduction attempt sounds very unlikely. Why should the German Reich have kidnapped a prominent and respected citizen of a neighboring country who they wanted to keep in benevolent neutrality? Not even during the occupation of Denmark did the Gestapo insist on the extradition of Jensen, who spent the war years in a Danish prison. Nor is there the slightest hint of such a plan in the Gestapo files, in which Richard Krebs's reports were recorded.

Wollweber describes Krebs's arrival in Copenhagen differently than Jensen does. His version is all the more credible because it has been handed down twice - the first time in 1941 in Swedish detention to the Swedish security police and the second time from memories not intended for the public.

According to Erik Nørgaard, who had access to the Swedish files, Wollweber reported to the Swedish police "that Krebs immediately upon his arrival in Denmark told them about his new role with the Gestapo and then declared that he wanted to return to work for the Comintern, but in reality tried to continue his spying activities"[243]. Nørgaard was obviously irritated by this contradiction to Jensen's account, which the writer had presented as fact in his earlier publications. Nörgaard squared the circle by concluding that Krebs must have betrayed his informer role in consultation with the Gestapo.

Such an agreement though can be ruled out if one takes as fact what Wollweber was to tell the Swedish police three years later: "Wollweber did not confirm that he saw Krebs again in 1937. He only said about this time that Krebs had worked at ISH as the tool of another man who was demonstrably in the service of a foreign power. This man had been Adolf Schelley, who, as is well known, had been exposed in Moscow as a traitor and spy."[244]

Finally, here a brief quote of Wollweber´s memoirs which he wrote down after having been deposed as head of the Stasi, the East German secret police: "Krebs came to Copenhagen with a false document and declared upon his arrival that he had been recruited by the Gestapo. To gain confidence Krebs immediately presented the order allegedly given to him by the Gestapo, his documents and bank cheques. Between Krebs and me there were actually meetings, but since we didn't trust him, he was completely cut off from the outside world. Krebs was isolated."[245]

Both versions can't be right. Either, as Jensen reports, Richard Krebs received worthless information which he passed on to Hamburg, or, as Wollweber claims, he was completely isolated from the outside world.

In reality, from August 8 to September 27, 1937, a veritable flood of information poured out of Copenhagen, which was summarized by the Gestapo in Hamburg and passed on to Berlin. Gestapo headquarters filed away long reports with the most varied information: that Thomas Mann was chairman of an international antifascist society - which probably interested the Gestapo less -, information about the underground connections of the "Skania Hjaelp" to Germany (which were already known after the arrest of a courier), about Comintern ship connections, about a Scotland Yard office in Hamburg, about the exposing of a spy, about the Danish freethinker society, internationally active Communists, Scandinavian seafarers' functionaries, about aid to Spain and so on and so forth. Already for the first delivery the courier from Hamburg must have needed a small suitcase. On August 5, agent S50 (the other, more frequent code name for Richard Krebs was "Erka") sent the Gestapo the *Deutsche Volkszeitung*, the *Communist International*, Issue 6, seven more brochures, including "On the Particularities of the Spanish Revolution," "Destroy Trotskyism," and 13 camouflaged brochures.

On 7 September, the Hamburg Gestapo needed no less than seven pages to inform headquarters of the latest news received from Erka. On top "Erka" had sent 11 brochures.

This flood is an indication that the alleged informer, just like the hero of *Out of the Night*, was used to mislead the Gestapo with a mixture of truth, half-truth and fiction. All the while Richard Krebs must have been – just as Wollweber was to write - completely isolated in Copenhagen, for he never learned of Bem's arrest. How likely is it that Krebs, who had not even been told the truth about his friend, had gathered this huge amount of information himself?

As already described in the Beilich case, the reports of an agent, who in reality works for the opposite side, do not in themselves provide any indication of his double play. In order not to damage the credibility of a double agent, a secret service will always take care never to let him deliver verifiably false information, but only such that have a certain dose of truth or at least likelihood. If the opposite side is given false information, it is only given false information that it cannot verify.

The truthfulness and intention of a double agent's reports can only be deduced by comparing the state of knowledge of both parties. With the reports of agent "Erka" this is often impossible. How can we check after 60 years whether Jensen's ship liaison officers, which "Erka" listed in his first report on 5 August, actually played the role he reported they did? Other reports by "Erkas" could hardly be called secret. For example, Bert Brecht's collaboration with the journal *Das Wort*, which was edited by Lion Feuchtwanger, or the congress of the Danish Stokers Union.

One of the reports which on first sight would seem to reveal that Richard Krebs was a "real" agent on closer analysis proves the exact opposite:

"Hamburg the 21.8.1937

Subject: Richard Jensen Denmark

Through the stepson of Jensen, whose tongue could be loosened by alcohol, the following became known concerning the functions of Richard Jensen:

Official: Head of the Stokers Union in Copenhagen, member of the City Council, member of the leadership of the central Danish trade union cartel, member of the Politburo of the Central Committee of the CP Denmark;

Unofficial: Central contact point for all international people travelling from the USSR to Western Europe. Probably in such a way that these people travel via Finland and Sweden to Copenhagen using legal papers. At Jensen, their legal passports are exchanged for false ones, and only here do they receive their written or oral instructions and other material.

Jensen receives all kinds of mail destined for Moscow in order to be forwarded from there by special couriers and liaisons (without using the regular mail service). Where these threads converge, i.e. where the clearance office for these things is, the agent has not yet been able to determine; Jensen's apartment does not serve such purposes. The official distribution centre for illegal German literature is located in Copenhagen, Larsbjörnstr. 15."[246]

What seems absolutely "real" at first glance and was certainly calculated to appear so, turns out to be a bunch of old news on closer inspection. After all, Jensen's role in the accommodation of international functionaries was well known to the Gestapo through Albert Walter, Copenhagen's relay function was an old hat and passport forgery as well.

Furthermore, the Gestapo had not only captured Richard Krebs, but also other German Communists with papers that came from Jensen. Another agent, a Danish political police officer and a strict anti-Communist, reported barely three months later that it was very unlikely that Jensen would be involved in passport forgery.[247] Richard Jensen's role in arms shipments to Spain went far beyond that, as Nørgaard writes in his publications, in which he relies heavily on Jensen's own statements. "It soon became clear that Jensen had become one of the most valuable men in the established weapons network for Spain. Where others got stuck in unmanageable difficulties, Jensen managed in a short time to dispose of a fleet of new ships, all manned with reliable people, to direct ships all over Europe in a labyrinthine way, to load and reload them and to smuggle large quantities of ammunition to Spain. Through a clever transaction involving Sweden, Jensen managed to buy rifles and ammunition in Hamburg."[248]

If "Erka" had really succeeded in "loosening the tongue" of Martin Jensen, his father's bodyguard, then he really could have provided the Gestapo with valuable information. But since Richard Krebs only learned about Richard Jensen's activities after the war, "Erkas" report must be regarded as clever disinformation.

Just as Beilich's statements about Hermine were misleading by assigning an important role to a woman who had long since turned her back on communism, so too must a certain intention be suspected in Erka's reports. Reading the analysis of Erkas reports by the Gestapo one is struck by the fact that the only potentially explosive information that Erka had to communicate about the communist underground in Germany was the liaison work of Skania Hjaelp. A fact that – as the Gestapo suspiciously noted – had been known by them for a long time.

On the other hand, those messages referring to the British secret service and the ITF, the old adversary of ISH, were accurate and completely new to the Gestapo.

In order to understand what role the Agent "Erka" really played, one must know that the German section had practically ceased to exist even before the dissolution of the ISH. "Comrade Pirate", Hermann Knüfken, had mutinied in mid-1935 against the leadership of the ISH, had pulled the majority to his side and had led them into the ITF. He and his comrades had succeeded in the unique feat of "outstripping the party in terms of the number of members and political influence in an entire professional sector".[249] With characteristic momentum, the experienced mutineer set his followers the goal of bringing about revolts like those of 1918 at the outbreak of war. The fact that these plans, which at first sight sound like the fantasies of a megalomaniac, were not entirely far-fetched is confirmed by the Gestapo, which closely observed the mood in Hamburg.

Whereas the rejection of the Führer was clearly noticeable in the Hamburg shipyards, the mood among the seamen was even worse. Exposed neither to constant propaganda nor to the permanent threat of the Gestapo, most were openly opposed to the new regime. That is confirmed by contemporary witnesses, who remember that even Nazis preferred not to denounce dissenters if they did not want to go overboard during the next voyage.[250] Knüfken and his small group of activists succeeded from their base in Antwerp in winning 300 confidants on German ships and in attracting the majority of former members of the German section of the ISH to their side.

The concealment of the group, which like the insurgents of 1918 worked without any formal structure, was done to such perfection that the German authorities had no idea before Richard Krebs's arrival in Copenhagen. Behind any agitation they still suspected the ISH. Thus, as the historian Dieter Nelles writes, "in a 1937 study by the German Labour Front on 'Disturbances to Economic Peace in Maritime Navigation' ... five pages were devoted to the 'tactics of the Comintern' and a whole two sentences to the ITF".[251]

Erka explained to the Gestapo their mistake. Already his second delivery contained information that electrified the Secret Police: "The ISH has been liquidated; its sections joined the national sections of the ITF which resulted in an extraordinary radicalization. It goes without saying that former leading ISH officials have also been deployed and are working to increasingly lead the ISH into communist waters. [252]

That this report had the desired effect can be inferred from a letter by the Gestapo headquarter dated 9 November 1937: "At the beginning of September it became known here that the ISH had ceased to exist on Moscow's orders. It was absorbed into the ITF. This measure has resulted in an extraordinary radicalisation of leading ITF circles. (…)

If there is any further information on this matter there, I would ask that a report be sent."[253]

By breaking with the Comintern Knüfken and his people had committed a sin that warranted the death penalty. But as it was they were out of reach of Stalin´s executioners. All that was left was to to denounce the renegades as Gestapo collaborators. Wollweber himself travelled to Edo Fimmen, the ITF leader to tell him so. But by doing that he only aroused the mistrust of the old revolutionary, who now supported the Antwerp group even more.

For Knüfken the situation was much more dangerous than for his comrades-in-arms. As one of the men who had helped set up the OMS network, he knew too many secrets.

As he had already barely survived an investigation by the Soviet secret police he knew perfectly well which danger he was in. But he was one of the very few former members of the Soviet Sevret Services who managed to survive.

Maybe a vow of silence saved his head. This is indicated by the passage in his memoirs about his imprisonment in the Soviet Union, which is worded such that it does not allow any conclusions about the author.

In addition, the old fox was not as easy to finish off as the leadership of the ISH might have hoped. After denouncing him in vain as a Gestapo agent, a comrade was sent out in 1936 to control Knüfken's correspondence. It turned out that Knüfken had intelligence contacts.

The "Comrade Pirate" claimed that it was the GPU with which he was in contact. The controller flinched at the mention of the dreaded secret police and wrote a letter to Moscow to find out if that was true. Unfortunately, only this letter, but not the answer, is contained in Knüfken's cadre file, and so it is unclear whether Knüfken was just bluffing.

That Knüfken collaborated with the British secret service from 1936 is certain, however. During the Thirties for the British Knüfken became more and more important. When he was arrested in Sweden in 1940 while exploring the destruction of the same railway that had led Richard Krebs to Norway in 1933, the British secret service used all diplomatic means to prevent his extradition to Germany. Knüfken's activity for the British was suspected relatively early; Adolf had already reported this at the beginning of 1936 after his arrival in Moscow.

Only the Gestapo didn't know about it yet. It was only through "Erka" that they were made aware of this on 21.8.1937. The double agent announced that he had accidentally read a letter dated January 1, 1937, in which a certain Grebjakow reported "that Knüfken had worked for the Scotland Yard for years and days and was also paid from there"[254].

Ernst Wollweber was the man in whom the Gestapo was interested in the most. They had lost sight of him when he went to the Soviet Union in 1935. What he did there exactly, and whether he was also targeted during the purges has remained unknown. In 1937 at any rate - this has been proven many times and described in detail by himself in his memoirs - he no longer had anything to do with trade union work or agitation against the Third Reich. The man who, according to the Soviet secret service officer Soya Voskressenskaja, had already worked for the Soviet secret service in the early 1920s and had been "shut down" when he was elected to the Central Committee of the KPD, was now organizing a worldwide series of attacks on the shipping of the Axis powers on behalf of Stalin and with the support of the Soviet secret services, which would later earn him the moniker "King of the Saboteurs". He recruited his staff from ISH Northern and Central European cadres, who, just like himself, retired from any open work. The Latvian Ernest Lambert alias Michael Avotin or Avatin, whom Richard Krebs had accommodated as a stowaway on the Montpellier during his first trip on behalf of IPK Transport, played an important role. When Richard Krebs arrived in Copenhagen, the sabotage organisation was already in action.

Did Wollweber only follow the rules of conspiracy or did he not trust Richard Krebs for completely different, possibly personal reasons? Was he aware, in the paranoid atmosphere of those years, of the dangers that for him personally proceeded from too close a contact with Richard Krebs? In any case, the former prisoner did not receive the slightest information about the new field of activity of his former boss. Otherwise, he would later not have hesitated a minute to make it public.

Nevertheless, Richard Krebs apparently came just in time to Copenhagen for Wollweber to distract the Gestapo from his new field of activity. About the ITF and Knüfken, the alleged Gestapo informer reported interesting and correct facts, whereas everything that he wrote about Wollweber was misleading or even outright wrong.

Thus, in the reports "Erkas" summarized by the Hamburg Gestapo for Berlin, no personal meeting of the Agent with Wollweber is reported anywhere, although according to all participants such meetings took place. In the first report by "Erka" there is the following passage about Ernst Wollweber: "The previous director of the ISH in Copenhagen Ernst Wollweber was deposed during the purges after the VII World Congress. He was ill for a long time and is now in Leningrad."[255]

The next message "Erkas" about Wollweber seems to contradict the thesis that Richard Krebs gave false information.

"Wollweber, Ernst has been back from Leningrad for 3 months and works as instructor of the Comintern for Norway and Sweden under the code name 'Valentin'. As such he is soon in Oslo, soon in Stockholm. He is married in Oslo to the Norwegian 'Kitty' née Andresen and is fluent in Scandinavian. Wollweber is said to have got quite fat."[256]

In reality, this was another clever hoax. Wollweber was by no means an instructor of the Comintern. On the contrary, since communists were observed everywhere by the police he had to completely avoid contact with party circles when setting up his sabotage organization. He had indeed married a Norwegian, but not Kitty Andresen. However, Kitty Andresen was already known to the Gestapo as a Norwegian Communist, which added further credibility to the report. This had undoubtedly been intended. From a later statement by Richard Krebs one can reconstruct how this message came about.

In 1950, at the beginning of the Cold War, the American CIC compiled all the information that could be found in *Out of the Night* and asked Richard Krebs for any other details he remembered about Wollweber. According to *Out of the Night* Wollweber was married to the sister of Arthur Samsing when Valtin met him in Copenhagen. Here now the minutes of his statement 13 years later:

"Krebs assumes that the story that Wollweber married Sylvia Samsing is true. He concludes this from the excitement that arose in Copenhagen when he mentioned that Kraus had sent him a message saying that such a report was available and asking him to check it out."[257]

The reason for the report by "Erka" was thus a contract by the Gestapo to check some information. Obviously, the Gestapo already knew that Wollweber was no longer in the Soviet Union, as reported by "Erka. To deny the content of Kraus' message to "Erka" outright would have endangered the credibility of the double agent. So the true patrons of "Erka" compiled a report that sounded plausible and distracted the Gestapo from Wollweber's actual mission. To ascribe the wrong woman to Wollweber was not difficult because the Gestapo's information contained a small but substantial error: Wollweber was not married to the sister of the famous Norwegian communist, but to his sister-in-law. This is the only scene from the long-distance duel between the Soviet and German secret services that the two of them carried out by using "Erka", which we can reconstruct. Since the files of the Hamburg Gestapo were burned during the Second World War, we will never know how many other of Erka´s reports came about in a similar way.

Richard Krebs no longer plays along

In *Out of the Night* the hero is received by Jensen with all honours. At first willingly, then more and more hesitantly, he transmits to the Gestapo the material that Avatin's people put together for him.

Insisting time and again to get Firelei out of Germany, he is always put off. The only one who supports him is the man of action, Avatin, who is thrilled by every action against the hated Gestapo. Behind Wollweber´s back Avatin provides him with bogus material for a trip to Germany, i.e. documents with apparently explosive information, which, in the event of arrest by the Gestapo, are intended to provide him with an alibi for his stay in the Third Reich. Valtin is arrested as soon as he enters the country. Avatin's material saves him. He returns to Copenhagen and soon afterwards informs the Gestapo that Wollweber will soon travel to Sonderburg near the German border. This is meant to induce the Gestapo to put together a kidnapping squad, which Avatin's people in turn were supposed to ambush. The members of Gestapo were then to be exchanged for an important Soviet agent. After this plan has failed, a Gestapo agent, whom Valtin had lured to Copenhagen with a false report, is kidnapped. Valtin then signs off by informing the Gestapo that he will soon travel to the Soviet Union. He fears that otherwise the Gestapo will discover his double play and take revenge on his wife.

His "signing off" leads to a violent confrontation with "two of the most powerful figures of the Soviet secret service and the Comintern", Wollweber and the Finn Otto Kuusinen.

"Kuusinen shrank back... He had always had the reputation of being a coward. My fists, after all, were still those of a sailor. ... Wollweber remarked that I sought to use the Westbureau as a means for the solution of my private difficulties. Private difficulties! ' I snarled into Wollweber's face. ' The thousands of comrades in the Nazi concentration camps would like to hear that! The ones who had their heads chopped off, the ones who were hanged, cut to pieces, beaten to death. The ones who died with the cry, 'Long live the Communist Party!' They all would like to hear that—the attitude of Comrade Wollweber, their leader, who sits on safe ground on a salary of six hundred dollars a month."

After this argument Valtin is first put on ice but then sent to Rotterdam. There, he works as an instructor for the last time, until he is given the task of playing an "unreliable" comrade into the hands of the Gestapo. He sabotages this order, is denounced and called back to Denmark. Then follows a final, fateful confrontation with Wollweber, which ends with Valtin being detained in Jensen's country house.

The reality was probably far less spectacular. The scene with Wollweber and Kuusinen, the angry accusations and the conflict over Firelei cannot have taken place in this form. On the one hand, it is completely out of the question that Richard Krebs even dared to suggest smuggling his wife, who was considered a traitor, out of Germany. On the other hand, Wollweber, who under the code name "Anton" was travelling all over Scandinavia and Western Europe in order to organize a large number of bomb attacks, would hardly have got involved in a dispute with the double agent Richard Krebs.

Richard Krebs himself was to tell the CIC a few months before his death, that he saw Wollweber no more than two or three times and always under extreme security measures. The same applied to Avatin, the right hand of Wollweber. The only one he met regularly was Richard Jensen, who occasionally gave him a hundred crowns. He kept contact with him through the office of the Danish Stokers Union.

He had no idea what Wollweber, Avatin and Jensen were really up to. It was only clear to him that Jensen, despite his prominence in public, was no more than a tool for Avatin and Wollweber. And Richard Krebs, as one may add today, therefore no more than the tool of a tool. Through Jensen he got all the brochures and lists of names, the true and false messages to be send to the Gestapo, that were compiled by Avatin and his people.

Nevertheless, Jan Valtin's story has a true core. The moment when Richard Krebs stopped playing his double role is reflected in the files of the Gestapo. On September 28, 1937, the Hamburg Gestapo reported to the headquarters in Berlin that Agent "Erka" had set off for Moscow for a "conference of the leaders of the Communist factions in all notable seafarers' and dockers' associations in Europe, East Asia, and North America," which took place "under the leadership of the well-known Alfred Bem alias Adolf Schelley".[258] In addition to the agent, Erich Krewet, Wilhelm Siebert, and Mike Appelman were to take part from Germany.

Alfred Bem was probably already dead. Erich Krewet and probably also Mike Appelman were in the USA at that time, and Wilhelm Siebert had been admitted to a Leningrad remand prison a week earlier, on September 20, as the German Consulate General there reported to Germany shortly afterwards.

Only one person could be interested in the false report: the agent himself. The longer the game lasted, the more likely it was that the Gestapo would come onto his tricks. Waiting for this moment must have been nerve-wracking for Richard Krebs. What if the Gestapo found out that Wollweber was not married to Kitty Andresen, but to Samsing's sister-in-law, or that Avatin was not in Latvia, as reported by Erka, to reorganize the Communist Party there, but was traveling the ports of Scandinavia and Western Europe on Wollweber's behalf? If he continued like this, it would only be a matter of time before the secret police would take their revenge by turning on Hermine. Also the plan he had forged with his brother was then no longer feasible.

With the letter to Hamburg he had cut himself off and sufficiently explained his future silence without arousing any suspicion. Should the Gestapo never hear from him again, it was reasonable to assume that he had shared the fate of thousands of other German Communists who had made the mistake of fleeing from the Third Reich to the Soviet Union.

In fact, from this date on no more reports of "Erka" can be substantiated until the agent unexpectedly appeared in mid-November in the German embassy in Paris, made a short statement there, disappeared again and in February returned with a mysterious letter one last time.

The last dispute between Richard Krebs and the Comintern must have taken place between the "deregistration" of "Erka" and his appearance in Paris. Now Richard Krebs had become useless for Wollweber and Jensen.

The question was what to do with him. In no case could they simply let him go as he knew too much. In Moscow, the matter would have been settled quickly. A brief indictment for contact with the German secret police, a shot in the neck, and Richard Krebs would never have been heard from again.

In Copenhagen, however, a different approach had to be adopted. His contacts with the Gestapo could not be held against him, since, with the exception of the last report, they had taken place entirely in agreement with the Comintern. Neither Wollweber nor Jensen nor he himself later commented on exactly what he was accused of after his unauthorized deregistration from the Gestapo. Wollweber, who would tell the Swedes his rather lame story of the alleged connection between agent Richard Krebs and spy Alfred Bem in 1941, was to write in his memoirs about Krebs's Gestapo work, which had suddenly been uncovered. As did Jensen.

Jan Valtin's story of the comrade that he was ordered to play into the hands of the Gestapo in Rotterdam cannot be true either: There wasn´t enough time for a Rotterdam interlude between his "deregistration" on 26 September and his appearance in Paris in mid-November.

It must have been another, much harsher and above all more apt accusation that was brought against him: the accusation of covering a traitor. For if he tried to justify his arbitrary action with anything, it would certainly have been with fear for his wife. And that's when they had him. According to all the rules of the illegal KPD he would have had to break off any contact with her. That he not only didn´t do that but on top refused to continue his double play because of her, afflicted him with the odium of the traitor. In this respect, Jan Valtin's report is correct: after the letter to the Gestapo, there had been a wild argument about Firelei, but it went differently than described in the book. And only someone to whom the rules of the illegal KPD had passed into flesh and blood, who deeply affirmed and understood the necessity of insisting on the observance of such rules, who had learned all his life not to deal with "traitors", could be so deeply affected by this accusation that he should angrily deny it for the rest of his life, even turn it into its opposite.

There are various clues to the assumption that this was indeed the charge against him. Richard Jensen wrote in 1948 in *Frem I Lyset,* his refutation of *Out of the Night,* that Hermine Krebs did not die in a concentration camp, as claimed in the book, but married an SA man. It was an incoherent assertion that contributed nothing to his portrayal of the "actual" course of Richard Krebs's Gestapo activity. It is only understandable as a gloating allusion to the true story and Richard Krebs as its addressee.

Ernst Wollweber, told the Swedes in 1940 that Richard Krebs had not been trusted anyway because of his connection with the "bourgeois" Hermine.

Richard Krebs himself never reported what he was accused of in Copenhagen. He approached his sore point, the accusations against his wife, only once and shortly before his own death when he reported to the CIC, that Wollweber had called his wife a traitor in Copenhagen. But he immediately - as if the Communist hunters of the CIC had been in the least interested in the long dead Hermine Krebs - added that this had not been true.

Getaway

According to Jensen's memories and the protocol of the CIC, no official verdict had been reached after the indictment. As Jensen later reported to historian Erik Nørgaard, however, unofficially the decision had already been taken. Only the verdict was not to be carried out in Denmark. In order not to cause the "informer" to flee, Richard Krebs was informed that his case was still pending. From then on, Richard Krebs was under constant surveillance. It must have been some of the darkest weeks of his life.

For the foreseeable future, it was impossible for his wife and child to escape with the help of his brother. Then there was something else that tortured him as well.

Richard Krebs, whatever heretical thoughts he might had time and again, was literally a child of the Comintern. After his father's death, Richard Krebs, not yet seventeen years old, had joined the party and then spent three years almost uninterruptedly on its missions. Without ever betraying the party he started an indefinite prison sentence at the age of twenty and had postponed his dream of becoming a writer in order to be able to fully work for the Comintern again. As an adult, he had hardly known a home other than the company of his comrades. He was emotionally bound to the communist world movement to an extent that is otherwise only known among followers of obscure sects. Many of the thousands of German and foreign Communists who in the Soviet Union were under the flimsiest of pretexts arrested, tortured and handed over to the hell of the Camps died shouting "Long live communism".

As much as he elevates his alter ego Jan Valtin, who takes up the fight with the Comintern on his own and wins with his escape, as much as he underlines the autonomy of his hero - *Out of the Night* shows that it wasn´t him who made the final break. The reviewers of the first edition as well as literary scholar Michael Rohrwasser, who analyzed the text 50 years later, emphasize that the book neither presents a conversion nor a learning process, despite all the disillusioning experiences of the protagonist.

In *Out of the Night* Valtin is accused of "deliberately organizing acts of sabotage against the *apparatus* in Hitler's Germany", and has to fear for his life. Now he is forced to turn his back on the Comintern. "I struggled with myself. I cursed myself as a weakling in a frantic search for excuses to justify my crumbling faith. At eighteen, I had felt like a giant. At twenty-one, it was simple: "Pitch the grenade into the face of the counter-revolution!" At twenty-two, I had circled the globe in Comintern service, gaunt, hungry, fierce—and proud of it! At twenty-nine, the police departments of half a dozen nations hunted me as the Comintern's chief troublemaker on the waterfronts of Europe. At thirty-one, I was at work transforming Hitler's prisons into schools of proletarian internationalism. And now, at thirty-three, I found myself asking: Has all this been a falsehood, a fraud, a dismal spook? No man can strip himself of his skin."

In fact, an emotional bond was to remain that, turned negative, also determined the rest of his life.

Jensen and Wollweber largely agree on the end of the career of agent "Erka" or agent no. 51.

In his memoirs Ernst Wollweber writes about Richard Krebs: "The variant of bringing him to Spain was worked out. With the help of Danish sailors he was brought to Paris. In Paris he managed to jump out of the bus and run into the German embassy."[259]

When Richard Krebs, according to Jensen, expressed the wish to go to Spain to fight in the civil war there, he and his comrades were happy to comply. "I expected that if we sent him south, there would be others who would do what was necessary with him. ... With the same boat I sent a young comrade to watch out. I also travelled to Paris myself and delivered a picture of Krebs to my connections and oriented them as to what kind of man he was. Four days after my return, I received a message that Krebs had escaped his guards in a metro station."[260]

Combining the reports of Wollweber and Jensen and the next report of "Erka" to the Gestapo which came from Paris, the following picture emerges: After Jensen and Wollweber had told Krebs that his case was still pending and was only to be decided in Spain they dared to send him across Europe under relatively loose surveillance. Richard Krebs pretended to believe them. Had he really gone to Spain, his fate would have been sealed. In the republican camp the Communists had asserted themselves with Soviet help and unleashed a terror against all dissenters that in no wise was different from what was happening in the Soviet Union. Thousands of anarchists, alleged and real Trotskyists, and supporters of the left-socialist POUM, in short, anyone on the left who did not believe in the all-encompassing wisdom of Stalin and his policies, was arrested, tortured and executed. A word from Jensen would have sufficed, and Richard Krebs would never have returned.

In Paris Richard Krebs then did what all attacks against him were to later cite as proof of his being an agent of the Gestapo: He rescued himself by entering the German embassy. In order not to prove his enemies right he was never to mention this episode. In *Out of the Night*, there only remained a strangely unmotivated journey to Paris.

It is from Paris that "Erka" send his last message to the Gestapo. Unlike the previous reports, it is very short and sounds as if it had been written under time pressure. Richard Krebs must have handed it in a few days before November 28, 1937, since that is the day when he was for the first time branded as a Gestapo agent.

"Deter is currently a trade union specialist at the Central Committee in Paris. He talked to me for five minutes. He said that the present affair could break Ernst Wollweber's neck because of his 'earlier connection with Holstein and Hermann' (Kurt Beilich). I'll keep pushing in that direction. The personal fights within the CC seem to be quite bitter in nature. Franz Pietrzak (Bremen) currently representing in Stockholm"[261]

Perhaps Deter, a former leading German ISH cadre, was actually a trade union specialist at the CC in Paris at that time.

However, it is hardly credible that any official party authority in Paris had the slightest idea of what Wollweber was up to at that time. Nor is it at all likely that any of the German functionaries who were then collectively dreading a call to Moscow would have had the clout to break the neck of Wollweber, who enjoyed much more effective protection. It is finally impossible that Richard Krebs would have had any knowledge of the inner workings of the German CC.

There is only one explanation for these (rather sensational) falsehoods: Richard Krebs entered the German Embassy and revealed his connection with the Gestapo. He must have been referred to the local representative of the Gestapo. The agent had to explain to him, why he, by turning to an official German institution, had risked his exposure. He could not reveal the truth - that he had already been "uncovered" and slated for liquidation- since the Gestapo would have immediately ordered the now useless spy back to Germany.

In order to retain the Gestapo's trust, which was the prerequisite for the escape of wife and child, Richard Krebs had to remain "Erka" for them. That meant he had to provide new information. Since he knew nothing concrete about Wollweber's activity, he was forced to make something up. It was important that it fit the previous messages of agent "Erka". For example, intrigues related to the distribution of posts after the merger of ITF and ISH.

His maneuver was a success. It was a long time before the Gestapo realized that they had been fed misinformation. On 23 April 1938 the secret police still believed that Ernst Wollweber was working as a Comintern instructor under the code name "Valentin" and "married to 'Kitty' née Andreesen".[262]

With one mysterious exception, this was the last time that the Gestapo received a report from "Erka". On leaving the embassy Richard Krebs must have stated that he is now travelling to Spain. The Gestapo headquarters in Berlin noted on 10 December in connection with the unification of ISH and ITF: "According to information from Gestapo Hamburg, he is currently in Spain. Since only agent 'Erka' can provide information about the ISH, there is no need to ask Hamburg at the moment."[263]

Richard Krebs's second attempt at signing off with the Gestapo without arousing their suspicion had - at least temporarily - succeeded.

Instead of heading south, Richard Krebs travelled north on an unknown route. In Belgium he contacted the Knüfken group. In a letter dated November 25, 1937, a member of the group, Hans Jahn, mentions a German refugee who can only have been Richard Krebs: "The appearance of a former senior CP official, who about six weeks ago has served his four-year prison sentence for high treason, gives me reason to convey a few words from his report to you. Since his family is still in the realm, these few words are intended only for you. In addition to his experiences in the various penitentiaries, the mood of the political prisoners, he also shared his experiences about the countless interrogations by Gestapo officials. All higher Gestapo officials seem to be in the know that neither C.P. nor S.P. are any longer able to carry out mass work in G. This is also supported by the fact that mass arrests and mass trials, as they took place a year ago, have virtually ceased."[264]

Four weeks later Richard Krebs was given a place on the "Ary Lensen" by Knüfken. She was an English ship that set sail on January 1 from Ghent in the direction of Newport News, a small port not far from the military port of Norfolk. He arrived there on 3 February 1938. After checking his personal details, it was established that he had been expelled in 1929 on the condition that he never enter the USA again. He received a strict ban on going ashore and an obligation to leave the USA with the same ship.

But as the "Ary Lensen" took on no cargo Krebs' stay on board dragged on for weeks.

On February 3, 1938, Hermann Knüfken wrote to ITF Chairman Edo Fimmen, enclosing a newspaper clipping showing the photo from Richard Krebs's Gestapo identity card: "Meanwhile, news enclosed here. So Richard Krebs was made a Gestapo informer after all. ... We are of the opinion that if R. Krebs were an informer and actually worked for the Gestapo, then various Comintern people must be watching their steps. This boy is in the know and also knows where the skeletons are buried. But because he diverted from the party line and might make some damaging disclosures they have branded him an informer.

If you have a chance to investigate, do what you can. Maybe the Parisians can tell you the reason for their suspicion?

After all, he is a comrade who had received almost 4 years and, unlike others, behaved very well, both in pre-trial detention and in prison."[265]

On the 21st of February that is less than three weeks after Knüfken's letter to Fimmen, a last report by "Erka" arrived in Berlin. In addition to many trivialities and false statement, it contained a wealth of detailed information about the Knüfken group. Most was completely new to the Gestapo and parts of it were cited in indictments against some members of the group after their arrest at the beginning of World War II.

This report and the fact that he had apparently concealed his double play in Antwerp seem at first glance to prove that Richard Krebs was a "real" agent of the Gestapo.

However, the reasons for the concealment of his work for the Gestapo and, indirectly, for the GPU are obvious. Neither could he afford to shake the confidence of Knüfken on whose help he relied, nor could he risk any delay that would have resulted in the disclosure of his double-cross.

Moreover, it is very doubtful that the report actually comes from Richard Krebs. Already the date raises serious doubts. Even if one assumes that the report first went to Hamburg and only then to Berlin, there is no conclusive explanation for why it should have lasted almost eight weeks until the last report "Erkas" from Belgium arrived in Berlin, as it can hardly have come from the USA. First, a letter - assuming it had been sent on February 3, 1938, the day of Richard Krebs's arrival in Newport News, and addressed to Inspector Kraus – could not have arrived in Berlin from the east coast of the United States via Hamburg in just 18 days. Secondly, the Gestapo searched in vain for him over the next few months. If they had had a postmark as a clue, they would not have send informers to search for him in Antwerp.

Finally, the report could not have been in Krebs' interest, as he had led the secret police to believe that he was on his way to Spain.

Not only the dating, the report itself is mysterious. It comprises eight typewriter pages and has been preserved in its original form, together with a six-page evaluation dated 23 April 1938.

It begins: "Since the liquidation of ISH, the ITF has been the only international organisation of transport workers with a membership that is more than 10 times stronger than that of the ISH". The report continues with a history of the Knüfken group and their break with the ISH and includes a detailed description of the Antwerp organization.

About the unification efforts of the ITF and ISH the report claims that Edo Fimmen had exposed "Wollweber, Deter, Atschkanow and Schelley ... as factionalists" at a conference in Paris. [266]

The part about Knüfken and his people is mostly true, the section about the ISH people and Wollweber is clearly not.

So far, the report could have come from Richard Krebs. The passages about Knüfken and his people would probably correspond to his level of knowledge. However, there is no obvious reason why he should have continued to spread false information about Wollweber.

If the first five pages already raise doubts as to whether Richard Krebs was their author, this applies all the more to several passages of the last three pages. Especially the following passage makes no sense at all.

"Members of the Lehmann Group in Antwerp are the following:
1) the former Secretary of the Railway Section of the General Union in Duisburg
2) a certain 'Karl' from Hamburg.
Personal description: About 36 years old, medium sized, slim, with blond hair and slightly curved nose, sailor. He is said to have appeared in Antwerp soon after the national uprising, with the information that he had been sent as an agent by the Hamburg Gestapo. He's a former KPD member who then joined the Lehman Group."

Kurt Lehmann was the second leading personality of the Antwerp Group. An outsider might have therefore also described it as the "Lehmann group. Furthermore there was only one member of the ITF Group to whom the description under 1) applied: the very Hans Jahn, who was the first to report the arrival of Krebs in Antwerp.

Finally, mentioned "Karl from Hamburg" could be no one else but Knüfken himself, as the Gestapo soon discovered. The description fitted him perfectly, and moreover, as the secret police later found out, "Karl" was the alias which he had used in Antwerp. Assuming that Richard Krebs had written the report to keep the Gestapo quiet, protect his wife, and continue to pursue his plan to get them out of Germany: what would have been the point of describing Knüfken and Jahn, but not naming them?

The report concludes with an explicit reference to Wollweber's supposedly minor importance: "It is interesting that not a single sailor functionary of note is available to the Wollweber-Deter group today".

The discrepancies must have soon become apparent. Agent "Erka" didn't know the legendary Knüfken? In fact, the last letter concerning Krebs that is known from the files of the Gestapo indicate that the Paris report was seen as his last "real" information.

After the publication of *Out of the Night, the* embassy in Washington asked for information about the author and the secret police answered:

"While serving his sentence, K. repeatedly regretted his actions and expressed himself to the effect that he had broken with communism. After serving his sentence, he was therefore given the opportunity to make good his misconduct towards Germany. Krebs then tried to get back into the ISH. He allegedly did not succeed because he was called a Gestapo agent. After some time K. appeared in Paris and wanted to be recruited for the International Brigade in Spain. But in reality he travelled via London to the USA."107[267]

The last word on the Agent "Erka" probably belongs to Ernst Wollweber. Nørgaard writes in *Krigen for Krigen*: "In 1941 Wollweber told the Swedish police that he knew that Krebs had arrived in America in the spring of 1938. Towards the end of his time in Copenhagen, he had reported the old revolutionary sailor Hermann Knüfken to the Gestapo."[268]

How did Wollweber know that? Is that how one might explain the last report of "Erka"? Had one of the secret channels of "Erka", been used to divert the Gestapo's attention one last time from Wollweber's organization and onto the group of Knüfken?

If one presumes that "Erkas" last report was put together just like the reports that came from Copenhagen to Hamburg in August and September, then Wollweber and his people must have known about internals of the Knüfken group. And that was certainly the case. *Paa Törn*, the magazine of the Scandinavian seaman's clubs in the USA, had already published a profile of him before Richard Krebs's arrival in the USA. Furthermore *Paa Törn* reported that he had last been in Antwerp and was now on his way to the USA.109 Where did this information come from, if not from within the Knüfken group? And who had transferred it to the USA with such speed, if not the communist secret apparatus?

The Gestapo though was to stay in the dark for a long time. On 29 March 1939 a certain Eiler Pontopiddan, who was suspected of pro-German espionage, was interrogated in Copenhagen. When asked about who he had collected material on, he replied: "About communists like Wollweber, a man named Richard Krebs, all Danish communists and many others."[269]

It was not until 1941 and the publication of *Out of the Night,* that the Gestapo finally knew for certain what had happened to agent "Erka". The conclusion though that "Erka" had betrayed him was one at which Inspector Kraus was to arrive at much earlier.

PART IV America

Hiding in New York

After his arrival at Newport News on February 3, 1938, the ship moved to Norfolk, a much larger port a few miles away. Week after week passed without it being foreseeable when and with what goal the "Ary Lensen" would set sail again. Richard Krebs stayed on board and was kept busy with the usual work that captains find for their crew if there is nothing else to do: bracing the bream, painting the deck and cleaning the galley. Suddenly, on March 6th, he disappeared from the ship. Already on March 9th he was in New York where he registered with an employment agency under the name Jan Valtin which he was – alternating with Eric Holmberg - to use for the next few years.

The year after his arrival in New York is in some ways unusually well documented. In the hope of one day being able to achieve legal residence Richard Krebs kept all receipts for work done, registrations with a private employment agency, a.s.o. It is therefore possible to reconstruct almost to a day how he made a living.

Everything else has to be laboriously put together from the most diverse sources as only a few statements about the central events during this time, the most bitter of his life so far, have been handed down to us. Only shortly before his death would he reveal a few details to the CIC. His silence was caused by a file concerning the "espionage case of Richard Krebs" that the FBI of Richmond, Virginia opened on the 20th of April.

The file, which was passed on to the US Naval Secret Service and is therefore preserved without the usual inscriptions in FBI files, contains in translation seven letters in German, two postcards and two handwritten notes, that were obviously made by Richard Krebs himself. There is also an excerpt from the Scandinavian seafarers' magazine *Paa Törn*, with a photo of Richard Krebs's Gestapo identity card. Four of the letters are from Hermine Krebs and one from Hans Felix Jeschke, a friend in Ghent who belonged to the Knüfken group. Richard Krebs probably already knew the sailor from his days in Hamburg. Another very personal letter came from an unknown person in Belgium and then there are two postcards from Hugo Krebs.

The first letter is from Hermine. It is dated 6 January in Bremen, Germany, signed with Fitsch and without adressee.

"You evil one. Again you destroyed my castle in the air, but wait until I can use my legs again. I hope that in four weeks I have recovered enough to be able to visit you, and then I will grab you by the ears. You can count on it. Do what you think is right. Today I know too little about you and the circumstances. Stay healthy and be a little brave. Give enough and give wisely - but give up carrying letters around with you for fourteen days. The waiting is terrible .

P.S. Write to Stove, the village postal clerk"[270]

She sent the next letter on January 31. Now she called him Braun.

"I don't know where and how this letter will reach you, and you can imagine what it means for me not to hear from you for weeks.

My heart and soul are so hurt that I have not been in the mood to write the whole time. ... I don't visit anyone anymore, and my only sunshine is Tau (that's the child). I can't do anything bigger for now. Every now and then I suffer from rheumatic pain in my leg, but it's straight again. My nerves have suffered considerably during this disease, and for two sleepless nights I had heart depression at the thought of the future. It would be very easy if this suffering did not oppress me. It's just the way it is, and I have to go on despite everything. ...

You're suggesting I come, but right now I just can't. I haven't recovered that far yet.

Today I'm asking you to come yourself. Nothing stands in the way. You can come back. We should finally clarify the matter and create a good basis. I just can't stand it. I'm not good for anything because there's no hope for the future. And how happy, how hopeful I was for Christmas. Listen, Braun: If you think about my happiness and my worries, about Tau and me, then make it possible to come. ...«

On February 25th, she had written to him again:

"My dear Braun

A few days ago I received your letter. It was bad weeks of waiting, bad weeks in every way. How nice it is that you like your life so much now. You write about it in a way that makes me regret not being a sailor.

... Listen - I was able to walk well again. Then the suffering came back, and I had to have the leg subjected to a 'Chaiselougine', a radiation treatment. I knew the hip again wasn't okay. The leg must be given complete rest for four weeks. The day after tomorrow three weeks will be over and then only one, and I can start all over again. ... You must therefore forgo my visit. I can't come before May under any circumstances. For a whole year I will not be able to lift, carry or do heavy work. The pain is terrible when the leg is dislocated. When you put it back in, you pass out. ... All this must be endured. When an impenetrable darkness darkens the future and the present has nothing to offer, what may drive, encourage, or force oneself? ...«

Two postcards with unknown date of dispatch were from his brother Hugo.

"Dear Richard

I hope you get that greeting even though you're out somewhere. Until December 22, I was on U.S. [illegible] Unity and searched in vain for a particular sailor. Today I came to the S.S. Drake, and I will stay there until the end of March. Then the sailors set off again in the direction of the Baltic Sea, and then I will probably reach my full sailing time. We're still five months short. I've often thought about our boat. I was accommodated in A. at the place of Saint Anna. Nobody knew you there. I wish you good sailing. Leave the 'Eastern Companions' to the left."

"Dear Richard

I am very grateful to you for the card from the fourth of March from Norfolk. I've written to you in Ghent several times. As far as I'm concerned, we could go 'west' tomorrow, but I have to wait for the 2000 U [illegible] I'm supposed to get. There's nothing I can do before then, and nobody should know anything before the start. It'd be idiotic to sail a vessel that is not seaworthy. I'm thinking of a fishing boat from the Baltic Sea. Not fast and complicated, but stable. One of the first Danish ports would be a possible meeting point. Write how you feel about it. Also in terms of equipment and so on.

Greetings

Your Peps"

Hugo's daughter Martina remembers from her childhood that Jan Krebs, the son of Richard and Hermine, talked with her father for hours long after the war about plans to secretly bring him and his mother out of Germany. Plans somebody familiar with the circumstances can easily read from the letters of Fitsch and Peps.

Richard Krebs was probably in contact with his wife and brother via a Belgian address. A long letter from Hans Felix Jeschke dated 1 March from Ghent indicates that he must have entrusted his address to him. Jeschke writes that he has passed on Richard Krebs's address to "Karl", i.e. to Knüfken, who urgently wants to speak to him about the "commune".

"Maybe you don't know yet that the commune describes you in their publications as an informer and what not and distributes photos of you. You can see what primitive methods these crooks use. Unfortunately, you sacrificed the four precious years of your life that you spent behind curtains in vain for these crooks. In any case you now know that Karl from the group will instruct you. Furthermore I hope old boy that with you and 'your past' everything goes well. I will give you an address so that your mail will always reach me until I tell you a new one. I also hope that I will soon have disappeared from cursed Ghent and will not fall into the hands of the gendarmes. ...

Hans Felix

Be careful of the commune"[271]

This was not the only attempt to contact Richard Krebs by Knüfken and his goup. A letter from Edo Fimmen a year and a half later states that the chairman of the ITF had also tried to reach him several times via New York contacts. Always in vain.

Let's go back to Richard Krebs's situation in Norfolk at the beginning of March. The "Ary Lensen" did not and did not move from the spot. She'd been anchored for a month. Everything was possible: that she, as hoped, sailed into neutral waters - best of all into the English-speaking Caribbean - or suddenly got the order to pick up cargo in one of the Axis countries. Walking off deck and disappearing into the U.S. was dangerous because the chances of ever being legalized there were minimal. One possibility, though, he might have had. A possibility that would explain why Fimmen and Knüfken tried to reach him again and again. In the conglomeration of incoherent, right and wrong information that makes up the last "Erka" report, there is a strange passage about someone who can only have been Richard Krebs: "Some time ago a hamburger appeared in Antwerp and contacted the ITF. A conference took place in which Edo Fimmen, Lehmann, Knüfken and the Hamburger took part, and in which Fimmen proposed to send the Hamburger to New York as representative of the German section of the ITF, since he had become aware through his confidants in the vicinity of Achkanow (Leningrad) and Jensen that the Hamburger had broken with Moscow. Fimmen showed great interest in information from the circle of ISH officials Wollweber-Deter-Jensen and about their activities behind the scenes. The hamburger said he had to think about it because he was illegal in America. Fimmen promised to install him as an American because he had connections in New York."[272]

If Richard Krebs was the one from Hamburg, why didn't he accept the offer but stayed on deck for more than a month at the "Ary Lensen"? Probably because work for the ITF did not fit into his plans for the time being, as he had to avoid any kind of attention. His greatest fear must have been the Gestapo finding out that he had not travelled from Paris to Spain at all, but was in the USA. After all, the plans for his wife and child depended on the German secret police not knowing the truth about agent "Erka".

And there was another reason for his restraint: he had to assume that the ITF could not offer him security from the Soviet secret police. After all, he had been in the business long enough to know that in the Knüfken group there were probably one or two German sailors who had only pretended to have turned away from the KPD. Possibly this assumption had already become a certainty in Norfolk, when Krebs learned of the warning against him that *Paa Törn*, the magazine of the Scandinavian seaman's clubs in the USA, had already issued in January. The profile stated that the "Gestapo agent" was on his way to the USA - information that could have only had come from within the Knüfken group.

Nevertheless, Richard Krebs left for New York on March 6. He probably had no other choice. In 1941 he told the immigration authorities that he had heard that the "Ary Lensen" would soon set sail for Italy.

After his arrival in the metropolis, Richard Krebs took the risk and contacted former ISH cadres. He could have received the addresses only in Antwerp from Knüfken himself or from members of his group. One of them was Max Bareck, the special courier who had brought him money every week from Berlin to subsidize ISH units all over the world. Max Bareck was now caretaker in a Manhattan apartment building. Here Richard Krebs found temporary shelter. Already after a few weeks the Soviet secret police or communists, who worked for them, had discovered the

"Gestapo spy". Possibly the information came from Bareck himself. Here one must keep in mind that all former communists who were legally in the USA could be blackmailed with their past. After all, at that time everyone who wanted to enter the USA had to sign that they had never been a Communist. They searched Richard Krebs's room and took Hermine's letters with them. This is all apparent from some of the statements he made to the CIC in a completely different context.[273]

It is mysterious how the letters fell into the hands of the FBI in Richmond at the end of April, more than a thousand kilometres from New York. There's not a clue in the file itself. In the absence of other explanations, one must assume that those who had taken the letters had found them useless as they could not make any sense of them. Finally they came up with the idea of playing them to the FBI. In order to get more attention for the mysterious letters, they added the excerpt from *Paa Törn*. Richmond was chosen because the FBI there was responsible for Norfolk, the port the "Ary Lensen" had moved to after her arrival at Newport News. At that time Norfolk was one of the largest naval bases in the USA and was therefore intensively monitored. At the same time, it was also the last place where American authorities had registered the presence of a certain Richard Krebs. The desired effect occurred: The naval intelligence service was also involved in the investigation.

But the game didn't quite work out. Compared to Europe, where the whole world was preparing for the next war, the USA was not yet exercising any increased vigilance. FBI and naval intelligence concluded that Krebs had obviously been active as an intelligence agent in Europe, but as far as could be seen not in the USA. On 24 August 1938 the case was closed again.

After the search of his room Richard Krebs had to disappear again.

He was now completely on his own. In his later, likewise autobiographical novel *Castle in the Sand*, he described how an illegal immigrant of these years made it through New York. At night, when the weather permitted, he slept on a park bench, otherwise, wrapped in a coat, at the entrance to the subway stations, or spent the night bending over a coffee in one of the fast food restaurants open 24 hours a day.

In the morning he went to the neighborhood around Sixth Avenue on Lower Eastside, where there were a number of employment agencies. He hoped to find work there in a hotel as a painter, dishwasher or sidekick, as a hotel job usually also brought a place to sleep in some broom closet.

But he had to be careful. Not only *Paa Törn*, but also *Schiffahrt*, an organ of German sailors loyal to the Communist Party in New York, and the *Daily Worker*, the daily newspaper of the American Communist Party, had meanwhile published his picture and called him a "Gestapo informer". Shortly after the file was opened in Richmond, on May 5, 1938, the *Daily Worker* wrote:

"Richard Krebs, one of the top people with the Gestapo - the German secret service, has been seen twice this week on Staten Island -in St. George and in New Brighton. Krebs, who was caught in Paris as a Nazi spy, fled to Antwerp and escaped on an English freighter, on which he signed on as a seaman. The „Daily Worker" discovered that he left the ship in Norfolk, Virginia and then disappeared for a while. The appearance of Krebs in Staten Island gives weight to the suspicion that the meeting place for a Nazi spy ring exists here. The judiciary has been informed : Krebs is of average height, speaks English fluently and is about 30 years old.."

His future friend Benjamin Gitlow, top official of the American Communist Party in the late 1920s and later, like Richard Krebs himself, demonized as a renegade, writes in his memoirs that these unnamed informants of the *Daily Worker* didn´t just twice "discover" the German refugee as if by chance. The Soviet secret service had kidnapped Richard Krebs to Staten Island, a large, densely populated island off Manhattan in the middle of the shipping channel, and locked him in a woodshed. "There he was alert enough to knock over an oil lamp, start a fire and escape in the confusion that had arisen. The story of the *Daily Worker* was written to hide the OGPU's bungling and the fact that it had established itself in Staten Island for the same reason as the Gestapo: to spy on American shipping."[274]

Richard Krebs transferred this episode to Jan Valtin. In *Out of the Night* he lets his hero escape in exactly the same way from Jensen's country house, where he was arrested after his refusal to further follow orders. It is characteristic of Richard Krebs, for whom - after many years on ships, in prison and as a Comintern agent – it had become second nature never to show weakness that his hero sets himself free from Jensen's country house instead of admitting his own helplessness and that he had had no other option but to turn to the German embassy in Paris, which had saved him from certain death in Spain.

His employment slips show that Richard Krebs worked in a hotel in the Bronx district of New York from March 11 to March 18, 1938. On 31 March, when he started his next job, he had left the city. This time he had found a job as a painter in Rockaway Beach, a small village on the coast at that time.

It was not until June that he returned to New York City.

He had managed to cover his tracks, as the article of 5 May 1938 was the last one to appear about him in the communist press. Only with the release of *Out of the Night* were his enemies to get back on his track.

After the search of his room and the narrow escape on Staten Island the contact with Hermine must have broken off. An undated letter from Fitsch, the last of her to him that the espionage file Richard Krebs contains, was most likely also his last contact with her.

"(...) My room will be vacated tomorrow, and the sky will be open to me. I will once again pull together all my strength and energy and fight for a place in the sun with my armour, which warms me and without which I cannot live. In four weeks Tau will travel to the Baltic Sea with Grandma and spend the rest of the summer there according to your wishes. And then what? Then I and Tau will travel to Hamburg, and I will attend the Hanseatic Drawing School there. Do you understand what this means to me? Ha, this should prove to you that the old Fitsch is full of sparkling ideas, full of the old energy. And then, on to a place where one can get equipped and take aim at the final goal. (...) Yes, I'm happy again. Therefore you should pursue your goal with undiminished energy. My God, darling, if one day you should triumph, triumph. 'And we have triumphed despite all that.' This will be a day of incomparable celebration. As far as my journey to you is concerned, you will have to wait a little longer. This leg is the devil himself, and all I can do about it is flick my finger. - Look, I am unable to visit Peps, but I will write to him. He was never here again. Well, my song, greet me the sea and the sun and tell him that I am also slowly humming the melody. Take care. Braun, don't forget us, and don't forget what it means when someone has to wait six weeks for a letter from you.

Love from both your strays

Fitsch"[275]

A cousin of Hermine Krebs, who was sixteen when she died, remembers that before her death she went with her son to Hamburg and attended a drawing school there. A small brown Gestapo file card dated 17 June 1938 with the inscription "Richard Krebs" and "ISH functionary" and the information "supposed to be on an English ship"[276] indicates that Inspector Kraus was no longer waiting for news from agent "Erka". Richard Krebs must have cheated him. What could be more logical than interrogating his wife who had remained in Germany? On December 4, Richard Krebs had found work in a small town outside New York, he wrote to a relative of his mother who lived in the Midwest of the USA:

"Far Bookaway N.Y.

Dear Margarete

Yesterday a letter from Germany came into my hands. Hermine is dead.

Had she never met me, she would still be alive. Her going strikes me harder than the death of my mother. After she had left prison in 1936, she was ridden with illness. Adolf Hitler´s gift to one of his land´s fairest daughters. Nervous breakdown, heart trouble, general depression. Her joyful spirit was murdered there. For nineteen months, between superb but frustrated efforts of will to be her old self again, she made the rounds of hospitals and doctors. - Then suddenly, she died, simply died.

Her heart was noble. She loved beauty and harmony and has never hurt a creature in her whole life. She hated arrogance and the dogmas of self-proclaimed authority. She's been the best thing in my life, and I've been the best thing in hers. She loved her son tenderly and degraded herself to win him back. So I am here, lonelier than ever, and cannot even put a flower onto her grave. White lilies she liked most of all.

She didn't believe in God or heaven. She believed in the struggle for a decent life here on Mother Earth, which now surrounds her all around; definitively, irrevocably; and I see her cold and white and rigid in the earth; her face looks calm and sweet and a little astonished at her sudden and unjust end and above her I see the cold, flat landscape and the icy northwest wind singing in the tops of the naked trees. He's singing a song I've heard her sing a hundred times: Greet me the green earth ...

There is Jan our son. He is six now. We had planned to make him an architect, or an engineer, or a builder of ships, or even a simple artisan. Someone who makes things which are good. He is with her parents. They are very good to him. Too good! Make him a wilful sissy. Too old to understand youth. And next year the school will have him and make him a miserable yes man of gangster Hitler for life. Never.

I want him here. This land is good. It will be good to him. And it gives my blasted existence a slender purpose.

There are two ways:

1. Someone in this country adopts him, and has him come over. Soon, as soon as possible. I might marry some good girl and send her over to get him. To be

considered: as soon as the Gestapo learns that it is I who wants him, Jan will be a hostage in one of their accursed asylums.

2. I go over and kidnap him.

Please give me your advice. I have no one to speak to about this problem. What would be the formalities for an adoption? Court decision here, or in Germany? Consular decision? I have no idea about the red tape involved; always liked direct action best.

All pre-1933 photos of Hermine have been destroyed in the raids. I have not one. But I remember that some were sent to you 1930 and later. I beg you to let me have them. Copies at least. I need them. Especially the snap of Hermine, hands thrown up in the wind on the rocks of Heligoland.

The day Hitler came to power, my mother died. My friends died under the executioner's hatchet; some by suicide, others were tortured to death. The rest was buried alive. My brother was burned alive under the command of Göring. And now this. I find it grotesque that I'm still alive.

Your R.

My address: Will reach you separately. If you don't get anything, use the old address. Destroy this and write nothing about me."[277]

According to her death certificate Hermine Krebs died at the age of 33 years on 15.11.1938 in the general hospital Barmbeck near Hamburg from a rare blood disease similar to leukemia. Her cousin reports that in her family it was always said that she had succumbed to the consequences of imprisonment and concentration camps.

Richard Krebs was never to overcome the guilt of her early death. Not only had he been the one who had led her into the KPD - with his double play he had handed her to the Gestapo the moment she was slowly recovering.

Shortly thereafter Richard Krebs wrote in a letter to his mentor and former journalism lecturer in San Quentin, Arthur L. Price:

"I have not written anything new. I am sick of it. But I shall write again. Had various hard labour jobs and gave them up. Outside I look strong and able. But inside I am bust. Besides when the hearing is smashed a man is utterly alone. Now I have a dog, an Irish setter, rust brown and long haired and ten weeks old. „Smoke". He shares my meals and sleeps on my blanket and tears things up when I am away. But he is honestly, riotously happy when I come back home.

We live under the roof in a tenement among the Negroes of Harlem. Next week we are going to have a Christmas tree. The last one I had was Bremen in 1931."[278]

Shortly after Richard Krebs wrote this letter, he found work as a painter for a real estate company on Eighth Avenue.

Three months later, in March 1939, Richard Krebs himself was close to death. The destitute refugee was admitted to a New York hospital with pneumonia and pleurisy. If there hadn´t been a German doctor there to treat him with the just discovered penicillin he, according to his second wife, wouldn't have survived. This doctor, Friedrich Rost, was not only a philanthropist, but also had connections to the circle around Robert Bek-Gran, a German anarchist who had already come to the USA in the mid-twenties. After his release, Richard Krebs found temporary accommodation there.

A new beginning

Robert Bek-Gran was a painter, writer and lover of Chinese literature, whose small print shop in Manhattan contributed only insignificantly to the family income. This was mainly disputed by his wife Mary Watson, a native American. Bek-Gran came from a Munich family of artists, had participated in the short-lived Munich Soviet Republic in 1919 and emigrated to the USA in the mid-twenties. He was a man who made little fuss about his person and left many a riddle, since he used to destroy personal papers. He resembled his friend, the mysterious B. Traven, who has been confused with him several times. The fact that he had already met the famous writer in Munich, that he had promised him to keep the secret of his origin, and that he kept this promise, was known only to his immediate family.[279] Robert Bek-Gran remained a communist after his entry into the United States, until he openly turned against the Stalinist dictatorship in the mid-1930s. He founded the German-language magazine *Gegen den Strom* (against the current) and was the first to print the passage from Kurt Tucholsky's farewell letter to Arnold Zweig, which dealt with Stalin. Above all, with *Gegen den Strom,* he conducted a campaign against attempts to transform the German-American Cultural Association into a so-called front organization, an outwardly independent organization operating against Hitler under the cloak of the "People's Front," but in reality dominated by Communists. This fight, led by him and a small group of New York individualists, ultimately failed because of the superiority of their well-organized opponents. A statement by Richard Krebs's second wife Abigail suggests that some of Bek-Gran's activities will remain in the dark. She remembered that he was in contact with an underground organization in New York Harbor that was engaged in violent confrontations with both Nazis and Communists. "These people used to wear bracelets with razor blades. For example, they went with the stevedores to the docks and onto the ships. If someone didn't like that, there was a fight, and these people were thrown off the pier or beaten off the deck. It was pretty rough. Sometimes there was a murder. (...) It was just not generally known, there was never anything about it in the newspapers, because it was secret."[280]

With Bek-Gran and his circle, Richard Krebs had for the first time after his arrival in America found contact with people whom he could trust unreservedly. When Krebs was brought from the hospital to Bek-Gran, he was "sick in body and soul"[281], as Bek-Gran's wife Mary Watson later recalled. Both first solved his most urgent problem: they procured a refugee ID card for him through a German Christian refugee organization, which was issued in his real name. Although this paper was signed by Cordel Hull, the then secretary of state, it did not imply any right of residence. At best, it was suitable to get through a cursory examination.

After recovering from his severe pneumonia, Richard Krebs traveled to the Catskills, a low mountain range in the western state of New York, lived there for a few weeks in a tent, and began writing seriously. He had drawn a line under his previous life. Now he tried to deal with the death of his wife and the separation from the Comintern.

Richard Krebs had not voluntarily broken away from the Comintern. It wasn't until he was in mortal danger that he took flight. He more resembled a Soviet functionary like General Walter Krivitzki than intellectuals like Arthur Koestler or Manès Sperber. Krivitzki, head of Soviet Military Intelligence for Western Europe, had escaped to prevent his execution in Moscow. The aforementioned writers on the other hand, no less convinced and committed communists made the break on their own after long deliberations.

In his novel *Darkness at Noon* the former Communist Arthur Koestler was to find a plausible explanation for the greatest mystery that the Moscow trials posed to contemporaries. Why had the old Bolsheviks, the heroes and leaders of the revolution, who had so often come into contact with death that they called themselves "dead on vacation," confessed to the most absurd and hair-raising accusations? To plans to poison Lenin, to have been spies of the Okhrana, the tsarist secret police and then spies of the British? If one excludes revolutionary leaders "who, like Radek, only wanted to save their lives, and those who, like Zinoviev, were mentally broken" – "there still remained a hard core of men ... with a revolutionary past of thirty, forty years, veterans of tsarist prisons and Siberian exile, whose complete and joyful humiliation remained inexplicable".

In *Darkness at Noon* Arthur Koestler was to intuitively grasp what former GPU officer Walter Krivitzki would later write from personal experience in his book *I was Stalin's Agent*: the secret police had appealed to the defendants' party conscience until they admitted "that no Bolshevik group was strong enough to reform the party machine from within or overthrow Stalin's leadership. There really was deep dissatisfaction in the country, but fighting from outside the Bolshevik ranks would have meant the end of the Bolshevik dictatorship. (...)

The examining magistrate and the prisoner agreed that all Bolshevists must subordinate their will and thoughts to the will and thoughts of the Party. They agreed that to serve the party they would rather suffer death and dishonor than endanger the dictatorship of the party. It was up to the party whether it later wanted to pay tribute to their self-sacrifice."

Richard Krebs had also been a "dead man on vacation". Already as a teenager he had adopted the credo "The Party First". The unconditional belief in the historical mission of the party, which justified all victims in the name of a "bright future", had led him halfway around the world as well as to the prisons of the USA and the Third Reich. Despite his sobering experiences, he had stayed until the bitter end. Arthur

Koestler described the seven years of his party membership as the "best years" of his life "because of the unconditional devotion that filled them". Such a sentence could also have come from Richard Krebs, who had dedicated his entire adult life to working for the party.

Richard Krebs was only able to overcome his forced farewell and the demonization as Gestapo agent after he had drawn a clear line. The story of the death of Bert Adrian shows how much this had burdened him. The address on the front page - 148 Avenue - indicates that it was written before his serious illness, when he lived in Harlem. Here Richard Krebs not only pleads guilty to his wife, but also assumes the role of traitor on her behalf and is executed. It's like he wanted to go back in time to die instead of her.

His first publication under the pseudonym Jan Valtin appeared in the magazine *Ken* under the title "Hitler's Slaughterhouse: the living hell of Ploetzensee". After this description of the central execution site of the Third Reich, he published "A pillar of the Komintern", the sketch of a certain Ernst, which was easily recognizable as Ernst Wollweber.

Richard Krebs could not live off the few dollars he received for these publications. In June as well as in October and November he once again hired himself out as a painter.

In November 1939 the *American Mercury* printed "Comintern Agent", a description of the work of a Comintern instructor. This is how Richard Krebs got to know Eugene Lyons, the editor of the journal. The former communist and employee of the Soviet news agency in New York first made a name for himself with a book about the *Sacco and Vanzetti* scandal that was translated into most European languages. In *Assignment in Utopia,* a fascinating account of his time as a correspondent for a news agency in the Soviet Union in the early Thirties, Eugene Lyons describes his growing disillusionment with Soviet reality.

During his rare travels to the USA it had become increasingly difficult for him to conceal his doubts about the success of the Soviet experiment from his comrades. In the book he harshly criticized Western colleagues in Moscow who looked with contempt at the ill-dressed masses in the Soviet capital. Even worse they were careful not to write the truth about the millions who died during collectivization because they feared for their accreditation. His special scorn was reserved for the correspondent of the *New York Times* who liked to cite omelette thesis - to make an omelette you have to break the raw eggs - as a reason to hide the famine.

Lyons, who in *Assignment in Utopia* reported on the approval the lack of trade union rights in the Soviet Union found among American industrialists, continued to be a socialist. At the same time he was a bitter opponent of the American CP, which had gained such an influence in the USA in the 1930s that it went down as the "red decade" in American historiography.

The influence of Communism in the US had grown with the complete collapse of American-style laissez-faire capitalism. Following the 1929 stock market crash, President Roosevelt and his team, the so-called New Dealers, had had to save capitalism from itself. Roosevelt's predecessor in the office of president, Herbert Hoover, had reacted to the crisis and the drop in tax revenues by reducing government spending. Thereby weakening the economy even more Hoover had stood idly by while industry used the crisis to make further cuts in the already miserable pay of its workers. The resulting drop in demand exacerbated the crisis and fuelled social unrest.

The New Dealers increased government spending, introduced a series of social laws for the first time in US history, and strengthened trade unions. They collaborated with the CP of the USA, the only force on the left that remained after the smashing of the IWW in the 1920s. In the course of this collaboration, a number of disguised Communists managed to gain a foothold in the Washington bureaucracy. As American historians were able to prove after the opening of the Moscow archives in the early 1990s, a network existed in the capital of the USA at the end of the 1930s that worked for the secret services of the Soviet Union and imperceptibly influenced government policy.

The hardest and most bitter opponents of the Communists, apart from reactionary businessmen who rejected the whole New Deal, were Trotskyists and former party members who were better informed than the public about Stalin's dictatorship. They had experienced themselves how the Comintern dealt with renegades. The hatred that Stalin's murder actions in the Soviet Union and during the Spanish Civil War had engendered among them went so far that Leon Trotsky had agreed to testify before the "Congressional Committee on Un-American Activities". His murder prevented that.

Richard Krebs came into contact with these circles through the publication of Comintern Agent and Lyons' intercession. For the first meeting with Ben Mandel, an investigator at the "Congress Committee for Un-American Activities", who had belonged to the Central Committee of the American Communist Party until 1929, Krebs chose a meeting place under the large L in 114th Street in Manhattan. There, if necessary, he could have quickly vanished into the crowd. After Mandel, he met a number of other ex-communists from Lyons' circle of acquaintances. Among them were the well-known humorist, Trotsky biographer and supporter Max Eastman, who broke with his mentor's ideas in 1941, the Trotsky translator Malamud, who later became his closest friend and was to give Krebs Trotzky´s winter coat after the latter´s assasiation. To this circle also belonged Benjamin Gitlow the former vice-presidential candidate of the U.S. Communist Party, who had separated from the party in the early 1930s.

In his memoirs, Gitlow described how he met Richard Krebs.

"In 1940, a large, handsome, nervous young man established contact with a small anticommunist circle in New York who dared to stand against the towering wave of pro-Soviet and pro-Communist sentiment in the country. He had a story to tell and wanted their help and advice. Looking at the hounded, frightened man no one could foresee that a year later that man, Richard J. Krebs, writing under the pen name Jan Valtin, would produce a fictionalized autobiography of his experiences as a communist waterfront agent that would sell more than 700,000 times.

For two years after the Staten Island incident, the OGPU tried to track down Valtin. Whenever the trail got hot, changing his name as he got new quarters.

Once among friends, fear left the hounded young man. He liked to talk about his adventures and exploits, colouring the dramtic incidents, giving them substance and interest. Listeners often tried to fathom the mind of a young man who boasted about deeds of violence and murder that frightened and disturbed the listener.

What most listeners forgot was that Valtin reflected the thoughts and mood of the movement he had just left behind. Although he wanted to spread to spread the shocking story about the National Socialism of Hitler and Communism of Stalin, he could not stamp the past out of his mind nor could he suddenly change and alter the psychological grooves that years of communist association had channeled through the sensitive cells of his brain." [282]

At that time Richard Krebs also met Isaac Don Levine who was to be of the greatest importance for his future. A Russian born Jew he had returned there after the revolution and wrote a book about this world-historical event. At first enthusiastic about the coup, Isaac Don Levine had already turned against the Bolsheviks in the 1920s and was now one of the leading publicists in the USA. He has published in the Hearst press, the largest and most influential U.S. newspaper chain, sat on the board of the Book-of-the-Month Club, the book ring with the largest circulation, and had good connections to Hollywood; among other things, he wrote scripts for the film studios for blockbusters such as Jack London's *Call of the Wilderness*. When Richard Krebs showed him a bundle of notes, the preliminary work for a planned book with autobiographical background, Levine immediately sensed a potential bestseller. To make sure that the book was not the tale of an impostor, he had Richard Krebs write down the events in Copenhagen in detail and had the text checked by the State Department in Washington. After the officials had informed him that the description of Richard Jensen and Wollweber and their role in the Comintern corresponded to their own findings, Levine returned to New York satisfied. Levine himself had never heard of the two, though he had spent twenty years studying communism.[283]

On December 23, Levine gave the final go-ahead for *Out of the Night*. He and Ben Mandel provided Richard Krebs with a monthly scholarship. Freed from money worries, he moved to the Bek-Grans country house in Stanford, Connecticut, where he filled over 1000 typewritten pages in seven months, painting the Bek-Grans house on the side. During his stay in Stanford he met the 16-year-old Abigail Harris, who supervised the two children of the Bek-Grans in the summer.

Abigail Harris came from a wealthy Jewish family; her grandfather had been a well-known rabbi. Her mother and herself were secular Jews and belonged to the intellectual milieu of Manhattan in which European immigrants felt most at ease. When Abigail Harris saw Richard Krebs for the first time, she had already met many Europeans like him. Her mother and the Bek-Grans belonged to a small circle of New Yorkers who signed affidavits for refugees from Europe, which enabled their entry into the US. Europeans, who were illegally in the USA also found shelter with Abigail's mother. Bek-Gran took them to her, and she hid them in the attic. Since there was no toilet there, Abigail's task was to empty the chamber pot twice a day.

The tall girl fell in love with the mysterious German. Sixty years later, she remembered her first encounter:

" Richard and I got to talking 'cos I was visiting there and he was there and he had a big dog and I was interested in dogs and first we started talking about the dog and later we started talking about literature and he asked me what books I was interested in. I was just finished reading Joseph Conrad's Heart of Darkness I believe it was, but anyway there was a trilogy of Joseph Conrad which I had read and enjoyed very much and I'd also read a lot of John Gallsworthy. Well these were both two authors that Richard had cared very much about, so we started talking literature and when the children had gone to bed that night after dinner, he asked, Richard asked me to go down to the brook, there was a brook across the street which has been there, it used to be an old mill stream and eh, so we walked down to the brook together, there had been a dam that he had made and they used to go swimming there with the little children and I think we took a dip, I can't remember, but then we sat and talked by the side of the brook and he put his arm around me."[284]

Out of the Night

With *Out of the Night*, an angry manifesto against the inhuman practices of the Comintern and the cynicism of its functionaries, Richard Krebs went on the counterattack . The identification with the simple comrades, the anonymous and unbending fighters against the Nazi dictatorship, however, had remained. For murders committed by the Nazis he used the term "brutal murder", for murders of his comrades the more neutral "assassination". Asked for an explanation at a press conference after the publication he replied that the "eggshells" of communist terminology had not yet fallen off him. In truth, it wasn't just the eggshells of terminology that still clung to him.

Richard Krebs describes Valtin as a communist with the "right", proletarian origin. The "spot" in his own biography, his bourgeois background and the "betrayal" of his lover, was omitted in the description of his alter ego. He didn't want to admit his own weakness, his role as a plaything between the GPU and the Gestapo and his escape into the German embassy in Paris, nor that of Firelei, which he passed on to posterity not as a desperate mother, but as a hard communist. This showed that he had adopted the standards of his former comrades. He had internalized the basic maxims of illegal activity in the merciless male world of seafaring and later in the prisons and concentration camps of Germany: the commandment never to expose himself, never to have any contact with traitors, even if it was his own wife, to observe the rules of conspiracy at all costs. Thus the process of coming to terms with his traumatic experiences, which had begun with his retreat into the mountains of the Catskills, already bore the seeds of failure.

After Richard Krebs had moved from the house of the German emigrant Bek-Gran to that of the experienced Hollywood author and ghost writer Don Levine in the late summer of 1940, his fictional hero Jan Valtin was given the finishing touches. Don Levine knew exactly what a book and his hero had to be like in order to achieve a bestselling success in America. While Valtin's proletarian background with his father in the Soldiers' Council was due to the author's efforts not to offer his former comrades any point of attack, Valtin's transformation into the ubiquitous functionary, who personally receives his instructions from Dimitroff, was probably due to Levine's interventions.

The background of Krebs's work as an instructor, his long and for an American audience tiring discussions of intrigues and ideological quarrels within the party were either greatly simplified or faded out. To keep the reader in breathless suspense, Valtin experiences a series of events of which Richard Krebs had only learned in conversation.

The same applies to important stages in the development of the Comintern. Thus Valtin is present at the decision in Moscow that preceded the official founding of ISH, although Richard Krebs was at that time attending the shipping school in Bremen, and so the hero of *Out of the Night* conducts the strike of the German sailors in Leningrad, while Richard Krebs was at that time in Hamburg. Robert Bek-Gran, who knew the original manuscript, was indignant when the book appeared. In a letter he is said to have asked Richard Krebs: "Come down from your wooden horse and forget acting the hero."[285] He told a journalist that Valtin's story was made up of the experiences of several others, and that a middling functionary had been elevated to a man who was on intimate terms with the leaders of the Comintern. The story of a party worker, who had in reality been a sacrificial pawn, had become a hero legend. At least the book should have been preceded by the hint that the original manuscript had been written down in one piece and that its discrepancies could be explained by gaps in memory. And as the author had not been able to curb his lively imagination, there were a number of misinterpretations.

Robert Bek-Gran was never to forgive Richard Krebs for the changes to the manuscript. With him Richard Krebs lost a friend who knew what the German refugee had really left behind. From now on he was surrounded only by people for whom his past in Germany was a distant rumour and who considered Jan Valtin's accounts of his origins and youth to be those of the author.

Richard Krebs probably had allowed Don Levine's interventions because he was dependent on the help of the influential publicist in every respect. He needed him to find a publisher and his connections to Washington to survive the storm that would arise after the publication. Should the immigration authorities become aware of him and investigate his case more closely, the document obtained through Bek-Gran would not have been of any use to him, as he had been absolutely banned from entering the country since his deportation in 1929. Because Richard Krebs knew how little his chances of legalizing himself in the USA were, he had applied for an immigration permit at the Santo Domingo embassy in the summer of 1939. The request had been rejected.

Neither Richard Krebs nor Levine himself were ever to admit to the latter's interventions in *Out of the Night*. Richard Krebs wanted to avoid the impression that he was not the actual author, and Levine had - as it turned out - legitimate fears that the book could become the subject of court proceedings. Levine was paid well for his work on the manuscript. After the publication, he not only received the 10 percent that he would have been entitled to as an agent and editor, but a total of 35 percent of all revenues.

In order to promote sales, *Out of the Night* was marketed as absolutely authentic. After the publication of the novel, the question immediately arose as to what influence Don Levine had had on the final form of the book. The communist press in particular declared that the book could only be a work of Goebbels or the production of a collective of authors led by Levine. A German sailor was supposedly not capable of such sophisticated English.

Of course, that was a lot of exaggeration. Although it is not possible to trace in detail the interventions of Don Levine, since the original manuscript was stolen from the Library of Congress in the late forties by unknown persons, it is certain that the novel is the work of Richard Krebs. Both the short stories he wrote in San Quentin and the notes, miniatures and short stories written after his escape from Europe show him to be an independent and gifted writer; many of their motifs and storylines can be found in the first chapters of *Out of the Night*.

There is no doubt that Richard Krebs, who had lost his social environment by fleeing, reinvented himself to a certain extent with the figure of Valtin. It is not unusual for the first work of a writer to be autobiographical. In Richard Krebs' case though that later became his undoing, as *Out of the Night* was sold to the American public as the author's life story. Accordingly he first became the voluntary prisoner and two years later, after his opponents had uncovered some of the contradictions, the victim of his own invention.

Jan Valtin was a hero without fear and blame with mental and physical gifts that bordered on the improbable. With his rise and fall, he embodied a hero, like the American public loved. The political history of the protagonist largely corresponded to that of the author, with one major difference: Valtin's activity as an instructor was not limited to the ISH, but extended to the entire party organization of the countries in which he was deployed. The fact that Jan Valtin used the mechanisms of the internal exercise of power, which Richard Krebs had become acquainted with in the ISH, against the leaders of the party organizations of Norway and Great Britain, increased the significance of its protagonist and intensified the accusation against the dictatorship of Stalin, as it was exercised abroad by means of the Comintern.

The suspenseful narration and its colourful and vivid descriptions milieu of sailors, prostitutes and harbours, social struggles and secret service intrigues make up the strength of the book. Although questionable or unverifiable in many details, *Out of the Night* is a unique contemporary historical document. After all, the author was one of the few who survived their service in the Comintern of those years, and he was the only one to report on it with little spare to himself. Most of the other Comintern cadres who survived the persecutions of Stalin and Hitler were given high positions in one of satellite states established by the Soviet Union after the war. Whatever they wrote about their past was either embellished or strongly censored.

The weakness of the book lies in the lack of an inner life of the characters. Their motives and development are largely ignored and they tend to be good or evil, black or white. Accordingly, but also in order to spare them from possible harm, those comprades who were closest to him were not mentioned at all or only in coded form. His most important friend and patron along with Atschkanow and Walter, Alfred Bem, is absorbed in the figure of Wollweber; in *Out of the Night,* the latter also occupies the position in the ISH, which in reality was held by Bem. Hildegard Thingstrup, whom he names after his sister Cilly in the book, is the lover of Wollweber and not of Bem. A whole series of his former comrades, whose fate was actually quite different, had Richard Krebs disappear into Hitler's concentration camps or end up in Stalin's camps. Sometimes, however, he happened to be right.

Quantities in *Out of the Night are* often greatly exaggerated. The circulation of the leaflets mentioned is ten times higher than in reality, and during his first time in the Fuhlsbüttel concentration camp, not 24 Communists died on Christmas night 1933, but two.

The most astonishing "correction" in the alleged autobiography concerns the hero's prison sentence. In the Red Navy trial Jan Valtin is sentenced to 10 years in prison, so that after the second trial for treason he has to serve a total of 13 years. Most likely this change was due to the action of Levine. The PR professional could imagine how Richard Krebs's relatively mild judgement of four years would affect the American public. On the one hand, there would have been questions why Valtin, the top functionary, got off so lightly; on the other hand, Hitler's terror state would have seemed almost harmless, considering the harsh verdicts handed down by American courts against IWW activists after the First World War.

Out of the Night was launched with a large advertising budget and discussed as a lead story in the literary supplements of the most important newspapers. Not least, because the tragic love story between the hero and Firelei, who dies in a concentration camp, was first-class propaganda when Roosevelt had the greatest difficulty in convincing a skeptical American public to take part in the war. During the Hitler-Stalin Pact, the other thrust of the book, the accusation of Stalin's dictatorship and the cynicism of Comintern functionaries, was no less valuable from a propagandistic point of view.

How much the success of the book depended on the political situation at the time of its publication became apparent when the USA entered the war on the side of the Soviet Union. The same media that had highly praised book and author were to condemn them both at the end of 1942.

In November 1940 Richard Krebs returned to New York. There he met again with Abigail Harris. She remembered that he lived in a "very dangerous area" on the seventh floor and used the name Eric Holmberg. Only on the day of the wedding, the 1st of December 1940, did she learn her husband's real family name.

Out of the Night had just been released by Alliance, a renowned house in which many German exiled authors published. The unabridged first edition already caused a sensation.

The *New York Times* opened its literary supplement under the title "The Life of a Revolutionary - An Agent of Moscow and Victim of the Gestapo tells His Story" and dedicated one and a half pages to the book. "Apart from its value as a dramatic portrayal of personal experiences, Valtin's book sheds light on an international underworld that emerged in the shadow of totalitarian dictatorships (...) Generally speaking, the author is not afraid to call a spade a spade. His book is not for the squeamish as sex and brutality play an important role. Valtin falls into the hands of the Gestapo, and the depiction of the torture to which he and other prisoners were subjected is the most horrible thing the reviewer has ever read about this terrible subject." The review concludes with the following sentence: "The book unfolds a gruesome, repulsive panorama of murder, espionage and intrigue in a world where no one trusts anyone, thus providing a fairly accurate picture of daily life in a totalitarian society."[286]

The communist newspaper *New Masses* titled its review "Out of the Sewer". "The anti-Soviet experts of Hearst sponsor the book of a Nazi agent. The 'Book-of-the-Month-Club' is advertising a fake to the public."[287]

The communist philosopher Ernst Bloch described *Out of the Night* in the exile magazine *Freies Deutschland* as an "open dirt and trash novel"[288].

The reviews of those critics who did not judge the book from a political point of view alone were mostly quite positive. Pearl S. Buck rated *Out of the Night* as unique, lively and of high literary quality. H. G. Wells was also impressed. Even a reviewer as hostile as Karl Korsch, senior cadre in the early days of the KPD, emphasized "the truly epic quality" of those parts of the book "dealing with ships, ports, and seafarers".[289]

After all the persistent (and continuing) attacks on the book for its alleged "slandering" of the Communist movement it has slipped from memory that the greatest controversy on its publication was not caused by its description of the Comintern but by its report about conditions in the Third Reich.

Not surprisingly that, apart from the communist press, it was mainly newspapers from the conservative peace camp that rejected the book. After their experiences with the reports of German atrocities during the First World War, which had turned out to be vastly exaggerated, they considered Valtin's description of the conditions in German concentration camps to be nothing but propaganda.

An example of this attitude was the review in *Sribner's Commentary*.

"I can only say the basic idea, from a propagandist's point of view, has been so cleverly executed that I'm surprised no one else has come up with it. ... Mr. Valtin let´s his communists brethren off rather lightly. When he comes to speak of his suffering by Himmler, the hell-servant, he knows no stopping. In repulsive details he describes acts of the worst bestiality ... The modern war must be a people's war. ... Therefore one must sell this war to the people as one between good and evil."

The first edition at Alliance was followed in March by a shortened version for the Book-of-the-Month Club, which was the basis of all later editions and translations.

The book club of *Out of the Night* alone had a circulation of hundreds of thousands. Thus the novel was finally on its way to becoming the work with the highest circulation ever published by an ex-communist about his time in the party. After *Reader's Digest* in 1941 distributed an even more abridged edition of seven million copies, there was hardly an adult American who had not heard of Jan Valtin. The book remained at the top of the bestseller lists throughout the year.

British and Swedish editions appeared in 1941 and 1942 respectively - both with significant abbreviations: In the Swedish edition the chapters on Gestapo torture and concentration camps were missing, in the British edition the largest part of Valtins mission in Great Britain. Sweden then exercised benevolent neutrality toward her powerful neighbor Nazi Germany, and in Britain Her Majesty's government apparently thought it better for its subjects not to know about the total subversion of the English CP by Scotland Yard.

The hype surrounding his person, who took the form of a manhunt after being selected for the Book-of-the-Month Club, was fuelled by the author's persistent refusal to show his face. During this time, the left-wing New York daily *P.M.* sent one of its reporters on the heels of Valtin. Previously, a journalist named Roe had appeared in the newsroom claiming to have found out that *Out of the Night* was pure fiction, cobbled together by Isaac Don Levine, bestselling author Oliver LaFarge and a few others. Valtin was in reality Richard Krebs, a German terrorist, who was covered by the FBI as he had helped it to spy on radicals.

After days of research the reporter was able to find Valtin by chance. He described his encounter with the mysterious author:

"I sat for two hours on a sofa beside Valtin in a little back room down the hall of their railroad apartment. His wife sat opposite, close enough to pat Valtin´s knee every once in a while worshipfully. A dog sat at our feet - not the great Dane Life pictured - some type of mongrel; I don´t know dog types. Valtin is big, about six feet, and heavy and has wavy medium brown hair. His almost childlike Teutonic face is placid, but every once in a while it clouds up and you see violence and turbulence underneath. Once when he was quoting Dimitrov, in German, he scared the hell out of me. - I also think he´s frightened. - He´s deaf in one ear and every once in a while he either missed entirely or ignored my questions.

I think he is capable of damn near everything, including the writing of *Out of the Night*. He showed, in conversation, something of the same remarkable memory that the book implies. I don´t doubt he knows the Comintern business - and the Gestapo - inside out. That doesn´t absolve him of exaggeration or invention, of course.

Just before I left he patted his pocket and hinted that he had a permit to carry a pistol, that he was a good shot and if Roe - a communist journalist out to smear him- tried anything funny, he´d find out. His mother-in-law, who had come into the room a little while before, laughed this off with some remark about his not being as bad as that. - Valtin mentioned the FBI frequently, said they knew all about Roe, etc. He made it clear that he had powerful friends here now. Moreover, in times like these I don´t believe Richard Krebs, alias Jan Valtin, an alien revolutionary with a criminal record could get where he has in this country without the co-operation of the FBI."[290]

The article was a sensation and the first attempt to do justice to *Out of the Night* without either dismissing its content as fictional or believing it to be completely authentic. The author came to the following conclusion:

"I do not doubt that the description of the malicious underground activities in the book is true in principle.

I am sure that the book is being rammed down the throats of the public without questions being asked. Valtin's version of every detail is praised as if it were in the Bible. The advertising department of the *'Book-of-the-month Club'*, *Life* and *Reader's Digest* are apparently more interested in making our enemies untrustworthy than in raising enough skepticism.

However much of it may be true and how much invention, *Out of the Night* remains a frightening tale of deception and ambush. While trying to dig deeper, I came across other scams and pitfalls. No matter how long one may be investigating, one will not come any closer to the truth."

An American hero

For the first time in his life, Richard Krebs had more than enough money. With discomfort his young wife watched how freely he entertained acquaintances and friends from earlier days and which sums of money disappeared when they frequented the pubs and restaurants of Manhattan.

As another consequence of his sudden success the bestselling new author received a myriad of letters. Among them were lots of business proposals, like that of an insurance broker who made this "unbeatable" offer:

"After reading your book *Out of the Night*, it occurred to me that it might not be easy for you to get a life insurance policy. Since I have experience with any kind of risk, please have a talk with me."[291]

In the mountains of letters from this time there are marriage proposals and less moral offers, letters from old prison comrades from San Quentin, whom he supported as far as he could - one of them he hired as private secretary -, from real and alleged relatives, opponents and admirers. Faithfully, he tried to answer all of them. He sent 200 dollars to an unknown black man, whose brother had to leave the Third Reich as soon as possible but had no money to do so. From the "Comittee for a Jewish Army" to the "Workers' Defence League" or the "American Civil Liberties Union" he became a paying member of various associations.

The furor also reached the German embassy. The first letter was sent to Berlin on 24 February. "The publication of an autobiography of a former German communist agent, published under the title 'Out of the Night', is being accompanied with an advertising campaign that is unusually loud even for America. A sensational plot and numerous horror scenes, partly with an erotic aftertaste, promises the book a quick success with the broad readership. The publishers anticipate this by unusually high initial editions (200000 copies). Moreover, it may be assumed with certainty this that the publication has received financial backing from interested parties, since it contains effective propaganda against National Socialism, and secondarily also against Communism. ... 'LIFE' magazine initiated an extensive series of articles about the book by publishing a full-page photograph of its author with his face concealed. Despite the relatively high price, 'Out of the Night' is a huge success. It is currently a topic of conversation everywhere and therefore has a strong propagandistic effect. A film version is to be expected."[292]

On March 27 Richard Krebs gave his first interview on the radio. *P.M.* ironically titled is report about the transmission "Valtin is crazy about the good old USA". It went on: "Well, now it's over, and you can breathe a sigh of relief at WOL in Washington. Jan Valtin, the eloquent Book of the Month refugee from the OGPU, sneaked into town, spoke to the nation from a secret hideout and escaped without a shot being fired. What Jan Valtin had to say was nothing new for the readers of 'Out of the Night'. But the sound of his voice - genuine, robust and with a strange accent reminiscent of Erich von Stroheim - was enough to make the show a real sensation, especially for those who had previously thought that Jan Valtin was the German accent of Isaac Don Levine. ... Mr. Valtin rumbled over the nation's radios like a secret agent from the Jack Armstrong show.(...) Mr. Valtin explained that he wrote 'Out of the Night' not to make money, but 'to warn the Americans'."[293]

This first transmission was followed by numerous others. After America's most prominent radio man, Walter Winchell, had gotten wind that Valtin was married and to whom he was married, there was a small scandal, since Abigail was only 17. She was immediately expelled from school. She was already pregnant and in July she had her first child, a son called Conrad Freeman.

The former fanatical communist had found a new ideological home. Being identified one-to-one with his hero Jan Valtin and feted up and down the continent, he, like many other former Communists, succumbed to the temptation to "change to the other extreme or convert to a religion," as Artur Koestler put it. It was not a religion that Ri-chard Krebs had found, but the interviews from that period identify him as a man who believed in the *American way of life* with similar fervor as he had in the *Communist Manifesto* before.

At the end of his first radio interview he piously declared: "I tell you that there is more freedom and tolerance in San Quentin today than on the whole European continent."[294] To a radio interviewer who asked him if, after his experiences in Germany, it didn't seem like a dream to him to be in America now, he replied: "Well, it is not a dream. I find life in America very real, but I would say what I experienced in America was much more fantastic than anything related in Out of the Night. I'm glad I'm in America and glad to be living among free people."[295]

After a reporter from *Sacramento Bee* had found out that Jan Valtin was none other than the former convict Richard Krebs, who had been banned from entering the United States for life, he got a first inkling of what was still to come. For now his prominence saved him. According to the letter of the law his marriage to Abigail would not have protected him from deportation. Nevertheless, he had to face the immigration authorities, an institution which traditionally has extensive powers in the USA and against whose decisions a non-citizen had practically no legal remedy. Like all other employees of the various authorities who were to scrutinize him in the coming years, these officials were basing their questioning on *Out of the Night*. Perusing the book for suitable passages they examined him above all for his "moral" suitability as an immigrant. The author of *Out of the Night* had done himself no favours with his description of life in European ports as well as the acquaintance of the hero with various prostitutes. In addition in America perjury was seen as immoral and judged accordingly to an extent that was unknown in more cynical Europe. Again and again his interrogators were to drag up the various lies that Valtin had told Dutch, British or Swedish policemen.

During the first interrogation by the Immigration Department on April 17, 1941, he was accused of having entered illegally, although he had signed in 1929, never to enter the soil of the United States again. Further of having upon his entry belonged to an organization that planned the overthrow of the United States, and of having committed "morally questionable" acts in the past.

Anyone else would have been interned and deported to Germany. Still Richard Krebs was interrogated for several days. In connection with Valtins memorable declaration of commitment to the Gestapo in *Out of the Night*, there was this dialogue:

"Do you admit that when you signed this undertaking and allegedly gave up your membership of the Communist Party, you did not act with honest intent?

- I signed this declaration with an honest heart, as the signature would enable me to resume the fight against Hitler.

- Does your answer mean that you signed this declaration without any seriousness, or does it mean that you meant what you signed?

- I signed this declaration with the greatest seriousness to use the Gestapo's own methods in the struggle against Hitler's movement. I never have and I will never consider a commitment given to the Gestapo as given in good faith.

- And when you signed this Declaration of Commitment, did you intend to carry out any of what you committed yourself to in the Declaration?

- Not at all.

- So then you also claimed at that time that you were turning away from communism out of the same attitude of mind?"[296]

It went on like this for hours. On the basis of many passages of the alleged autobiography the officials felt sure that the interviewee was a notorious liar and by no means showed the moral aptitude demanded by a prospective American. The interrogation by immigration finally ended in a stay of deportation. A legally watertight status could not be achieved as long as the 1926 ruling and the accompanying immigration ban remained in force.

The uncovering of his true identity and the publication of the court records of 1926 had a further consequence. The communist press relied on a sentence taken out of context by the then twenty-year-old -"The Jew had made me angry"[297]- with which he had justified his assassination of Goodstein to the court in 1926 in order to present the author of *Out of the Night* as an anti-Semite. Morris L. Goodstein himself threatened a libel suit because he - contrary to whatever was written in the book – claimed not to have had any relations with Communists. Richard Krebs then sent a former fellow inmate to investigate Goodstein's past. He did not find out very much, but realized that he was not the only one interested in Goodstein. He recognized one of the other interested parties as a former customs investigator with whom he had once had an unpleasant collision. The former inmate of San Quentin, who recognized plain clothe policeman from afar, was guessing at the FBI as the man's current employer.

Long negotiations began with Morris L. Goodstein, who was interested above all in cash, and were not concluded until 1943. To his misfortune, the Soviet Union had in the meantime become a respected ally of the United States, so that alleged relations with Communists were no longer half as dishonorable as before the war. Goodstein had to settle for a relatively modest 500 dollars, where he could have gotten four times that amount two years earlier.[298]

The problem with his past in San Quentin was solved in other respects as well. His friends founded an "Aid Valtin Association", which put the governor of California, Culbert L. Olson, under such pressure that in 1941 he subsequently pardoned Richard Krebs for the act committed in 1926. Richard Krebs was granted a permanent residence permit.

Despite his enormous popularity and nationwide fame, Richard Krebs still lived in fear at first, as Abigail remembers. He feared both GPU and Gestapo, but the Soviet even more than the German secret police. In spring of 1941 the family dog, a large, harmless Danish mastiff, was stabbed to death by strangers.

When the two came home at night, her husband first searched all the cupboards, looked behind all doors and under all beds to make sure there was no assassin lurking somewhere. Once - the two were now living in a house near New York – a travelling salesman rang the doorbell who - according to a picture shown to her by the FBI - the then pregnant Abigail recognized as a foreign agent. In panic, she left the house and ran to a neighbor. Immediately the young family moved house. Also in New York Abigail was shadowed time and again. "I remember once a man chased me on the subway and I went straight to the FBI building on Wall Street.

I remember changing trains several times, but the man followed me and was back after every change. (...) Richard had dragged me into something I had no idea about before (...) Richard told me if I ever suspected that someone was following me, then I should drop something on the street, turn around and pick it up. If I then saw someone, I should take a different direction. If I was still followed, I'd know."[299]

Pretty soon Abigail had had enough of this life and the game of hide-and-seek of her husband, who only had himself photographed with his face concealed. She persuaded him to finally go public and to go on a lecture tour after his bestselling success. The better known and more famous he became, the less his enemies would dare to turn him into a martyr.

He followed that advice. One of the first performances in which he showed his face took place at the "National Press Club" in Washington at the end of May 1941. The Propaganda Secretary of the German Embassy reported to Berlin:

"I have received the following description of the evening from a participant, which I ask to be treated confidentially:

Valtin looks like a Hamburg dock worker, speaks very good, chosen English, albeit with a somewhat European accent. He speaks aloud like an agitator and merely made accusations without proving a single one. He claimed that the Gestapo and the GPU in America did not instigate strikes for the good of the workers, but for their own interests. Stalin himself does not believe in world revolution, but only wants to strengthen his own position. The GPU has agents in every American industry, a total of at least 300 men. The Gestapo has informers in every German company in the USA. The Fifth Column movement must be fought by stronger methods, not only here, but all over the world. His whole speech moved along this line, without details, without examples.'"[300]

The press conference was the kick-off event for his statement to the "Committee for Un-American Activities", the so-called Dies Committee, which began a few days later.

After Richard Krebs's initial refusal, Levine first had to talk him into this performance, which his enemies rated with relish as further proof of his "informer nature". Dies, the chairman and namesake of the committee, was an influential and powerful congressman of the Democrats, the party of the president. He was a man who Richard Krebs had to bring to his side as there was a plan to grant him citizenship by a congressional resolution.[301]

Richard Krebs's statement lasted two days and filled 50 pages of the official transcript. It was equally about the activities of the Gestapo and the Soviet secret service in the USA. As one would expect from Richard Krebs's state of knowledge, his statements about German intelligence work were both more current and more accurate.

One of his statements, that the Gestapo forced anyone released from prison or concentration camp to commit themselves to the secret police and that the Gesatpo sent agents disguised as refugees abroad, corresponded to the facts, but provoked angry reactions among German exiles. The social democrat *Neue Volkszeitung*, published in New York, wrote on 14 June that the "former Gestapo agent" had remained true to himself in one respect: "in the sovereign contempt of all that is called morality in politics". They found it extremely displeasing that "in this country there is a veritable cult around Krebs-Valtin" and that "respected men and women show themselves publicly with him".

Richard Krebs replied with a long letter to the editor, the Social Democrat Friedrich Stampfer, in which he expressed the opinion that there could be no harsher condemnation of the Nazis than the disclosure of precisely this inhuman practice.[302] Stampfer could not be convinced.

Perhaps because Richard Krebs had written to him in English. He thus distanced himself from the editor of the *Neue Volkszeitung*, an important representative of the German emigration. He thereby also once again underlined how much he believed that he had left his past behind him. The fact that Richard Krebs, with his appearance before the Dies Committee, had now also upset the non-Communist parts of the German exile community was unpleasant, but remained without further consequences. Something else did not remain without consequences: With his statement he had incurred the aversion of J. Edgar Hoover, the powerful boss of the FBI.

First Shadows

In the autumn of 1939, Richard Krebs was once again in the focus of the Federal Police. The FBI file of Erich Krewet, a comrade from Hamburg days, contains a letter from New York FBI agent Foxworth, who informed J. Edgar Hoover on October 12, 1939 about the observations of an unknown informant:

"In connection with information from the confidential informant, it is reported that he has successfully contacted a certain Jan Walten. The preliminary information regarding Walten, as it comes from [blackened], shows that Walten was a member of the Comintern and carried out confidential missions for the Soviet Control Commission, the OGPU, and Soviet Military Intelligence Service. In this capacity he instigated Communist strikes and riots in Europe and the United States. ... [Blackened] reports that Walten has considerable information about the Gestapo and the GPU, but is afraid for his life (...)

His description is according to personal observation the following:
Age about thirty
Size 8 feet 1 inches
Weight   130 pounds
Building   medium
Hair   black
Eyes   dark
Facial features   coarse
Teeth   two or three missing on the right upper jaw
Walten doesn't seem to speak very good English. His posture is quite awkward."[303]

Since Richard Krebs was just being introduced to Eugene Lyons' circle at the time, it seems safe to assume that it was one of those strict antistalinists who drew the FBI's attention to him. Possibly even with his consent, for what could be more natural than to turn to the federal police himself before the FBI took action against him on the basis of reports in the communist press or of an anonymous denunciation.

Possibly J. Edgar Hoover might have remembered the name Richard Krebs from the letter of 1939; with his appearance before the congressional committee though this name suddenly got a special meaning for him. On May 31, 1941, Thomsen, the propaganda secretary of the German Embassy in Washington, sent a telegram to his superiors in Berlin:

"Richard Julius Hermann Krebs, alias Jan Valtin, whose book of hate and actrocity *Out of the Night* is currently the most widely read book with over 400,000 sold, is recently also appearing before the Dies Committee talking about alleged 5th column activity in the USA. In addition to his sadistic scare stories about the maltreatment in German concentration camps Krebs also tells fantastic lies about German espionage in America, which are believed by a heated audience.

As I learn confidentially, Government Secret Police Chief Edgar Hoover is very angry that Congressman Dies Krebs is using this to make cheap propaganda for himself and his committee. The Ministry of Justice also intended to deport Krebs as a notorious criminal who had been sentenced to several years' imprisonment for robbery, and had already initiated proceedings against him. Albeit it does not dare to touch him now, as long as he is doing such brilliant service for Roosevelt's propaganda and as long as there isn´t stronger evidence incriminating him. American contacts have confidentially indicated to me that Hoover is interested in detailed information from Germany on the criminal career of Krebs. Welcome would be information on previous prison sentences for sex crimes, incitement to murder and manslaughter, arson and the like. Propagandistic possibilities of such information would be also evaluated by me or my confidants."[304]

Had Thomsen only used the head of the FBI as an excuse to persuade the Gestapo to release material, or had J. Edgar Hoover actually made contact with the representative of a power that had rather bad relations with the USA?

When Earl Haynes an American historian and specialist on the CPUSA was asked about this letter, he immediately believed it possible that J. Edgar Hoover could have made such a request.

J. Edgar Hoover was a power hungry man and unsurpassed in the art of bureaucratic intrigue. He did everything he could to expand the reach of the FBI, which was only founded in 1934 and still had no more than 800 agents in 1937.

For him, the "Congress Committee for Un-American Activities", equipped with its own investigators and a large apparatus, was an undesirable competitor for money and influence. With its investigations of Soviet and German activities in the US it was interfering in matters that Hoover considered to be the very domain of the federal police. Because Hoover could not openly take action against the committee, he took his anger out on its informants. According to Earl Haynes Richard Krebs was not an isolated case in this respect.

The slightly sour answer, by the way, with which the Gestapo replied to the request from Washington, was rather lacking from a propagandistic point of view. Yes, Richard Krebs had repeatedly stated during his imprisonment that he had turned his back on communism. The Gestapo had given him the opportunity to make amends for his misdeeds. Krebs had then tried to rejoin the ISH abroad, but this had failed because he had been called a Gestapo agent for unknown reasons. Finally he had wanted to join the International Brigades in Paris, but in reality left for the USA via London.[305]

Richard Krebs later made no secret of his contacts with the FBI. After a long list of all the jobs he'd done since his arrival, he also mentioned his contact with the FBI when he was questioned by Immigration in 1941.

"In October 1939, FBI agents approached me for the first time, asking for my assistance in their task of fighting subversive activities in America. I gave this support as best I could on many occasions, and the FBI repeatedly thanked me for my cooperation."[306]

As the CIC, the Counter Intelligence Corps of the US army, was astonished to note in 1950 after requesting his FBI file, the FBI never questioned Richard Krebs thoroughly about his past. Since many pages in Krebs's FBI file are blackened or even missing, it is impossible to determine to the last which information he provided. However, some of it can be reconstructed from files of the FBI which appear in the inventories of other authorities. At least about Erich Krewet, the man whose FBI file contains the first information about him, Richard Krebs reported everything he knew. That was not surprising, since Erich Krewet was in close contact with a group of German communists in New York who had denounced Krebs as a Gestapo agent in their magazine *Schiffahrt*. Richard Krebs certainly took the opportunity and told the FBI everything else he had heard about followers of Hitler as well as Communists.

Richard Krebs was to believe until the end of his life (a belief the FBI did nothing to dispel) that these brave protectors of American democracy were on his side. Reality was different.

Although the FBI agents with whom he had to deal, as on the occasion of his internment as a suspicious foreigner in 1942, were always friendly and affable towards him, the many letters by J. Edgar Hoover about Richard Krebs speak a different language. As far as Richard Krebs was concerned, J. Edgar Hoover was not prepared to say a single good word.

For instance when asked by the United States Attorney General on the 11th of October 1941, whether Richard Krebs has completely detached himself from all ties to Communists or Nazis and whether he has been helpful to the Department of Justice in any way, Hoover replied; "to point one, the FBI cannot say whether Krebs has severed all ties to Communists or Nazis because it has not made such a statement to a representative of this agency. ... In particular, point two is now dealt with: Agents in this office have occasionally talked to Krebs. During such conversations, he never provided any information that was new to the office or that the office had not yet known. During these talks it also turned out that Krebs had no information about communist activities after 33 when he became an outward member of the Nazi movement."[307]

Hoover possibly wanted to deliberately harm Richard Krebs by claiming that he had already become a member of the Hitler movement in 1933. This is supported by several further letters to the Alien Enemy Control Unit, which in 1942 asked Hoover for his opinion regarding an internment of Richard Krebs as an alleged Gestapo agent. Hoover's answer was always the same: he had no information that contradicted the assumption that Richard Krebs was a German agent.

It wasn't just his appearance before the Dies Committee with which Richard Krebs had incurred Hoover's dislike. Wanting to be a good American Richard Krebs had been far too open to immigration in 1941. Without having been prompted he also volunteered the following about his relations with the FBI:

"In November 1939, I was invited to the FBI's New York office, where Mr. Foxworth, then the agent in charge, offered me work on a weekly basis. I refused on the grounds that I had no information to sell, but that I would work with them to the best of my knowledge whenever necessary."[308]

If this statement was already quite naïve, Krebs was obviously reporting an offer by the FBI to become a paid informer, a later statement was all the more so. At the tribunal in 1942 that was to decide on his interment he stated in public that the FBI had wanted to hire him in New York as an informer, but that he had refused. Richard Krebs obviously did not imagine that the FBI would be as unwilling to have its methods exposed as its European counterparts. This statement forced Hoover to officially announce that "the infiltration of individuals into subversive organizations is contrary to FBI policy and there has never been any such offer to him"[309].

Richard Krebs was never to find out what had happened behind the scenes after his appearance before the Dies Committee. But he was to experience the effects.

Summer and autumn 1941 were some of the happiest months of his life. With the book income he bought a fruit farm in Montville, Connecticut, where his second son was born at the end of July. After the pardon in California, he had permanent residence in the United States of America. He had become a famous, universally renowned man who was completely identified with the hero of his novel. The "hounded, frightened young man," whom Benjamin Gitlow had met in 1939, had within two years become a self-confident *All American hero*, whom the rich and famous were seeking out. Not all encounters were to the satisfaction of both sides.

There was a collision with Henry Ford, the car industrialist and notorious anti-Semite. Richard Krebs was willing to warn of communism on a radio station of the "Ford Corporation", but only on the condition that he also gave speeches against Hitler, which the "Ford Corporation" was to broadcast into the Third Reich. Since Ford did not agree to this condition, the project fell apart.

In the fall, Richard Krebs went on a lecture and reading tour that took him from Ohio to Wisconsin, Michigan, Illinois, Massachusetts, Minnesota, Pennsylvania, Connecticut, Oklahoma, Texas, and Louisiana. On December 7, 1941 he was in Texas when all radio stations of the USA interrupted their program with the news of the Japanese attack on Pearl Harbour.

The past returns

The very next day Richard Krebs volunteered for the war. But if he had hoped that his knowledge of Europe would be used, he was thoroughly mistaken. He was now primarily a member of an enemy nation. Besides, his attacks on Stalin were no longer welcome. Overnight Josef Stalin, the bloodthirsty mastermind of world revolution, had become good "Uncle Joe", the slightly disreputable but legitimate leader of the heroic Russian nation in the defensive struggle against German barbarism. The Communist Party of the USA, which had already felt an upswing after the German invasion of the Soviet Union and the end of the pact between the two dictators, was about to reach its greatest influence in American domestic politics. Hollywood immediately ended all negotiations about a film version of *Out of the Night*. Maybe the viewer has been spared a lot, as a script proposal shows.

"One day, when Firelei and Valtin (who has taken off from his underground duties for an hour) enjoy themselves on the beach, they are harassed by Wollwegen who has an eye on Firelei. Wollwegen reports that Valtin is in love. "Grab his girl and you'll have Valtin in your hand." ... The conspirators interrupt Göring just as he is making his famous cannons-instead-of- butter speech. Shortly after, the submarine base is blown up. The Gestapo is now focusing on catching Valtin. The manhunt reaches its climax. Against this background, and in order not to lose Valtin, Firelei decides to join the underground. After that follow underground adventures in which Firelei takes part, with Wollwegen appearing here and there in a dark and mysterious way ..."[310]

By the way, Wollweber was changed to Wollwegen, because Hollywood feared a lawsuit. Who knew if Wollweber wouldn't, like his arch-enemy Valtin, one day also make an appearance in Hollywood?

Richard Krebs wanted the defeat of Germany and had always demanded the war entry of the USA. But even after Pearl Harbour he continued to warn of the intentions of the Soviet Union, which was now an ally. Others, for instance Don Levine, were more astute. After Pearl Harbour, the USSR was no longer an issue for him. He started on a biography of an American hero, Air Force General Billy Mitchell.[311]

Nine month later Richard Krebs was arrested. Until then he was in a state of limbo. On the one hand, he was still popular enough to receive invitations to lectures anywhere in the USA and the Department of Finance used his rhetorical skills to sell war bonds. In August, September and October he lectured several times in front of thousands of listeners. He himself invested not only the requested 10 percent, but as much as 20 percent of his assets in such bonds.

On the other hand, his freedom of movement was severely restricted as he needed a permit for each of these trips. In addition, his dream of a quiet life on the farm he had bought in Connecticut was shattered.

By chance, that farm was located near a submarine base and a large power plant, prompting its neighbors to submit a flood of petitions to the authorities, which were faithfully investigated by the FBI. As it turned out, none of these denunciations had any factual background; they were based solely on the fact that Richard Krebs was German and the author of *Out of the Night*, which provoked wild speculation among the neighbors. One man even wrote that the location of his house was perfect for sending light signals to German submarines.

After the rumor began to spread in the small town of Montville that he had painted his house white only to signal the location of the naval base to German submarines, as well as having added a window to better observe ship movements, he gave up and sold the farm in June 1942. He then moved to another small town, Bethel in the same state.

At the end of January he had already written to a friend:

"Dear Dorothy

I do get permission to travel for lecture purposes, although much energy and many hours of efforts have to be given, in one way or another, to conform with the requirements and untie the „Red Tape". - I shall not be able to go ahead with the new book on my „Political Journey" under present circumstances. One needs solitude, which I have not got; and peace of mind, which I have not, either. I would have to go away into the distant woods somewhere - and for that, too, Government permission would be required. Therefore I am postponing all writing efforts until summer comes. I am leaving here today for the Mid-West. I expect to return about the middle of March. It seems silly to be telling Americans the things they ought to know about Hitler in order to be able to fight him better, when the Government elected by Americans classes people, who were fighting Hitler long before America began to fight him, as „alien enemies". It almost brings one into the attitude of „What the hell is the use?" [312]

In 1942 Jan Valtin published a book and two major articles. The negotiations had been conducted by his new agent, John Schaffner. There had been problems with Levine because of the income from the translations of *Out of the Night*; problems that would continue in the years to come. Moreover, Richard Krebs wanted to finally get rid of any suspicion that he was not a permanent writer in his own right, but the German accent of Levine.

Bend in the River was a collection of his short stories already written in San Quentin, preceded by a series of autobiographical notes. In contrast to *Out of the Night*, where the life of the hero in the Californian penitentiary hardly filled a page, here he gave a full panoply of his time there and dealt with his nightmarish experiences, which, in addition to his academic and literary successes, had shaped his three-year stay in prison. Critics' reactions ranged from a patronizing "not bad for a budding writer" in the *New York Times* to "the best non-English native speaker writer" in the *Los Angeles Times*.[313]

He didn´t do himself any favors with two longer articles. One was an "ABC of sabotage", a description of the various techniques for paralyzing or even sinking a ship with the simplest of means.[314] It was disseminated by the US Navy as training material, but also aroused distrust against him as a potential saboteur. The other publication showed that he was still unable or unwilling to understand his situation as a dubious foreigner. The text appeared in the July issue of *Reader's Digest* under the title "No revolt in Europe – Unless we promote it". This article was based on his fear that the Communists would take advantage of the foreseeable decline of German rule in Europe to take the lead in the resistance and, after the war, to gain power in Western Europe. Therefore the democracies should copy communist techniques and organize the resistance themselves. In listing what to do, he drew on his experience as an instructor for the Comintern.

Assassinations were to be organized to provoke mass resistance after the inevitable reprisals by the Germans. Valtin proposed to found small cells of conspirators and to propagate sabotage in war factories. Concerning the Germans, he saw them as sentimental and their behavior as fluctuating between cruelty and subservience. To undermine their morale he advised the use of threatening propaganda.

Richard Krebs was not aware that although he might have been a "real" American in his own eyes, in the eyes of many Americans he was nothing but a former double agent of dubious origin, who made too much noise.

With this article Richard Krebs gave an old acquaintance a golden opportunity. On 28 July 1942, Erich Krewet sent an open letter to *Reader's Digest* from a Californian internment camp.

"Richard, I read your article "no revolt in Europe" in *Reader's Digest*. Because you are beginning to interfere in the politics of the future with this article, I have to break my promise (never to write to you) and remind you that your bluffing is ending now. When I read your book *Out of the Night*, I was ashamed that I ever knew you. Some people who knew some chapters were missing from the book asked me to write those chapters. I refused for three reasons. 1) Because I didn't think you were important and valuable enough to be worthy of an answer, 2) because I don't intend to hand over some people to the Gestapo and the executioner by clarifying your fantastic statements, and 3) because, although you're not worth anything, I still have no interest to help to send you to the Nazis by exposing your phony story."[315]

He also made fun of Krebs' sabotage proposals and put them in the long history of terrorist acts that had never led to anything. Besides, thereby Krewet, who was himself suspected of being a saboteur, announced that he would never consider such methods. The propaganda that Richard Krebs proposed regarding Germany inspired Krewet to commit himself to Roosevelt and his four freedoms. These were the true values the war was fought for and Valtin´s proposals the exact opposite. "You still think and preach the old civil war tactics. - Create a situation without hope and any prospect of help, and then scream loudly, louder than the rest, until the masses belong to you." With that he led to a conclusion that had it all:

"So better forget your headline articles and understand that you're nothing but a nuisance. Just as you have been a menace to all who ever came into contact with you. Do you remember the list that led to the arrest of 26 Nazi opponents in Hamburg, including Herma? Do you remember the 28th of February before the Supreme Court in Hamburg and the man who testified for the Gestapo? Do you remember the men who gave you their money, helped you to freedom and now sit in a concentration camp, although you could have helped them with a few thousand dollars of your dirty money? Do you remember those who trusted you and who you delivered to the Nazis for $3 a book?

You have your physical freedom, your family and your security. But keep your hands off politics. Too many people have suffered too much because of you. Too many honest workers have slipped into the abyss because of you. But no more. Be satisfied with what you have."

Erich Krewet and Richard Krebs were old rivals. Five years older than the son of a captain, Erich Krewet was of the very working class in which Richard Krebs had placed the childhood of his hero Jan Valtin. A sailor by profession, Erich Krewet had spent the twenties, when he was not at sea, along the North Sea coast of Germany. In 1931, when Richard Krebs emerged in Hamburg seemingly out of nowhere and immediately received the key post of local interclub leader, Erich Krewet was already an established member of the KPD and head of the party cell shipping. Although this organization united all Communist seamen, it was subordinate to the KPD and thus of relatively minor importance in the port, where the ISH played the leading role. According to Richard Krebs, Krewet was outraged that a man unknown in Hamburg was preferred to him in leading the Interklub. All the more so since Erich Krewet also had literary ambitions and was involved in at least one play that was performed in the Interklub at the time. Obviously the two had not been good friends already in Hamburg.

Erich Krewet was a man of considerable personal courage who, even after Hitler's seizure of power, tried to agitate the seamen waiting for work at the Hamburg waterfront. He was well-known in the port and after various arrests been officially identified as a communist already in the Weimar Republic.[316]

He was arrested in May 1933 and tried on 28 February 1934 in the so-called Interclub trial. This trial was about the underground printing plant that Richard Krebs had set up with his wife and other Interclub staff prior to his departure for Sweden.

On that last day of February 1934, Erich Krewet and three other Communists stood before the judge. As witnesses were summoned two Gestapo men, a certain Julius Emmerich, a former communist who now worked for the Gestapo, and Richard Krebs.

In his open letter to *Reader's Digest* Erich Krewet had alluded to this trial. Krewet was not that naive to believe that *Reader's Digest* would publish the letter and disavow his own author. The real addressee was an office in Washington to which all letters from the camp were forwarded. The "Enemy Alien Control Unit" was an authority founded after the outbreak of war. It was subordinate to the Attorney General and was meant to control foreigners of "hostile nationality" and if necessary to intern them. It´s staff was largely made up of immigration officers who were still riled by the carte blanche issued to the prominent author Valtin, as well as some lawyers from civil life.

Responsible for Richard Krebs as well as Erich Krewet was a lawyer named Burling. After having read Krewet's letter and having reviewed Krebs's file containing the negative assessments of immigration officials, Burling flew to California to find out what Krewet's allusions in the open letter were all about.

That Richard Krebs had testified at the interclub trial without mentioning it in his book was Krevet's first charge. Since Richard Krebs had tolerated that *Out of the Night* was seen as an autobiography, someone like Erich Krewet, who had known the author for a long time, could use any omission in the book against him.

Krewet substantiated these and all other charges by citing the opinion of the Hamburg court.

Only the indictment has survived in its entirety and of the opinion of the court just a few sentences which had been translated into English for use against Richard Krebs.

The indictment shows that Richard Krebs admitted to having set up the illegal print shop. He also talked a lot about the nature of the interclub and falsely claimed that it had been subordinated to the Einheitsverband, the German section of the ISH. Finally, he contrasted the ISH, which supposedly had only carried out "trade union work," with the "party cell shipping" as a political organization of the KPD. Krebs also claimed that there had been "frequent and considerable conflicts between the ISH and the KPD". Here he had pulled the leg of the prosecution. There had indeed been constant trouble between KPD and ISH. The reason, however, was solely a struggle for power and by no means a contradiction due to the trade union character of one organization and the political character of the other.

Obviously Richard Krebs wanted to distract from the true balance of power. On the one hand, the Gestapo was meant to conclude from his subordinate role in the KPD that Richard Krebs himself was of minor importance. On the other hand, he did not want to give the Gestapo any clues about the secret organization in the port of Hamburg.

It is in this context that Krebs's testimony about Erich Krewet has to be seen. He confirmed a statement by Emmerich, a former comrade of the two who had told the public prosecutor the common knowledge fact that Krewet was "not a functionary of the Interclub, but the leader of the ... party cell shipping ". Moreover, Richard Krebs claimed that he had "informed Krewet of his imminent escape, whereupon Krewet told him not to go. As representative of the KPD Krewet is said to have observed and influenced the activities of the interclub."[317]

As a helmsman and communist, Richard Krebs was of course also a member of the party cell shipping. Thus Krewet was his superior in the KPD, which in practice played no role whatsoever as Krebs was an instructor of the ISH. The "escape" Richard Krebs spoke of was his departure for Sweden, where he was about to organize a strike. If Richard Krebs had only been a simple member of the KPD, he indeed would have had to ask Erich Krewet for permission before his trip.

Krebs had further misled the prosecution by claiming that Erich Krewet hat tried to influence the work of the Interclub in a communist way. He thus gave the impression that the Interclub had been an independent, non-partisan organization.

Erich Krewet, of course, knew that most of what the former leader of the Interclub had said was wrong. As a good communist, however, he would hardly have drawn the Gestapo's attention to the true state of things in the port of Hamburg. Did he take the testimony of Krebs personal?

Krewet confided to one of the American officials who was investigating Richard Krebs that he was ultimately quite happy to be sentenced and transferred to a normal prison, as he had previously been in a concentration camp.[318] Had he been acquitted, he would certainly not have been released, but sent back to a concentration camp.

In addition, Krebs' testimony about Krewet referred to the leadership of a party cell which he had "committed" before the first law amendment of the Third Reich. The sentence was therefore relatively light. In fact, he was sentenced to "only" one year and nine months in prison.

At the Red Navy trial a few months later, Krewet was to return the favor and exonerate Richard Krebs. Erich Krewet confirmed that it was indeed him, who is mentioned in *Out of the Night* as militant trade unionist Erich K who gave this particular statement that might have saved Richard Krebs from the hangman.

Despite all of that, Erich Krewet used Richard Krebs´ testimony at the Interclub trial as evidence that he had worked with the Gestapo from the very beginning. Burling, who had rushed from Washington, eagerly picked up on this. To further bolster his accusation Krewet also provided him with the opinion of the court. These papers are not contained in the file. To reconstruct Richard Krebs testimony one must therefore refer to the few literal quotes which Burling picked out to use against Richard Krebs.

Apparently, he repeated his assertion, known from the indictment that the ISH was a non-partisan trade union, which Krewet had tried to turn Communist. Further the opinion of the court states that Erich Krewet was convicted due to the testimony of Krebs and Emmerich.

On the basis of these German court papers as well as the alleged autobiography of Richard Krebs Erich Krewet came up with the following story: He himself had been nothing but a trade unionist who had worked in the non-partisan Interclub. That he had not been a communist could also be inferred from the very passage in *Out of the Night* in which he was described as a militant trade unionist. After Hitler had come to power, some members of the Interclub, including himself, had installed an underground printing plant. This had been discovered, and strangely enough, more than twenty people were arrested the next day in the apartment of Krebs, where - as previously arranged - they had all met after the bust. This was supposedly the true background to the episode in *Out of the Night*, in which Firelei, after barely escaping a raid, sent all sorts of apolitical acquaintances into her apartment to get her screaming child out. As written in the book a lot of people had indeed been arrested there. But in reality they had been Antinazis who had met in Krebs's apartment after the raid.

Erich Krewet had no compunction to use the most sordid means as long as it served to incriminate Richard Krebs. Burling noted: "Krewet stated to me privately, but refused to testify, that on the night of the raid on Herma Krebs´ apartment he learned of what was going on because the raid in some way became rumored about, and he in some way managed to warn Herma Krebs. He further states that on that night he asked Herma Krebs where Richard Krebs was and that she said he had been gone for several weeks; she did not know where he was and was not sure she could trust him. Krewet stated that his reason for refusing to testify to this was that he did not think it right to testify to some speculation about a man made by his wife."[319]

Commenting on his exculpatory testimony at the Red Navy trial, Krewet said that one day he had been unexpectedly taken out of prison and brought into the courtroom. There he was asked whether Richard Krebs had taken part in the conference at which the attack on the SA was decided. Krewet stated that he knew nothing about it. Months later, he learned that Richard Krebs's plan had been to let him answer this question in the negative. A negation would have implied his participation in the conference. Suspicion would have then fallen on him, Erich Krewet and he would have been in danger of being executed instead of Richard Krebs.

How can one explain these outrageous accusations?

Was it, as Richard Krebs believed, a Communist plot against him? This cannot be ruled out, but Erich Krewet also had enough personal motives.

After his release from German prison, he had travelled to Antwerp, where he worked with the Knüfken group for a short time until he was hired by a German ship sailing to Brazil where he jumped ship. Then he made his way to the US[320], where he worked as a speaker and organizer for the "German-American Cultural Association" and the Antidefamation League. He travelled across the country and gradually gained a significant reputation as an agitator against Nazi propaganda among German-Americans.

An excellent speaker who could express himself well in English, he also gave numerous lectures at trade union meetings, where he reported on his time in concentration camps and the abolition of all freedom of association in Germany. In autumn 1936 he came to San Francisco, where he met a young pianist with whom he soon had a child. Later they got married, and from then on he stayed mainly on the west coast. With the help of his wife, who improved the English of his manuscripts, he published short stories about the prisons and concentration camps of Hitler Germany, which appeared in such prestigious journals as *Esquire*.

The climax of his activity on the West Coast was the call for a half-hour general strike against the repression of trade unions in Germany that was supported by the Maritime Union of the Pacific. More than 30,000 seamen and dockworkers participated. The ITF leader, Edo Fimmen, was so enthusiastic about Krevet's activities that he appointed him his official representative at American water transport unions. A letter from Fimmen to Krewet shows that he considered him an ally against Communist subversion of his union. Erich Krewet writes in his own memoirs that he had had difficulties with Communists from the beginning of his activities in the USA and had already broken with the CP in 1938.[321]

For Erich Krewet, those few years in the second half of the thirties must have, in retrospect, been some of the best of his life. He wrote his (unpublished) memoirs in

1957 when he was too old for seafaring and living penniless back in Hamburg. He understandably skipped a few darker dots. For it is rather doubtful whether Erich Krewet had been completely truthful to Edo Fimmen. In that first report in Krewet's FBI file, in which an unknown informant drew the attention of the federal police to "Jan Walten", the same informant reported about Krewet that he was a representative of the Comintern on the west coast of the USA. The informant furthermore reported that Krewet was successfully subverting foreign workers' associations. It is a matter of record that Erich Krewet was a regional director of the "German-American Cultural Association", at precisely the time that this organization was – against the fierce resistance of Richard Krebs's friend Bek-Gran - taken over by communists. Finally, as can be seen from his FBI file, Krewet maintained close relations with a group of German sailors loyal to Moscow in New York, who in 1938 denounced Richard Krebs as a Gestapo agent in their journal *Schiffahrt*.

In November 1939, Erich Krewet was arrested for the first time in the US. Belgian authorities suspected him of being in contact with unknown perpetrators who had recently blown up a German ship in the port of San Francisco. Erich Krewet most probably had nothing to do with this, but as FBI informants, among them Krebs, had called him a fanatical communist his release was delayed. Finally set free in February 1940 he was promptly arrested again as a potential saboteur after Pearl Harbour.

For Erich Krewet, who had counteracted Nazi propaganda in the USA like few others, it was the greatest possible insult to be imprisoned with self professed Nazis. With growing bitterness, he watched as his old rival Richard Krebs was touring the US selling war bonds. This riled him all the more as Erich Krewet very well knew that, contrary to what the American public had been told, his old acquaintance and the hero of *Out of the Night* were not identical.

While Krewets own marriage was breaking up during his imprisonment the newly married Richard Krebs had become the happy father of a newborn child, as one could gather from the gossip columns. One of the last sentences in his open letter conveys his bitterness: "You have your physical freedom, your family and your security"

After his open letter, Krewet very soon found himself on familiar terms with Burling of the Enemy Alien Control Unit, who came to believe that the designation of Erich Krewet as a Communist was only due to false statements of Richard Krebs, which he first made in court in Germany and later to the FBI in New York.

Whether Erich Krewet was a communist plant in the ITF as well as in the "German-American Cultural Alliance" or not - in the internment camp he had probably ceased to be one. He gave extensive testimony to the FBI about Communists he had met as ITF representatives on the West Coast. He described the well-known labor leader Harry Bridges, who had led the general strike in San Francisco in 1934, as a secret Communist, which has been confirmed after the opening of the Moscow archives.[322] He even claimed to know who Bridges' superior in the party was. Last but not least, Erich Krewet warned the FBI about his mother-in-law, who was probably also a Communist.[323]

Krewet thereby gained the favor of the FBI who was later to deny any suggestion that Krewet ever had been a Communist. Accordingly Burling referred to the FBI when he described his main witness against Richard Krebs as an exemplary honest, non partisan trade unionist. [324]

On November 24, 1942, Richard Krebs was arrested at the breakfast table and interned as a Gestapo agent on Ellis Island. The *Daily Worker*, the newspaper of the Communist Party of the USA, triumphed and quoted from his indictment: "It is possible that Richard Krebs was active as a Nazi agent for the last five years (...) His life so far has been so marked by violence, intrigues and betrayal that one can hardly assume that today he is absolutely trustworthy. (...) The evidence presented does not allow the conclusion that Krebs has been a person of good moral character during the last five years. (...) An independent investigation has shown that in 1934, at a time when he was allegedly working against the Nazis, he was in fact a witness for the prosecution when a member of the ISH was sentenced for high treason."[325]

Other press organs switched their tone. *The American Hebrew*, a conservative Jewish newspaper, wrote that Richard Krebs was now being exposed as a Nazi agent:"The Valtin case is comparable to that of Rasputin. "[326] The governor of California Olson, who had pardoned Richard Krebs, published in his defense a list of names of all those who had urged him to make this disastrous decision.

Even in faraway Europe some found reason to cheer. In connection with the "hustle and bustle of Jewish emigrants who had fled Germany" and who had supposedly made themselves unpopular in England by their black market activities, the German news agency reported from Geneva that it now had been decided in the USA to "deport one of these 'guests' as soon as possible. ... Jan Valtin alias Richard Krebs ... This Jew ... was originally very celebrated when he wrote a book about alleged atrocities in Germany. Meanwhile, however, the successful author had to admit, as *Time* writes, that these were not only his own experiences, but that he had 'added the experiences of other men to make the book as effective as possible'. Yes, he was even called - one hears and is astonished - a forger, as he had committed the carelessness to also attack Bolshevists. ... With the proceeds of the book Krebs has acquired a beautiful villa in Connecticut, which he now has to exchange with Ellis Island, from where he is to be deported at the next opportunity."[327]

Under Nazi suspicion

The arrest was a shock to Richard Krebs. Although he had known about the suspicions against him, not in his worst dreams did it occur to him that he might be arrested as a potential Nazi agent. Five days after the arrest, he wrote a letter to Roger Baldwin, a personal friend and chairman of the American Civil Liberties Union:

"I am very glad that you wrote to me and that the ACLU will engage in the fight against my classification as a 'dangerous member of an enemy nation'." Richard Krebs then referred to his work for the war loan campaign, his advocacy for a war entry of the USA and mentioned that he had been told only a few days before his arrest that he would be accepted into the army.

"Therefore, you will understand why I was so upset when I was suddenly described as a potential 'Nazi agent' in a Justice Department press release. It was as if someone had broken into my house, thrown my baby against the wall, insulted my wife and set fire to our house."[328]

In a letter, probably also to Baldwin, he listed acquaintances, business partners and friends, a total of 18 people, and tried to assess how they would behave towards him now.

The only one he described as a friend without reservation was Charles Malamud, who had given him Trotsky's winter coat: "Charles Malamud is the most important translator of Slavic languages in this country. He is a very close personal friend, reliable, poor, but no cheapskate, and JV has the very best opinion of him. Disappeared last summer into the woods of Jersey to write a book, but could reappear at any moment.«

Ben Mandel, the investigator of the Dies committee who together with Levine had advanced him the money to write *Out of the Night*, he also described as a friend, with the restriction that he had a habit of sticking his nose into things that did not concern him.

Herbert H. Ross, an estate agent who negotiated the contract to buy the farm in the summer of 1942, was one of those he distrusted. "Be kind to him, but keep him at a distance. He's a parasite disguising himself as a friend. He's particularly fond of trying to sell my wife land and insurance when I'm not around."

Levine finally belonged to those people about whom he was unsure.

"Isaac Don Levine is the man who made me write 'Out of the Night'. He is a freelance journalist with great experience, very friendly, capable, but very cunning in business matters, and you never know if he will keep his promises. His good side is the great knowledge of the New York and Washington publishing circles. His bad side is his big hunger for money. For the sake of money, IDL [Isaac Don Levine] would not hesitate to break with his closest friends. (...) Since the Goodstein affair Levine has kept his distance from me, because he (my guess) does not want to bear the part of the costs that would correspond to his share of the profit."[329]

The decision on whether to intern a detained foreigner was taken after the involvement of a civic body that made a recommendation based on material submitted by the Enemy Alien Control Unit and after hearing the foreigner. The person concerned had no right to call in a lawyer, but could name reputation witnesses and defend himself. The final decision was made by the Attorney General, who generally followed the panel's recommendation.

Richard Krebs had no illusions about the attitude of the Justice Department officials toward him as he wrote to Baldwin: "Judging by the tone and nature of the press release issued by the Justice Department, I quote - The Department awaits the recommendation for internment - I am trying not to give in to false hopes about the final decision. However, I have great confidence in America as a country where a great liberal tradition is linked to the ideal of fair play".

One day after Richard Krebs's arrest, on November 25, the U.S. Attorney General telegraphed from Washington to California that Erich Krewet would be temporarily released on parole and asked whether Krewet was willing to come to Washington on state expense and testify regarding Richard Krebs. That was the moment Erich Krewet had been waiting for.

On 8 December, the hearing began before the Citizens' Panel, which consisted of three wealthy businessmen and two retired army officers.

Also permanently present during the four-day discussions were Burling of the Enemy Alien Control Unit, an FBI official who did not say a word and only took notes, and a Connecticut state attorney. The jury essentially had to decide whether Richard Krebs at the 1934 trial had testified to a well known fact i.e. that Krewet was a prominent Communist, or whether – to curry favor with the Gestapo - he had falsely denounced a non-partisan trade unionist.

Connecticut's honorable citizens were hopelessly overwhelmed by the minutes of the 1934 trial and the political situation in the Hamburg of those years. The air buzzed with difficult German words such as "Verkehrsbund", "Einheitsverband", "Einheitskomitee" and the like. German Rules of Procedure were discussed; namely whether the defendants were questioned first and then the witnesses, or vice versa. Finally, the two Germans were giving conflicting testimony about what they claimed to have heard about each other in prison, whether Julius Emmerich was an informer or not, etc. The battle swayed back and forth, with the state attorney, who was wary of Krewet, increasingly opposing the official from Washington, which later resulted in a series of disciplinary complaints against him.

Sometimes the man from Washington thought he could triumph, for example when Richard Krebs admitted that Krewet had asked him in prison to testify that he only knew him as a fellow sailor. This Krebs had refused. He had explained to Krewet that it was always best to admit as much of the truth as possible and only deny something if there was no proof to the contrary. Burling noted maliciously: "I then involved Krebs in a lengthy discussion about this particular technique of perjury, until it dawned on him that he was about to reveal his tactics in this trial."[330]

Sometimes the scales leaned against Krewet, as when the prosecutor from Connecticut asked him if he had ever been in the Soviet Union. Krewet first denied this, then stated that he had not understood the question correctly, and finally admitted to having been several times there as a sailor.

Finally, Burling brought Hermine's last letters to Richard Krebs into play. By them he wanted to prove that Richard Krebs had, contrary to his claims, been in contact with Germany since his arrival. As one FBI agent in attendance noted, "Mr. Krebs showed feelings for the first and only time during the entire trial and pretty much lost control of himself. He claimed that these letters had been stolen from him in New York".[331] Burling, who believed that Richard Krebs had betrayed his wife to the Gestapo and that her death was anything but certain, later contemptuously noted:

"Because of his antics, it seemed better to me not to ask him any more about the alleged death of his wife."[332]

Richard Krebs managed to keep his secret. Burling was for many decades the last one who tried to solve the mystery of the letters.

In the absence of conclusive evidence that Richard Krebs was a Gestapo agent, the outcome of the trial ultimately depended on the question of whether Erich Krewet was a credible witness. With the help of Krewet, Burling had been able to prove that the character of Valtin in *Out of the Night* was indeed, as Richard Krebs finally had to admit, not an autobiography in the strict sense of the word. In Burling's opinion, the author had thereby exposed himself as a liar. But the former military men among the jury did not concur. Happy to finally be able to contribute something substantial, they gave a little lesson in soldier's lore. From their days in the trenches in France, they remembered that their comrades, as soon as they had listened to some extraordinary experience, would retell it as if it had happened to them. In their eyes Krebs had, as an underground communist, also waged a kind of war.

The citizens' committee finally voted for release with probation.

Decisive for this decision was the undeniable fact that Erich Krewet had received one year and nine months for treason, while Richard Krebs had been sentenced to three years for the same offence. That seemed a little strange after all. Burling's assertion that in a fascist state, unlike in America, a crown witness would not be granted a reduction of sentence was not believed.

That Richard Krebs did not receive an unconditional acquittal was due to a character witness he had himself named. Don Levine, of all people, who after the beginning of the war had immediately stopped dealing with communism in order to write the biography of an "American hero", presented the author of *Out of the Night* as an unrestrained opportunist. Richard Krebs was loyal to America only because a writer could earn more in the USA than in any other country. Even when asked again, he did not deviate from this statement, which he made in the absence of the accused.

Normally, the Attorney General would have followed the panel's decision and released Richard Krebs. His own subordinates, the officials of the Enemy Alien Control Unit, beseeched him not do so. Burling wrote a twenty-page report in which he once again summarized all the arguments against him and Richard Krebs continued to be interned on Ellis Island. The majority of public opinion was against Richard Krebs. Some prominent publicists who thought they could sense a communist conspiracy were not able to change that.

Behind the scenes, a tug-of-war began that resulted in a myriad of memos, disciplinary complaints, and mutual accusations. Burling hacked into Cooley, the Connecticut attorney, who he blamed for the panel's decision, and Cooley fought back. Richard Krebs's character witnesses Eastman, Baldwin and Lyons publicly complained that they had been treated like criminals during their testimony. Burling replied that a Trotskyist like Eastman should not complain. After all, Trotskyists differed from Communists mainly in their rejection of Stalin's policy of peace toward the democracies. Moreover, he had been so considerate as not to mention to the conservative jury that Eastman was a nudist. Otherwise, he might even have won the hearing.

Even J. Edgar Hoover was involved in the controversy. Indignantly, he stated that he was not against, but for the internment of Richard Krebs. Burling, who believed the FBI had withheld evidence, had to apologize.[333]

In March 1943, Abigail wrote a moving letter to the Attorney General in which she affirmed her husband's innocence. After standing in front of Congress with a sign demanding the release of her husband, she was finally received by a staff member of the Enemy Alien Control Unit. According to her transcript, Richard Krebs was still considered a Nazi agent. His description of Nazi terror was supposed to have been subtle intimidation propaganda in Hitler's interest. They also did not believe that Richard Krebs would be sentenced to death in Germany. Finally the young woman was told that she was wrong to believe that her husband could not be a Nazi because he treated her and the child so lovingly. Many Nazis were the best husbands and fathers.

Abigail's intervention was useless. Richard Krebs remained in prison without a final decision having been made. His opponents in the "Enemy Alien Control Unit" always found new reasons for suspecting him to be a Gestapo agent. After the old arguments had been exhausted, an "independent" expert was called in, who now took a completely new direction. This time the passages from *Out of the Night*, which dealt with the inhuman conditions in the concentration camps of the Third Reich, were not anymore ignored, but interpreted as a sign of a particularly subtle propaganda. With these reports he had wanted to get compassion and sympathy from the Americans.

"In this context it is interesting how he quoted Hitler on 10.11.41 in Chicago: 'Propaganda is only good propaganda if it is not known as propaganda'.

The accused himself states: 'Nazi propaganda, and this is what Americans must learn, has as its object not the Nazification of the populations of other countries, but at sowing discord in the populations of other countries, as a necessary condition for their later defeat. People look around and don't see anyone screaming Hitler and conclude that there are no Nazis here."

So after Richard Krebs had gained the trust of the Americans, he set about sowing discord. By claiming for example, that Stalin had robbed banks on behalf of the party before the First World War.

"He will be able, unless most strictly censored, to impress Americans with fears and suspicions of Communism and the Russians in the very critical junctures right ahead of us, which demand collaboration with the Russians and confidence in the common future for all the United Nations.

Hatred of communists logically involves hatred of Russians, since the active practice of communism as a sort of religion, is the central characteristic of the interior life of Russia and the entire Soviet Union." [334]

Also after that letter, no decision was taken. The Attorney General, whose job it would have been to determine whether Richard Krebs posed a threat to U.S. security, did not want to antagonize neither Richard Krebs's supporters nor the Enemy Alien Control Unit. Thus Richard Krebs remained interned on Ellis Island.

No place, no where

On Ellis Island, prisoners of various nations were interned. The spectrum ranged from illegal Chinese immigrants, deserted sailors of all allied powers to radical Irish nationalists and professed supporters of Hitler. On the island, the political internees set the tone. Many guards shared the prejudices of the Nazis among their prisoners and worked openly with them. For 50 cents to one dollar you could smuggle out an uncensored letter and for fifteen to one hundred dollars you could get a look at the prison records. More than once Richard Krebs witnessed how non-whites, especially Chinese, were brutally maltreated by the guards and members of the Coast Guard.

Richard Krebs was threatened several times and the contents of his letters were passed on from the prison censor to his fellow prisoners. Only because he was moved to a single cell nothing worse happened. An FBI agent, who later dealt with these events, thought, however, that the segregation of Richard Krebs, whom he described as a "sturdily-built thug," could also have been a stroke of luck for the Nazis.[335]

Finally, at the end of May 1943, had the "Enemy Alien Control Unit" run out of reasons, no matter how harebrained, to continue interning Richard Krebs.

He had to be released on parole. The Richard Krebs, who left Ellis Island on May 28, 1943, was not the same man as before. His belief in America and its values, which he had upheld before his arrest with the same fervor as Communism before, had now been severely shaken. The hero of his post-war novel *Castles in the Sand* - an illegal refugee from Germany who under a false name laboriously builds up an existence as a farmer - falls victim to intrigues and a merciless bureaucracy after the war begins. The book ends with his attempt to escape from Ellis Island. He's shot by a guard.

"Daniel half sprang, half fell, from the top of the sea wall. Stumps of submerged piling hit his side as he entered the water. The pain was bad but he worked himself free of the stumps. He pushed off and he swam away from the Island and he heard the guard shout. The tide ran seaward. - Patches of oily film glistened under the stars. The chugging of the motor barge of the Jersey City wharves receded into the night. In the luminous darkness the shapes of anchored ships loomed up and drifted by and over the harbour waters came the sleepy thumping of chain cables in hawse pipes. The ebb tide carried Daniel in a south-easterly direction; and somewhere along his course the stars were blotted out by the mighty statue of a woman. The woman held aloft a torch that burned brighter than the brightest constellation. In the night she stood, enwrapped in an aura of magnificence and light, of pride and compassion, and light cascaded dimly over the letters of the message that was this woman's soul--*Give me your tired, your poor, your huddled masses, yearning to breath free....The wretched refuse of your teeming shore. Send these, the homeless, tempest-tossed, to me....*

The message was difficult to read at night. Yet had it been bright midday Daniel could not have read the words. He was drifting seaward. His limbs hung slack. His back was hunched up and his face was submerged. He was gazing down as though he searched for something at the bottom."[336]

In August Richard Krebs was drafted, although he was not an American citizen, and sent to an infantry training camp in Texas. His superiors found no reason to complain. He was an inconspicuous soldier who never expressed a political opinion, learnt eagerly and stayed away from others. Only when German prisoners of war made fun of the efficiency and discipline of the US army shortly before Christmas did he attract attention. "When he [] left the room, he for the time first showed that he had understood their conversation. With a grin, he told them that 'they should enjoy themselves as long as they could, since Congress had set the date for their hanging to the morning of the first day of Christmas'. [337] Richard Krebs got a reprimand for this evil joke. He was forbidden to ever again contact the prisoners of war without the permission of his superiors.

From the very beginning, he was under the watchful eye of the Army Counter Intelligence Corps, which had all the available files on him brought in, questioned his neighbors, friends, fellow soldiers, and superiors, and read all his letters. Last but not least, like all the authorities before, they dealt with *Out of the Night*. The result of all the effort was contradictory. In a February 1944 report, it says: "He is easy to get along with; good worker; of pleasant manners; loyal to his family and home; pleasant personality; good American; loyal American - not an opportunist; highly regarded by neighbors and acquaintances; follows with downright religious fervor all orders of the immigration authorities; open; honest," and in another one: "not trustworthy; an opportunist who would do anything to get ahead."[338] Albeit, Richard Krebs was sent to the Philippines in the spring of 1944 as an infantryman, where he was deployed in the jungle war against the Japanese.

He had his typewriter with him, and *Children of Yesterday*, a chronicle of the life and death of his unit, was published based on his daily notes after the war.[339] The jungle war in the Philippines exceeded in brutality anything American soldiers experienced in the Europe. Unlike the Wehrmacht, which, as far as Americans were concerned, adhered to the Geneva Convention in its own self-interest, the Japanese treated their prisoners with extreme cruelty. The Americans acted hardly different. One of the most gruesome episodes in *Children of Yesterday* describes how the author is supposed to bring a Japanese prisoner back to his unit. Already on the way there can he only with difficulty prevent Philippine civilians from killing him. Finally arriving he realizes that the prisoner will be handed over to local auxiliary troops and that his efforts to deliver him unharmed were ultimately in vain.

Children of Yesterday at times reads like the script of a splatter movie. Repeatedly the Japanese, who, cut off from their motherland, have run out of ammunition, attack their American opponents with anything that can be used as a weapon, Again and again they are mass slaughtered in their frontal attacks. Krebs describes vividly how the US soldiers, apart from the attacks by the Japanese, are particularly affected by the tropical climate and the traces of massacres of the civilian population which they encounter during their advance.

He also depicts the terrible fate of Japanese civilians, nurses, mechanics, officers' wives and children. Forced by their own compatriots, the fanatics, who lead the

Japanese troops to persevere without food in the jungle, they and their soldiers fall victim to the flamethrowers of the Americans or, after escape attempts, are mercilessly tortured to death by the local population.

In March 1945, while Richard Krebs's unit was struggling with the scattered remains of the Japanese army, his older sister Annemarie was dying in a Karlsbad hospital. The trained infant nurse had spent the war years serving in military hospitals before falling terminally ill at the end of 1944.

Annemarie, who had had to look after her younger siblings for years after the death of her father and the departure of the second Richard, remembered in her last moving letters to a friend in Bremen her few happy years after the others had left the house and before Hitler came to power. They were memories of a boat trip, some smaller trips to the Grunewald in Berlin and of the deep friendship she had with her pen friend. On the 19th of the month, she was dead.

After the end of the fighting in August 1945, Richard Krebs, who was still in the Philippines, began to search for his son Jan. He wrote to British and American army chaplains, official tracing services and the World Council of Churches in Geneva. It wasn't until 1946 that he received word. Jan lived on a farm near Bremen.

After Hermine's death he had stayed with his grandparents. When the youth was finally found, the grandfather was already dead, the grandmother half paralyzed and there wasn't anyone to take care of him anymore. After a lengthy correspondence, Richard Krebs finally succeeded in bringing his son to America. Abigail remembers that Jan was terribly thin when he arrived.

Richard Krebs had received the first news from Germany through relatives in the Midwest, who informed him in March 1946 that they had received a letter via the Red Cross. The news came from distant relatives and was very brief: "We are well despite having lost a lot of weight. House undamaged. Rolf prisoner of war, but healthy. Gertrude's all right. Lost everything. Fred unknown. Lutz fell. Fate of other relatives unknown. Communication impossible".[340]

A few months later he received a letter from his brother Hugo through his relatives in Iowa. He wrote right back:

"Dear Peps

I was so happy to get a sign of life from you. Your letter of May 31, sent to Dubuque, came from Aunt Wilhelmine today. I am glad to know that you are well and in good spirits, in spite of all misfortune. Do you know where Cilly is and how she's doing?

I've been running from pillar to post for months now to get back in touch with you over there. ...

I've heard of Annemarie's tragic death through Aunt Lilly. I'm so sorry. I'm so sorry. I haven't heard from Cilly.

Now about me - after I left Germany in 1937, the Hitler bandits made sure that I could not get in touch with you. I came to New York in 1938 on an English ship and got off. Worked in New York as a painter and handyman for two years, and with the money saved I bought a tent and moved into the woods with a dog and kerosene stove and started writing. After a year as a writer and back woods man, several magazines started publishing my work and I also wrote some books. One of my books had an effect on the Nazis like a red scarf on a bull. I had hit back to make up the bill for my years in the Gestapo concentration camps.

In 1940 I married an American girl. We got two boys, Conrad and Eric. Conrad is 5 now, and Eric is 1 year old. We have a house about 100 kilometers north of New York, with forest and fields, but I will move to the south of the country in a few months, where I just bought a house right on the coast. (...)

Yesterday I read in the newspaper that it will soon be possible to send parcels from here to Germany. Please write to me as soon as possible what you need most urgently and what kind of clothing (give size or measurements).

As soon as it's allowed, I'll send you what you need. Write to me in detail how you all are. With best regards from all of us and a firm handshake".[341]

When Richard Krebs wrote to his brother, he had become a father for the third time. In 1945 Abigail gave birth to her second and Richard's third son Eric. At the beginning of 1946 *Children of Yesterday* and *Castle in the Sand* had appeared. *Children of Yesterday* – a battle chronicle in diary form - attracted no further attention, while *Castle in the Sand* was discussed in all major newspapers. The reviews were mostly favourable, and although the book was not a great success, it was translated into seven languages.

Castle in the Sand is the story of a German concentration camp prisoner on the run and of the love between him and a Flemish girl who grew up in a brothel in Antwerp. Against the will of a pimp who has set his eyes on her, he takes her to America. There they live under a false name. After the birth of a child, they move from New York to the country and live on a small farm. At the beginning of the war, by chance they are discovered by the pimp who has also come to the USA. He denounces them to the authorities and they lose everything they have built up. The hero is brought to Ellis Island where he is shot during an escape attempt. Richard Krebs vividly describes their escape from Europe as stowaways, their early days as laborers in New York, and their efforts to build a new existence in a country in which, unlike Europe, nobody asks where you come from, but only what you are and what you can do. The tragic end of the two, who are crushed by a merciless bureaucracy after the beginning of the war, is described with oppressive precision. The book also has serious weaknesses. The reader does not learn why the hero was in a concentration camp, and the character of the pimp is overdone in its sheer malice.

As Abigail reports, in the first version it was communists who caused the ruin of the two heroes of the book. But as it was impossible to publish the original version in the Soviet-friendly climate immediately after the end of the war, Richard Krebs had been forced to insert the pimp.

In the summer of 1946 he gave up the house in Bethel, Connecticut, and moved with his family to the picturesque Chesapeake Bay south of the capital Washington and not far from Norfolk. He loved the house made of alluvial wood and the waters of the huge bay that stretches hundreds of miles inland. As in his youth at the mouth of the Weser he started sailing again, and from the summer of 1947 he lent boats to the few tourists who came to the then still very remote area.

For the now forty-year-old writer, the move could have marked the beginning of a quiet phase in his life. But he was not allowed to slowly recover from the last few years. He had brought a non-lethal but incurable virus from the Philippine trenches, the so-called Jungle Rot, which spread from the toes to the legs, spine and brain. Besides, his hearing loss had worsened. He was practically deaf in his right ear. In addition, there were the first depressions, which intensified in the following years. His wife remembers: "I think it was a result of not only concentration camp not only having been politically messed up not only having felt guilt at the loss of his wife Hermine not only worrying about the years that he had not spent with Jan not only the years in prison here in San Quentin and not only the war but if you put all that together plus the fact that there was so much publicity about him when the first book came out and the others had no notoriety at all he felt like he was a loser."[342]

The depression was compounded by quarrels with his young wife who, as a New Yorker, did not want to live at the end of the world.

After one of those collisions, he took the car and disappeared. Abigail, who was stuck by the water in the house without a car, was very worried about him. She called all his acquaintances and friends, her mother and even Don Levine, with whom he had not been on the best terms for a long time. No one knew where he was. Three days after he disappeared, policemen brought him back. He had been found lying completely naked on the roof of his car. According to Abigail, his first words when he was brought into the house were, "This place looks like a pigsty."

In the summer of 1948 Abigail took the children and moved to her mother in New York.

Long exchanges of letters between the two, some about final separation and others about reconciliation, could not save the marriage. In March of the following year, Abigail divorced him in Las Vegas. The two agreed that Richard would pay alimony and that the children would spend the summer with him. Already in April Richard Krebs wrote to a priest friend: "I have some news and a request. Against my protest Abby got a divorce last month. Our boys will come back to me this year in June. In order to keep my house together for her as well as for my inner balance, I will marry a good woman. It's Clara you've already met."[343]

Clara Medders was the daughter of a local shopkeeper and, although in her mid-thirties, had never been married. She became his third wife and the marriage was a last attempt to find inner peace. Forty years later - the now almost blind and destitute Clara Medders was still living in Betterton - she told German literary scholar Michael Rohrwasser about her two years with Richard Krebs: "At the beginning the priest wouldn't marry us, because Richard was regarded as a communist: we finally had to look for another priest and married in Aberdeen chapel. Even later people in the village always called him „the communist". Financially we weren't too well off, but apart from that it was a great time with him. Richard had the ability to forget terrible experiences and to love the good things. But he didn't really forget the bad things. Eric was his favourite son and the one whose appearance and behaviour resembled him most. He suffered from pangs of guilt towards Firelei and his mother who was Lutheran and disappointed about him becoming a communist."[344]

In 1947 the former soldier, who had returned with a medal for bravery, finally became an American citizen. The last papers in the several hundred page file of the Immigration Department are not about his alleged contacts to the Gestapo anymore.

Now the question was whether he was still a communist. This last fight against the distrust of the authorities deepened his disenchantment with America.

Richard Krebs for whom political convictions, the belief in a better world, for which he lived and fought, had always constituted the meaning of his life, had lost all illusions. Of his fervent commitment to "American values" and against the dictatorships of Hitler and Stalin, only an angry, hate-filled anti-communism remained.

When his son Jan brought a copy of the journal *Soviet Russia Today* home from his high school, he wrote an angry letter to the headmaster.

"Betterton, Maryland September 21, 1949.

Soviet Russia Today' has been described as subversive by the United States Attorney General. The editor, Jessica Smith, is described as a sponsor and member of 'one to ten pro-communist organisations'. While investigating the imprint, I found the names of the following communists:

Paul Robeson: member of more than 50 communist, subversive organizations
W.E.B. DuBois: Member of more than 11 communist organizations
I. Ehrenburg: Official Representative of Soviet Newspapers
Sidney Finkelstein: Member of 1 to 10 communist organisations
Corliss Lamont: Member of 41 to 50 communist front organizations. I could continue this list for a long time. There is no non-Russian author in *Soviet Russia Today* whose name cannot be found in the published lists of subversives by the Department of Justice or the US Congress.

It is probably not necessary to emphasize what damage such a publication can do to the brains of very young and receptive (and generally uncritical) readers."[345]

The scared headmaster promised to immediately remove Russia Today from the shelves.

In 1948/49 Richard Krebs collected material for various book projects. Among those which never came to fruition was a story about death row based on his experiences in San Quentin; a violent confrontation of fishermen at Chesapeake Bay over fishing grounds, and a novel about the German Revolution of 1918. *Wintertime* was completed, a book that emerged from the hundreds of testimonies and letters sent to him from Germany in return for just as many care packages.[346] It describes post-war Germany from the perspective of the letter writers, which are filtered by the image of Germany that the former concentration camp prisoner had retained. Remarkable are the haunting tableaus of poverty and destruction that the author draws of his fictitious Nordune, the scene of the plot. German authors who, like their readers, were already so accustomed to the destruction of their physical environment that they hardly noticed the extraordinary nature of the scenery, usually refrained from such detailed descriptions.

Wintertime tells the story of a tugboat captain who falls in love with a Baltic refugee girl and then gets in the middle of a power struggle between a network of old Nazis and fanatical communists, which ends with a bloody reckoning. The hero is send to prison as a murderer, and the girl loses her laboriously built home. The book is a drastic portrait of a morally delipidated society with some almost unbearably violent scenes. The American occupiers are portrayed as partly naïve and partly corrupted by their incomparably higher standard of living. Krebs himself saw the book, published at the beginning of 1950, as "the story of a man who fights for a piece of normality in a world that is completely out of joint". *Wintertime* was not a great success, although some critics were quite impressed. At that time Richard Krebs's depression had worsened so much that he decided to seek help.

"»7.1.1950 Dear Mr. Bond.

A year ago, I could hardly think properly, I wrote to a friend in New York - Mrs. Edna Mann, who urged me to go into psychiatric treatment. On January 14, 1949, she wrote and advised me to go to you. I believe Mrs. Mann wrote to you or spoke to you at the time.

However, in the hope and belief that I could solve my problems through my own efforts, I did not seek help from outside, but forced myself into a hard working routine, which helped for a while, but did not last. In June, the state of agonizing confusion returned and overlaid the desperate (and unsustainable) efforts to return to a normal and healthy routine.

My work is that of a writer and as such I have won a fair success. I have three bright sons whom I love. I do my writing under the pen name Jan Valtin. Circumstances are so that reason tells me that normal harmony and productivity need not be out of my reach. There are five people who depend on me. Yet, from week to week I seem to be sliding deeper into a sort of dead hole, and all efforts to stop the process appear useless.

I may characterise the nature of my difficulties as follows: Work difficulties, a fear of people which borders at times on panic, a great desire for solitude and a most primitive mode of live, a strong and almost constant feeling, that any step taken on any course in any direction is dead wrong, and a continuous --- almost daily---- struggle against the urge to end my life."[347]

Richard Krebs never started treatment. He accepted an invitation from the CIC (Counter Intelligence Corps of the US Army) to Germany, where he was interviewed for two weeks in the spring of 1950 about every detail of his work for the Comintern and about every cadre he had met during that time. He once again proved the almost uncanny personal memory that had so impressed the reporter of the New York newspaper *P.M.* in 1941. In the protocol, which comprises more than a hundred pages, there are hundreds of personal descriptions, including statements about the circumstances in which he had got to know the persons concerned, as well as precise estimates of their probable activity. The range went from "intelligent, unobtrusive, cosmopolitan, suitable for the apparatus" to "absolutely faithful, but more muscles than brain, typical man for the rough". It shows how much he had concealed from the Gestapo after his "conversion".

He made either no or misleading statements about his family history, Hermine's true fate and the prehistory of the 1926 assassination attempt. He saw no reason to give the CIC any material that could have been used against him. Almost all information about Richard Krebs himself must be derived from testimony he gave about others.

He had gained a cold distance to Wollweber and Jensen. He had left behind his angry hatred, the other side of a disappointed love. About Jensen he said it was conceivable that he would break away from communism because he had enough financial means and prestige in the Danish public to not be dependent on the CP. An apt assessment. Jensen did indeed turn away from the CP, but continued to play an important public role.

The CIC was most interested in Wollweber. Among other things, they discussed with his former subordinate the question of whether there would ever be the possibility of making him a turncoat. Richard Krebs considered this to be very unlikely, but conceivable under certain circumstances.

"If Wollweber has been able to build a little empire of his own, not too big, but sufficiently big to suit him, we would probably become a first class burocrat." If, in addition to the feeling of personal power thus acquired, a certain degree of exhaustion would occur after a very hard life, he might begin to weaken ideologically. Richard Krebs considered hatred to be the one emotion motivating Wollweber. He often said to his co-workers, "We must organize hatred."

If Wollweber's attachment to communism were to diminish, then it "this would probably take the form of a combination of his long-held disgust for everything and anyone non-communist with a newly found disgust for the communist movement. In such a mood he might be amenable to a suggestion that he work against communism, but the approach would have to come from someone he trusts completely." As is well known, Ernst Wollweber was never tempted. In 1953, after the uprising of 17 June, he became chief of the Stasi (Secret Police) of the GDR. He is widely credited to have developed it into the successful instrument of securing power for the East German Communists that it proved to be during the following decades.

In that regard one memory that Richard Krebs had of his former boss was to be prophetic: "Wollweber often spoke of what would happen if the Communists seized power. When comments were made how difficult it was to work in Germany and how thorough the Gestapo was in its man hunting, he remarked:' We will be far more thorough when we get to power.'"

When asked how Wollweber would react if he saw him again, Richard Krebs replied: "The only reaction would be a hard-boiled, sardonic grin and complete silence."[348]

How much the fight against communism had become the last meaning of his life is once again confirmed by his attitude to his main work *Out of the Night*.

Thirteen years later he judged it only by its value as a source of information about his former comrades. He scornfully dismissed it as "not written from an intelligence point of view, but for the entertainment of bored businessmen".[349]

Before his trip to Germany, his old friend Roger Baldwin had written to him:

"The trip to Germany is wonderful. Stay as long as you can. You can be very useful, although I'm sure you won't like what you'll find on both sides. German as well as American. You know that better than I do. But you can fix your own life. Maybe, as you say, your fears and your tendency to self-destruct will disappear. All this is so unconscious and independent of will that no one can predict it. But perhaps your desire to escape from yourself and your environment will be fulfilled and you can go about regulating your life at home."[350]

After his return Richard Krebs reported in a letter:

"The secret of my trip to Europe is no longer secret. I followed the invitation of a branch of Army Intelligence. I flew both routes, with short stopovers in the Azores and Iceland. In Germany I was provided with a German car and a chauffeur/bodyguard from the Midwest, who put a Colt in his shoulder holster for my safety. We drove around a lot, along the Iron Curtain and elsewhere, visiting about nine cities and the villages in between.

I talked to various people, starting with a German tugboat captain, who could have been my friend Martin Helm*. This man had been bombed out and was building between his journeys together with his wife a hut on the river near the edge of their port city.

Others were: Refugees, a scientist who had been Marshall Kesselring's intelligence officer in Italy, an artist, a librarian, a museum research assistant, a salesman, and many more.

As I had already thought, these people, their problems and views were familiar to me. The scenery - Hamburg, Bremen, Kassel, Darmstadt with its large fields of ruins - still provides a thousand cellar holes for the Martins and Lisas*. The black merchants with their dented suitcases are still hanging around at the railway stations and marketplaces.

Since the currency reform and the Marshall Plan, the stores have been full of goods again. Often enough only a dazzling shop window and above it four floors of burnt out ruin. Millions of families still live in one room. It was for me a return to the scenes from *Wintertime*, and if the whole book had been written in the middle of Germany, people and scenery would not have turned out any different. Although as a writer I would hardly have dared to use some of my own experiences in the book. For example, a former New York union boss, who now 'administers' a ring of spy hunters in a thousand-year-old German city; or a G.I. who arrests a well-known anti-Communist and sells him to the East.

Interesting, but generally not pleasant.

Now - back to work.

With best regards".[351]

After his journey, which had lasted barely three weeks, Richard Krebs lived again at Chesapeake Bay and tried to write, but did not get beyond beginnings. There was terrible news about his favorite sister Cilly, which he had seen one last time in Europe. She was terminally ill with a brain tumor and died in April without the medication he had sent to Frankfurt being able to help.

He spent the summer with his two younger sons, who had come to Maryland in accordance with the agreement with Abby, and in the autumn of 1950 he prepared for what he thought was at least a six-month stay in Germany. Don Levine had helped him get a commission from *Le Figaro* in Paris to do a travel report on the inner German border. The money for the contract, which was unusually well endowed, probably came from one of the American secret funds that served to influence European public opinion at the beginning of the Cold War.

---

* Character(s) in Wintertime

Before his departure he visited Don Levine once more. Richard Krebs had forgiven him for distancing himself during his internment on Ellis Island. The disputes over the income from *Out of the Night* also no longer played a role. Looking back, those months between the start of working on *Out of the Night* and the internment on Ellis Island appeared to him as the last happy time of his life. After their meeting, Levine wrote him a short note. He was touched by Richard Krebs's memories of those weeks at Levine's country estate in Danbury when they had both worked on the final version of *Out of the Night*. Levine assured him that he reciprocated these feelings, and concluded somewhat patronizingly: "I always thought that you were very talented and that with self-discipline you could achieve great things."[352]

The journey through Germany became a nightmare. During his short visit in spring Richard Krebs had taken note but ultimately disregarded the cooperation of the American officaldom with fanatical Nazis. He thought that he had left his past behind and was able to view German reality with the same inner distance as the Cold Warriors of the CIC. When he now travelled alone through Germany, this, as well as the assumption that he could identify with the Germans, proved to be an illusion. In *Wintertime* he had described Germany and its inhabitants from the point of view of his correspondents. Thus one of the secondary characters, the artist Marianne, who has lost a leg in a bombing raid, is portrayed with a lot of understanding. Embittered, resentful and full of hatred for the occupiers, she hides a former SS soldier and mass murderer who has remained true to his convictions.

The anti-communism of his correspondents, who after the horrors perpetrated by the Soviet army, feared nothing more than a communist takeover, had led Richard Krebs to believe that he could make their perspective his own.

No longer shielded by American escorts, the former concentration camp prisoner now became aware of the abyss that actually separated him not only from the majority of the German population but also from the spooks of the CIC. The latter were able to pass over the bloody crimes of the Nazi years in the interest of a new "anti-totalitarian" crusade. Not Richard Krebs, though. He could not reside in a country in which the majority had cheered Hitler only a few years before.

Back in Germany, he was no longer the American writer Jan Valtin, who had written in English to Friedrich Stampfer, the Socialist editor of the German newspaper *Neue Volkszeitung* in New York. He was again the German emigrant Richard Krebs, who felt just as alien in his former homeland as the majority of the other refugees, only a few of whom finally returned to Germany.

Several times a day he sent letters and postcards to Clara Medders. Soon after his arrival, he wrote:

"Then, in a frontier village, I spent a night in a tavern in the company of a true bunch of German hicks and talked and argued with them. Their energy and their ignorance and their „hurt pride" and their hatred of America is astounding. Out in the country districts some of them even still wear the old Nazi stormtrooper boots. - There, in the tavern a blonde giant gets up (after years of war and imprisonment) and shakes his big hairy fist into the murky night and roars: „Yah it's best for the Fatherland to DIE!" I asked him: „Hey fool, don't you think it's better to live for the

Fatherland?"- „No you American Coward, it's best to die!" What a bleak, Gothic, insane, heroic, gloomy and strange place this land will forever remain to me. I saw and heard what I came to find out - and it was somehow weird and frightening - and that's enough. Chesapeake is home."[353]

Already after six weeks Richard Krebs broke off his journey and arrived back in America at the end of November.

In his last publication, the article series for *Figaro*, which appeared posthumously in January 1951, his real feelings were not mentioned at all. In Richard Krebs´ long report on the Iron Curtain, there is not a word about the American collaboration with former Gestapo officers or about the impenitent Nazis he had met in West Germany. Nazis are only to be found in East Germany, who as red-painted brown shirts are involved in the establishment of the Kasernierten Volkspolizei, the forerunner of the National People's Army. Whereas in the early 1930s he had preferred to give up writing rather than to follow party guidelines, he now had - after the failure of his last hope to escape depression - neither the strength to look for new perspectives nor the strength to confront the sponsors of his trip to Germany.

He had lost faith in himself as a writer. Would he otherwise have made peace with Levine, a man for whom literary success was expressed in sales figures? Becoming indifferent, Richard Krebs delivered the commissioned piece. The anticommunist tone of the series of articles in *Figaro* was only a weak echo of his last, futile attempt to turn a political goal into a purpose in life. Deep down, he knew how little he had in common with saturated secret service types, who, after their victory over Nazi Germany, were now embarking on the next crusade.

Almost four weeks after his return, he fell ill with pneumonia, the same disease he had almost died of thirteen years ago after the news of Hermine's death. He was sent to a hospital in Betterton, Maryland. Clara Medders reports that he screamed in delirium that the Nazis were persecuting him again. In fear of death, the fevered man picked himself up again on New Year's Eve and ran a few steps before collapsing. On the morning of January 1, 1951, Richard Krebs was dead.

Peps wrote a letter of condolence to Clara:

"We couldn't believe, that the big, strong man had to part from life. He arrived here so healthy and beaming and was happy to see his old homeland again. He wanted to know and see everything. - He refused to miss spending my birthday on the 29th of October with me -

It's very hard for me dear sister-in-law to find the right words of consolation. It's also very difficult for me to know that the last of my brothers is dead with whom as a child I played and fought, ate and drank together."[354]

Many years had passed when John Schaffner, Richard Krebs's friend and agent who managed the gradually decreasing income from his books, wrote to Clara Medders, who was still living in the alluvial wood house at Cheasapeake Bay, asking her to look for some papers in connection with a business matter.

On April 15, 1967, she answered him:

"Dear John

I want to get rid of these things from you - they have worried me a lot because I really didn't know what to send you - I have enjoyed reading so much about Richard -

I have found more letters to me and loved them all anew! I even read your file and Roger Baldwin's. All this tells a story - what a *life,* and how his friends tried to help him! Instead of preparing myself for my journey, I read more and more - I should not have done it - I went through everything again. It fascinated me - but it took a lot of time and emotionally exhausted me. - What a time! - Remember how I was afraid the house in Betterton would burn down *before* we scattered Richard's ashes in Still Pond Creek? - I still remember when we went out on Richard's boat with two young friends to do what we thought was a sad job. - It was after a terrible thunderstorm - Then the calm, beautiful sea. Even the boys who knew the current here wondered in vain how to explain the large ring of flowers that was formed when we scattered the ashes - suddenly all the dancing, colorful flower heads gathered on the golden path of dusk - from a circle a straight line! Straight into the dusk - Nature's tribute to a good sailor!

There are hundreds of photos - from his baby days - in China - a sad family group photo - after the First World War - Richard in the army - Also enough of Jan's mother showing what happened to the beautiful, smiling girl. Many of Jan -If anyone is interested - I have written something more personal - but will not send it. - Will this help you?"[355]

On January 29, 1951, one month after his death, Clara Medders had written to friends about Richard Krebs's last days:

"Dear Billy, dear Jane

Your telegram has warmed my heart, and I thank you very much. R. was a good and tortured person. A man who was very much misunderstood. I met him in New York on November the 24th and he was taken ill at a cocktail party December the 27th. Those thirty days were beautiful - he worked well seemed to be happy and at peace. You perhaps know, how he always searched for peace - yet he seemed always to think he'd find it somewhere else, he was restless. But in his letters and cards which poured in from Europe, three or four daily, one day seven cards - he was homesick. And two weeks after his death, John Schaffner, our friend and agent, turned over a small blotter on his desk and found these eleven words in Richard's handwriting, which gave me great comfort - for I truly loved him --- „The never never land, never never land, is here, is here" --- Yes - I believe he found at last what he had searched for - he was at peace!."[356]

Epilogue

In 1957, the member of the Bundestag Albert Walter, who sat in parliament for the nationalist Deutsche Partei, turned to the *Verfassungsschutz*, the domestic secret service of the West German state, and put on record a strange request to be forwarded to the Americans. The reason was the planned release of *Out of the Night* in German. The now conservative, who, as one of the founders of the international communist seafarers' movement, had personally known Lenin, was concerned about his reputation in posterity. He wanted to put his version of the events surrounding Richard Krebs on record in order to refute the claim in *Out of the Night* that he had entered the Gestapo for fear for his mother. On 22 January, a certain employee of the *Verfassungsschutz* called Mehlen wrote to his counterpart at the CIC:

"In the following some of the claims of Albrecht [sic!] Walter:

- The author of the book in question, Krebs, went to Moscow shortly after the Nazis seized power, in early 33, where he received special training in communist underground work. This training was only given to very capable agitators. Krebs had secretly returned to Germany in 1934, had started a very effective underground work there and had been arrested in 1935.

In mid-1938 the Gestapo sent him to the USA as their agent, where he immediately entered the service of the Americans. Krebs had troubles there which he believed were caused by communist agents that were persecuting him the whole time because of his betrayal. (…) The book was not written by Krebs, but by a group of ex-communists, and Krebs only provided the biographical framework. (…) Krebs had earned millions of dollars with the book; had been back to Germany after the war, but Walter had had no contact with him (...)

What Krebs writes at the end of his book about him, Walter, and his relationship to the Gestapo is not true."[357]

The reaction of the Americans has remained unknown. However, the German translation of Out of the Night omitted any references to Albert Walter's later role as chief advisor to the Gestapo in maritime affairs.

The autobiographical novel translated as *Diary of Hell* was not a great success. The general public did not want to be reminded of a past that had just begun to be forgotten, and many reviewers were afraid of the book. Without being able to judge the most controversial part of the novel, the double play of the hero, one was afraid of getting compromised by association with the author. As long as the archives remained closed, Richard Krebs's companions were the only ones who could judge his report from the shadow world of Gestapo and GPU.

Strangely enough, in the same year when Albert Walter turned to the *Verfassungsschutz*, Ernst Wollweber, who had been rudely removed from his post as head of the East German Secret Police after having been involved in a plot against the then leadership of East Germany, began writing down his version of the events. Unlike Albert Walter, however, who at least managed to have Richard Krebs's book censored according to his wishes, the ostracized Ernst Wollweber had no choice but to entrust his version to posterity.

Only long after his death, after the fall of the Wall, did it become known. It is quoted in detail in this book.

One might add that Ernst Wollweber attributed the Soviet order to end the sabotage activities to the huge wave of publicity triggered by the publication of *Out of the Night*. Here, however, he was mistaken. In November 1940, when the book was published, Wollweber had already been in Swedish custody for a long time, where he, who his principals had quickly declared to be a Soviet citizen, happily survived all extradition requests of the Third Reich.

Strangely enough, Hermann Knüfken also survived the war in Swedish custody, with the difference that he was much more endangered by the constant extradition requests of German authorities due to a lack of foreign citizenship.

The Swedes, who as neutrals did not want to antagonize anyone, finally solved this problem by sending Hermann Knüfken to an institution for the mentally ill, where he survived the war under strict secrecy and the pseudonym "Friday".

After the war he settled in Great Britain and wrote down, probably in 1956, the memories of his time as "Captain Kidd of the Comintern".

Of the three Germans, Walter, Wollweber and himself, who had played leading roles in the communist seafaring movement as well as in Richard Krebs's life, Hermann Knüfken was probably the one with the most peaceful old age. After several years in the port of London, where he - according to his biographer Dieter Nelles - worked for a British secret service, he joined the conservative party and lived until 1965 peacefully in a house by the sea.

Much later, in 1989, when all those involved had long since died, the epoch that had shaped Richard Krebs's life finally came to an end. After the fall of the Wall and the collapse of the Soviet Union, archives opened up in East and West, allowing a new view of his life. Thereby the most personal secret of Richard Krebs, the true story of his love for Hermine Stöver, has come to light. Files of the British and Soviet secret services, which are not yet accessible may contain more revelations. But the very fact that these files are still closed points to the fact that the world of secret apparatusses and hidden manipulators has merely entered a new stage.

Richard Krebs had long believed that he had freed himself from the network of GPU and Gestapo. His autobiographical novel *Out of the Night was* preceded by the lines of the poet William Ernest Henley:

»Out of the Night that covers me,

Black as the pit from pole to pole,
I thank whatever gods maybe
For my unconquerable soul.«

The man who thanked the gods for his invincible soul, which had allowed him to escape the night, had to realize towards the end of his life that it had been easier to physically escape from the German and Soviet secret services than from their imprints, which he had involuntarily adopted. His longing for a free, self-determined life remained unfulfilled.

APPENDIX

Abbreviations

ADGB *Allgemeiner Deutscher Gewerkschaftsbund*, General German Trade Union (SPD)

CIC Counter Intelligence Corps

Cheka (Tcheka) Extraordinary Commission to Combat Counterrevolution and sabotage

Comintern Communist International

EKKI *Executivkomitee der Kommunistischen Internationale*, Executive Committee (of the Comintern)

FRG Federal Republic of Germany

Gestapo *Geheime Staatspolizei* Nazi secret police

GPU State Political Administration USSR Political secret service from 1922 to 1924, thenceforth OGPU

GRU *Gosudarstvenoye Razvedyvatelnoye Upravleniye* Soviet Military Intelligence Later SMERSH

IAH *Internationale Arbeiterhilfe (IAH)* International Workers' Aid

INO *Inostranny Otdel* The foreign branch of the Soviet S Secret Service

ISH International of Seamen and Harbor workers

ITF International Transport Workers' Federation

IWW	Industrial Workers of the World (Wobblies)
IP(A)C-Transport	International Propaganda (and Action) Committee of Transport Workers
KPD	*Kommunistische Partei Deutschlands* German Communist Party
KPAD	*Kommunistische Arbeiterpartei Deutschlands* Communist Workers Party of Germany
NEP	New Economic Policy
NSBO	*Nationalsozialistische Betriebs[zellen]organization* The National Socialistic Trade Union [Cells].
NSDAP	*Nationalsozialistische Deutsche Arbeiterpartei* The National Socialist German Workers' Party (The Nazi Party)
OMS	*Otdel Mezdunarodnoi Svyaz* International Liason Department (Comintern's intelligence service)
OPDG	*Oldenburg-Portugesische Dampfschiffahrtsgesellschaft*. A private German/Portugese shipping company
OGPU	*Obedinnoje gosudarstwennoje Uprravlenie* All-Union State Political Board
Profintern	Red International of Labor Unions Union equivalent of the Comintern
RGO	*Revolutionäre Gewerkschafts-opposition* Revolutionary Union Opposition
SA	*Sturmabteilung* Storm division, the Nazi brown shirts
SD	*Sicherheitsdienst* Secret service (of the SS)
SED	*Sozialistische Einheitspartei Deutschlands* The Socialist Unity Party of Germany (Governing party of the GDR)
SMM	Seamen's Minority Movement — the British equivalent to the *Einheitsverband*
SPD	*Sozialdemokratische Partei Deutschlands*

	German Social Democratic Party
SS	*Schutzstaffel* Defence squadron The German special police force, originally Hitler's personal bodyguards
WEB	Western European Bureau (of the Comintern)

ENDNOTES

[1] Protocol of the Interrogation of Richard Krebs' by the American Immigration Service, Deportation Hearings of 28.3.1941 (from the estate of Richard Krebs, Mudd Library, Princeton)
[2] National Archives Washington, Espionage Norfolk, 95-402
[3] Paa Törn of January 1938
[4] National Archives Washington, Espionage Norfolk, 95-402
[5] Michael Rohrwasser: Der Stalinismus und die Renegaten. Stuttgart: Metzler 1991, p. 188
[6] Lars Borgersrud: Wollweber-organisasjonen i Norge (Acta Humaniora 7). Oslo: Universitetsforlaget 1997 - German: Die Wollweber Organisation und Norwegen. Berlin: Dietz Verlag 2001; Richard Jensen: Frem i Lyset. Jan Valtin, Gestapo Agent 51. Copenhagen: Prior 1946; Erik Nørgaard: Krigen for Krigen. wool weaver organizations or skibssabotagerne. Ask the spanske borgerkrieg til besættelsen af Denmark. Lynge: Bogan 1986; ders.: Drømmen om verdensrevolutionen.. Fra den russiske revolution til Hitlers magtovertagelse. Lynge: Bogan 1985; ders.: Truslem om Krig: Komintern, Folkefront og 5. kolonne. Fra Hitlers magtovertagelse til de spanske borgerkrig. Lynge: Bogan 1985.
[7] The information on the family originates, if not separately indicated, from the ancestor passport of the Krebs family of 1936 or from the genealogy of the Schmitthenner family, both in family ownership.
[8] This as all other citations from „Out of the night" are taken from this online publication: http://www.prosperosisle.org/spip.php?article877
[9] 3Abigail Alderman, the second wife of Richard Krebs, in conversation with the authour
[10] Documents of the Bremer Seefahrtsschule (seafaring school). The author thanks Michael Rohrwasser and Peter Ober for the copies.
[11] 12Sebastian Haffner: Verrat. Deutschland 1918/19th Berlin: Publisher 1900, 1993, p. 151
[12] National Archives, RG 319 IRR Personal Name File; Box 124 BB. This is the signature for the two hundred page file of the CIC of the US Army on Richard Krebs. The file is not numbered continuously. In the following, either the exact date of the letter and/or the subfile from which the citation or evidence is taken is given as a guide. This quotation is taken from the subact "San Quentin prison records". The subfiles contain the alphabetically ordered statements that Richard Krebs made about his former comrades in 1950, hereinafter referred to as "statements about ...".
[13] CIC, "Summary of information", 18.8.1943
[14] Outbound, reprinted in: Bend in the River. New York: Alliance Book Corporation 1942, p.50;
[15] Magellans in the Bunker, p. 2 ff. (from the estate).

[16] Ibid p.1
[17] Bundesarchiv Berlin, holdings RAM 39.01, no. 2511, unpaginated
[18] Ibida, p. 118, London, 4.10.1920. The author thanks Hartmut Rübner for the copies from the Bundesarchiv Berlin
[19] Paul Borowiak: Unpublished manuscript on the resistance of seamen in the Third Reich (owned by the author).
[20] See Richard Krebs: Where and how to check the facts in Out of the Night (from the estate, 1941 or 1942). List with biographical stations of Richard Krebs and information about where you can check them. In this case verifiable by British immigration records in the port of Hull.
[21] Cited after Walter Tomin: Die Weimarer Republik. Hanover: Fackelträger-Verlag 1973, p. 123
[22] See Where and how to check the facts in Out of the Night
[23] ErnstToller: A youth in Germany. Reinbek: Rowohlt Paperback Publisher 1963, p. 110
[24] Victor Serge: Memoirs of a Revolutionary. London: Oxford University Press 1967, S. 159
[25] Bernd Kaufmann/Eckhard Reisener/Dieter Schwips: Der Nachrichstendienst der KPD 1919-1937. Berlin: Dietz Verlag 1993, p. 79
[26] Ibida p80
[27] Cited after Hartmut Rübner: Arbeit, Milieu und Konfliktverhalten. Syndicalism in shipping until the 1930s. In: Archiv für die Geschichte des Widerstands und der Arbeit, Issue 16/2001. Fernwald: Germinal Verlag, S. 183.
[28] First part of the quotation: Rübner, p. 183; second part from the unabridged original manuscript of the same text.
[29] Unpublished manuscript by Bernhard H. Bayerlein on the OMS, p. 23 ff.
[30] CIC, Statement on Hermann Knüfken, p. 52
[31] Unpublished memoirs of Hermann Knüfken
[32] Quoted after Dieter Nelles: Das abenteuerliche Leben des Hermann Knüfken. In: ÖTV-Report Seefahrt, Issue 3/September 1996, S. 13-22.
[33] Knüfken Memoirs
[34] Ibida
[35] CIC, statement about Daul-Sisters
[36] Ibid
[37] Cited after Bernd Kaufmann et al: KPD Nachrichtendienst, p. 87
[38] See: Down by the River, S.187, Juanita, S. 219 in: Bend in the River
[39] See Where and how to check the facts in Out of the Night, S. 2
[40] Ibid
[41] Ibid
[42] RCChIDNI 534/164/5
[43] Ibid sheet 25, letter of 2.5.1924
[44] Knüfken Memoirs
[45] In the biography of the most important actor of the INO (subdivision of the Soviet secret police responsible for foreign countries), the later defector Alexander Orlov relates about the relations between OMS and OGPU, that after Lenin's death there was a power struggle between Felix Dzershinski, the head of the Secret Police, and the leadership of the Komintern. The question was whether the OMS should continue to be responsible for the gathering of news from abroad and how much influence the OGPU

should have on the work of the Comintern. Not least because the Comintern had no notable successes in espionage, Felix Dsershinski won all along the line. (Oleg Zarew/John Costello: Der Super Agent. Vienna: Zsolnay 1993, p. 74.)

[46] Knüfken's statement of 28.6.40, P 423, Löp 2, SA/S Ar-chiv of the security police Stockhholm; CIC, statement about Avatin; BA-ZW, Z/C 14299, vol. 1-2, Agentn file "Erka", folder "Oststaaten", Lambert/Avatin. For Avatin see also Borgersrud.

[47] Magellans in the Bunker, p. 7 f.

[48] In defence he wrote Where and how to check the facts in Out of the Night

[49] See CIC, Summary of investigation

[50] Deportation Hearings, 18 March 1941, p. 33 ff

[51] See Where and how to check the facts in Out of the Night, S. 3

[52] Ibid

[53] CIC, San Quentin prison records

[54] Ibid

[55] CIC, 28.8.1943, and Paul Borowiak's interview with Ede Nikolajczik (in the author's possession).

[56] Bend in the River, p. 102 f

[57] Ibid p.72

[58] Gil Rankins: Jan Valtin in San Quentin. Manuscript from the estate of Richard Krebs, page 4 ff.

[59] Ibid

[60] Ibid page 6

[61] Bend in the River, S. 56

[62] .Ibid, p. 140. On McNamara see also Mike Davis: City of Quartz. New York: Vintage Books 1992, p. 32.

[63] Rankins: Jan Valtin in San Quentin, p. 8

[64] Bend in the River, p. 43.

[65] Rankins: Jan Valtin in San Quentin, p. 10

[66] Bend in the River, p. 32

[67] Ibid

[68] Ibid page, xxxi

[69] We only know about this way of transmission because Richard Krebs mentions it on a piece of paper in connection with a short sketch of Albert Walter. The address given on this sheet (88th Street) indicates that Krebs must have written the note in 1939 or early 1940.

[70] Bend in the River, p. 102

[71] Ibid p.210

[72] Ibid p. 215 f.

[73] Ibid p.210ff

[74] 1Friedrich Firsov: Die Säuberung im Komintern Apparat. In: Hermann Weber: Kommunisten verfolgen Kommunisten. Berlin: Academy Publisher 1993, p. 39 f.

[75] Cited after Alexander Vatlin: Die Komintern 1919-1929 Mainz: Decaton Verlag 1993, p. 179.

[76] Ibid p190

[77] Documents of the Bremer Seefahrtsschule as well as files from the Bremer Staatsarchiv are thanks to Peter Ober and Michael Rohrwasser

[78] Jorge Semprun: Was für ein schooner Sonntag. Frankfurt: Suhrkamp Taschenbuch 1984, p. 186.
[79] Ibid
[80] Arbeiterpolitik. Stuttgart, Vol. 11, No. 10 dated May 22, 58, p. 8 f. Following citations as „Arbeiterpolitik"
[81] CIC, statement about Gehrke
[82] See also Stephen Koch: Double Lives - Spies and Writers in the Secret Soviet War of Ideas against the West. New York: The Free Press 1994. First history of the IAH, for which files of the previously closed archive of the Comintern in Moscow were used.
[83] Richard Krebs to Arthur L. Price (from the estate).
[84] Compilation of excerpts from letters from Bremen in 1930/31 sent back to Richard Krebs by Arthur L. Price (from the estate).
[85] Arbeiterpolitik (see previous endnote)
[86] Staatsarchiv Bremen, 4,65-563, provided to the author by Michael Rohrwasser.
[87] Ibid
[88] Ibid
[89] Lagebericht der Gestapo Hamburg, 24.6.1939, Reports of the agents deployed in the Port of Hamburg and at the shipyards. Provided to the author by Karin Ney.
[90] About Alfred Bem see: Feliks Tych : Słownik Biograficzny Dzialaczy Polskiego Ruchu Robotniczego (Museum of the History of the Polish Revolutionary Movement, Vol. I, 1978), S. 139 f., as well as RCChIDNI, Kaderakte Polen 419, Alfred Stolarski aka Alfred Bem
[91] BA-ZW, Z/C 13936, vol. 8. Evaluation of a report by Erka 26.2.1938, Berlin, 23.4.1938
[92] CIC, statement about Alfred Bem
[93] Ibid
[94] RCChIDNI 534/5/221, page 4
[95] Staatsarchiv Bremen, 4.65-564.
[96] RCChIDNI 534/5/231, page 80
[97] RCChIDNI 534/5/227, page 21
[98] Ibid page 23/24
[99] Ibid 534/5/223, p. 134, report on strike preparation
[100] Cited from an unpublished manuscript by Paul Borowiak on the seamen's resistance (owned by the author)
[101] RCCHIDNI 534/5/223, pp. 48-66, report on the seamen's strike, 29.11.1931
[102] CIC, statement about Alfred Bem
[103] RCChIDNI 534/5/223, page 59
[104] Ibid p.60
[105] Ibid
[106] Ibid p. 61
[107] Ibid p. 64
[108] Ibid p. 66
[109] See Knüfken
[110] RCChIDNI 534/5/223, page 64
[111] The information is taken from Paul Borowiak's interview with Ede Nikolajczik
[112] RCChIDNI 534/5/223, page 66
[113] The author thanks Ruth Weihe for the information that some of these sailors were sent back to Germany after the Hitler-Stalin Pact.

[114] RCChIDNI 534/5/227, page 37 f
[115] Cf.Dieter Nelles: Jan Valtins Tagebuch der Hölle Journal 1999, Hamburg, No. 1 (1994), p. 19
[116] Letter from the German Consulate General in Leningrad to the German Embassy in Moscow dated 27 October 1931, p. 3. Political Archive of the Federal Foreign Office, made available to the author by Paul Borowiak.
[117] See RCChIDNI 534/5/231, Bl. 34, and CIC, The International of Seamen and Harbour Workers
[118] RCChIDNI 534/5/227, page 60
[119] Nelles: Jan Valtins Tagebuch der Hölle, p. 18
[120] RCChIDNI 534/5/231, page 38
[121] 51Cf. Franz Jung: Der Weg nach unten. Neuwied/Berlin: Luchterhand Verlag 1961, p. 145
[122] The German part, as is apparent from the text, dates from 1956, the English part from either the same year or the previous year. Knüfken describes the Soviet secret police as MWD; it was only called MWD from March 1953-March 1954. Then it was renamed KGB.
[123] CIC, testimony about Hugo Marx
[124] Cf. CIC, statement on Wilhelm Soltau; see also RCChIDNI 534/5/231, p. 34 for an attempt by the Hamburg party leadership to put Interklub under financial pressure by means of the "Einheit" stevedoring works
[125] Zoja Voskresenskaja: Pod psevdonimom Irina. Moscow: Sovremennik 1997, p. 143
[126] CIC, statement about Ernst Wollweber; there biographical information about Wollweber, which had been passed on by the British to the CIC
[127] On the conflicts between Bem and Wollweber see also RCChIDNI 534/5/234, p. 119, as well as Borgersrud, who bases his description of the conflict on Wollweber's memoirs; see Borgersrud: Die Wollweber-Organisation, p. 25.
[128] CIC Statement about Wollweber
[129] Interview of Paul Borowiak with Ede Nikolajczik
[130] Interview of the author with Helmut Warnke, late autumn 1995
[131] Quoted after Nelles: Jan Valtins Tagebuch der Hölle, p. 22
[132] SAPMO NJ/10324, page 12
[133] also Rohrwasser: Stalinismus, p. 221, and SAPMO R58/3440, p. 4
[134] CIC, testimony about George Mink
[135] See SAPMO NJ/14498, indictment and verdict Hermine (Stöver)
[136] The author thanks Peter Ober and Michael Rohrwasser for their address book research
[137] See Deportation Hearings Protocol
[138] Comintern Agent (from the estate), probably 1939
[139] Cited after G. M. Adibekov/E. N. Šachnazarova/K. K. Šikrinja: Organizacionnaja Struktura Kominterna 1919-1943. Moscow: Rosspen 1997, p. 138
[140] See Harvey Klehr/John Earl Haynes/Fridrikh Igorevich Firsov: The Secret World of American Communism (Annals of Communism). New Haven and London: Yale University Press 1995; Harvey Klehr/John Earl Haynes/ Kyril M. Anderson: The Soviet World of American Communism. New Haven and London, Yale University Press 1998
[141] On the Zinoviev affair, see Oleg Zarew/John Costello: Der Superagent. Vienna: Zsolnay 1993, p. 89. Information on British deciphering techniques comes from Barry McLoughlin

[142] RCChIDNI 534/5/223, page 92
[143] On the subject of the East Indian Seafarers' Association, see Krebs's statement to the Gestapo on George Hardy, BA-ZW, Z/C 14299
[144] RCChIDNI 534/5/227, page 60
[145] Hardy about Thompson cf., 534/5/231, pp. 15-17, and 534/5/236, pp. 3
[146] RCChIDNI 534/5/231, page 55
[147] Ibid page 60
[148] RCChIDNI 534/5/236 page 54
[149] Lars Borgersrud: Die Wollweber Organisation, p. 36
[150] RCChIDNI 534/5/236, page 53
[151] SAPMO R58/2161, page 14
[152] Bernd Kaufman et al: KPD Nachrichtendienst, p. 267
[153] This episode is described by Jan Valtin in Out of the Night; Richard Krebs retold it to his son Jan after the war (author's interview with Jan Krebs, California, early summer 1996)
[154] 91Cited after Dieter Nelles: WIderstand und international Solidarität. Essen: Klartext Verlag 2001, p. 134.
[155] Report on the Waterkant situation 11 September 1933, RCChIDNI 534/5/236, p. 111
[156] National Archives,Washington,146-13-3-14-3. Enemy Alien Control Unit,file Richard Krebs. Further cited as "Enemy Alien"
[157] RCChIDNI 534/5/236, page 53
[158] Enemy alien
[159] Lars Borgersrud: Nødvendig innsats. Oslo, Universitetsforlaget 1997. Chapter "Krebs to reiser til Norge"
[160] Ibid
[161] Gerhard Paul/Klaus-Michael Mallmann (Ed.): Die Gestapo, Mythos und Realität. Darmstadt: Wissenschaftliche Buchgesellschaft 1995, p. 104
[162] BA-ZW, Z/C 14299, vol. 1-2, Agent file "Erka", statement about Halvorsen
[163] Cf.indictment, criminal case against Popovics and comrades, Hamburg, 20.2.1934, p. 2 f.; made available to the author by Dieter Nelles
[164] CIC, testimony about Sabor
[165] Cited after Nelles: Widerstand, p. 132
[166] RCChIDNI 534/5/236, direct and circular letter, 8.5.1933
[167] Ibid, pp. 49 f.: Situation in Germany
[168] Ibid p 79
[169] Ibid
[170] About Hermine trip see SAPMO NJ/14498, indictment and verdict Hermine Stöver
[171] Cf. CIC, statements on Schmitt and Avatin
[172] Cf CIC, statement about Jensen; for the Danish ISH section see RCChINDNI 534/5/236, p. 53
[173] Statement about Jensen in BA-ZW, Z/C 14299, vol. 1-2
[174] The unpublished memoirs of Hildegard Thingstrup were made available to the author by Erik Nørgaard
[175] RCChIDNI, cadre file Poland 419, p. 37
[176] Ibid, p. 70, dated 24.11.1933.
[177] Cf CIC, statement on Hildegard Volkersen

[178] CIC statement about Wollweber
[179] Quoted after Nelles: Widerstand, p. 134
[180] Cf.Bernd Kaufmann et al: KPD Nachrichtendienst, p. 278
[181] Erik Nørgaard: Truslem om Krig: Comintern, Folkefront and 5th column. Fra Hitlers magtovertagelse til de spanske borger-krig Lynge: Bogan 1985, p. 78
[182] For Holstein, see SAPMO Sgy 30/1036/1, p. 53 ff., Wollweber memoirs
[183] Cf SAPMO NJ/1179/33, indictment and verdict against , Thingstrup and others
[184] SAPMO R58/2335, page 87
[185] SAPMO I 2/3/101, p. 137 f.
[186] Biographic note on Peter Kraus from Getrud Mayer: *Nacht über Hamburg.* Frankfurt/Main: Röderberg-Verlag 1971, p. 120, and Gerhard Paul/Klaus-Michael Mallmann (ed.): *Die Gestapo: Mythos und Realität*. P. 104.
[187] Enemy Alien Krebs, Burling report, p. 10
[188] SAPMO NJ/1179/33, P. 11 ff., accusation and verdict: Krebs, Thingstrup et al.
[189] SAPMO NJ/1179/33, P. 11 ff., accusation and verdict: Krebs, Thingstrup et al.
[190] Ibid, 13225/2, p. 15, recorded statement: Richard Krebs, 2.1.1934, following quotations also from same source, p. 2 ff.
[191] SAPMO NJ/10324, p. 19
[192] CIC, Statement on Nettkau.
[193] SAPMO NJ/1179/33, P. 47, Accusation and verdict: Krebs et al.
[194] Ibid, p. 37.
[195] Ibid, p. 40.
[196] Cf. Statement on Bem, BA-ZW, Z/C 14299, Vols. 1–2, 18.3.1937.
[197] Cf. SAPMO NJ/1179/33, last page.
[198] Erik Nørgaard: *Truslem om Krig*, p. 60.
[199] CIC, Statement on Beilich.
[200] SAPMO NJ/132225/2, 10.3.1934, minutes of interrogation: Hermann Beilich, p. 12.
[201] Ibid, p. 1.
[202] Nelles: *Jan Valtins Tagebuch der Hölle*, p. 26.
[203] Nelles: *Widerstand und internationale Solidarität*, p. 137.
[204] Nelles: *Widerstand und internationale Solidarität* (unpublished version). Dieter Nelles bases his argument on the prosecution records of the Hansa League High Court for the trial of Anneliese Beilich and Karl Grüninger, .9.2. 1937, in: BA-ZW 19046.
[205] Bundesarchiv Potsdam, PSt3, 26, P. 63 ff. Message to the Chief of Police (Political division), 8.14 1934.
[206] SAPMO NJ/14498, Prosecution document: Hermine Krebs, p. 7.
[207] Ibid, Verdict: Hermine Krebs, p. 9.
[208] Cf. Bernd Kaufmann et al: Der *Nachrichtendienst der KPD*, p. 420.
[209] CIC, Statement on Albert Walter.
[210] CIC, Statement on Herman Beilich.
[211] Ibid
[212] The Execution of Bert Adrian (unpublished), p. 9.
[213] Arthur Koestler: *The Invisible Writing, being the second volume of Arrow in the Blue*, New York, The MacMillan Company, 1954, p. 388
[214] SAPMO R58/ 2235, Report on the investigation document pertaining to Willendorf and others (Conspiracy to commit High Treason), Hamburg, November 24, 1936. (The naming of the Fuhlsbüttel investigation after Willendorf was an initial mistake. For technical reasons the Gestapo kept the name after having recognized their error.)

215 BA-ZW, Z/C 16125, Vol. 1,p. 6 a.
216 BA-ZW, Z/C 16125, Vol. 1,p. 6 a.
217 SAPMO R58/ 2235, p. 41, Report on the investigation document pertaining to Willendorf and others (Conspiracy to commit High Treason, Hamburg, November 24, 1936.
218 BA-ZW, Z/C 16125, Vol. 2, p. 10 f.
219 Cf. CIC, Statement on Karl Schaar
220 Semprun: *Was für ein schöner Sonntag*, p. 143.
221 SAPMO R58/ 2235, P. 79, final report and addenda on the Willendorf matter, Hamburg, 2. 22.1937.
222 Ibid, p. 81.
223 Ibid, p. 82.
224 Ibid, p. 79.
225 BA-ZW, Z/C 16125 Vol. 1, p. 29.
226 Ibid, P. 31f.

227 Ibid, vol.1-2, Agent file "Erka"
228 54Erik Nørgaard: An Gestapo agent sendes til Kobenhavn. In: Information. Copenhagen, 29.4.1985.
229 Bernd Kaufmann et al: KPD Nachrichtendienst, p. 406.
230 Luise Kraushaar,(ed): Deutsche Widerstandskämpfer 1933-1945. 2 vols. Berlin: Dietz Verlag 1970; Vol. 2, pp. 123-128.
231 CIC, testimony about Anton Saefkow
232 Letter of 4.12.1938 to Margaret (from the estate).
233"The Execution of Bert Adrian, p. 13.
234 63Cf . Bernd Kaufmann et al: KPD Nachrichtendienst, p. 414.
235 Gertrud Meyer: Nacht über Hamburg. Frankfurt/Main: Röderberg-Verlag, p. 128 f.
236 BA-ZW, Z/C 14299, vol. 1-2, quote from the report "Geldquellen der ISH".
237 BA-ZW, Z/C 14299, vol. 1-2.
238 CIC, testimony about Otto Kemnitz.
239 RCChIDNI, cadre file Poland 419, Alfred Stolarski alias Alfred Bem, p. 142.
240 Ibid page 137.
241 Nørgaard: Krigen for Krigen, p. 39 f.
242 Ibid p.40
243 Erik Nørgaard: A Gestapo agent senders til Kobenhavn.
244 Nørgaard: Krigen for Krigen, p. 43.
245 SAPMO, Sgy 30/1036/1, page 55, memorial file Wollweber.
246 BA-ZW, Z/C 14299, vol. 1-2.
247 SAPMO R58/2042, p. 363 ff., Subject: Agent Aage aus Kopenhagen, Lübeck, 1 November 1937.
248 Nørgaard: Krigen for Krigen, p. 20.
249 85Nelles: WIderstand, p. 154.
250 Ibid., Chapter IV.
251 Nelles: Jan Valtins Tagebuch, p. 36.
252 BA-ZW, Z/C 13936, vol. 8, Hamburg the 5.8.1937.
253 BA-ZW, Z/C 13936, vol. 8.
254 BA-ZW, Z/C 14299, vol. 1-2.
255 BA-ZW, Z/C 13936, vol. 8, Hamburg the 5.8.1937.

[256] BA-ZW, Z/C 14299, vol. 1-2, Hamburg the 30.8.1937.
[257] CIC, statement about Wollweber.
[258] BA-ZW, Z/C 13936-8, Agent file "Erka".
[259] SAPMO, Sgy 30/1036/1: Memorial file Wollweber, page 53.
[260] Nørgaard: Krigen for Krigen, p. 40.
[261] BA-ZW, Z/C 13936-8, Agent file "Erka", report of Agent "Erka" of 10. 12. 1937, Berlin, 18.12.1937.
[262] Ibid, Berlin, 23.4.1938, evaluation of the Erka report of 21.2.1938.
[263] Ibid, Berlin, 10.12.1937.
[264] Archive of Social Democracy of the Friedrich-Ebert-Stiftung, J 88, JSK 34. The author thanks Dieter Nelles for the copy of the letter.
[265] Modern records center, University of Warwick, 159/3/c/a/47. The author thanks Dieter Nelles for the copy.
[266] BA-ZW, Z/C 13936-8, Agentn file "Erka", Berlin, 26.2.1938, report of the V-person "Erka" of 21.2.1938.
[267] Politisches Archiv des Auswärtigen Amts, R 99929, Ausweisungsakte Richard Krebs, Letter of 23 June 1941 from the Chief of the Security Police and the SD. In the following Ausweisungsakte with date.
[268] Nørgaard: Krigen for Krigen, p. 59.
[269] Reader's letter from Richard Krebs to the editorial staff of the magazine The Call, 24.11.1946 (from the estate).
[270] National Archives, Washington, Espionage Norfolk 95-402
[271] Ibid, letter of 1.3.1938.
[272] BA-ZW, Z/C 13936-8, Agentn file "Erka", Berlin, 26.2.1938. From report of "Erka" of 21.2.1938.
[273] CIC, statement about Max Bareck.
[274] Benjamin Gitlow: Whole of their lives. New York: C. Scribner's Sons 1948, S. 328.
[275] National Archives, Washington, Espionage Norfolk 95–402.
[276] BA-ZW, Z/C 13936,
[277] From the estate.
[278] Letter of 6 December 1938 (from the estate).
[279] On Bek-Gran see Deutschsprachige Exilliteratur, Band 3, Teil 3, P. 3 Robert Bek-Gran (Ernst von Waldenfels). Zürich und München 2005
[280] Interview of the author with Abigail Alderman, summer 1996.
[281] Enemy Alien Krebs, 17.12.1942, FBI report, p. 20.
[282] Gitlow: Whole of their lives, S. 329.
[283] See Enemy Alien Krebs, 17.12.1942, FBI-Report, p. 20 f.
[284] Interview of the author with Abigail Alderman, summer 1996.
[285] P.M. 17.3.1941.
[286] 21 New York Times, 19 January 1941.
[287] New Masses, 4.3.1941.
[288] Ernst Bloch: "Verrat und Verräter", Freies Deutschland, I, No. 3, Jan. 15, 1942, p. 19.
[289] Karl Korsch (Pseudonym L. H.), »Revolution for what? A critical comment on Jan Valtin's Out of the Night«, Living Marxism, Chicago, V, Nr. 4, Spring 1941, P. 21–29..
[290] P.M., New York, »The truth about Jan Valtin«, 3.3.1941.
[291] Gerald Smith to Jan Valtin, 12.5.1942 (from the estate).
[292] Richard Krebs's expatriation file.

[293] PM, 17.3.1941.
[294] PM, 17.3.1941.
[295] .PM, 17.3.1 33Interview recording, private property Abigail Alderman, undated.
[296] Deportation Hearings protocol, p. 49 f
[297] CIC, San Quentin Prison Records.
[298] Cf.letter from Gil "Pat" Rankins to Richard Krebs, 4.10.1941, Rankins to Eckhart, 2.2.1942 (from the estate).
[299] Author's interview with Abigail Alderman, 1996.
[300] Richard Krebs's expatriation file, secret telegram, signed Thomsen, Washington, May 31, 1941.
[301] See letter Mandel to Levine 2. April 1941: »By the way. I just spoke to J. B. [Dies] He says you told him that V. would have nothing to do with the committee. If you did that it was unwise. He is sore about that ...« (from the estate).
[302] Neue Volkszeitung and letter of 16.6.1941 (from the estate).
[303] FBI file Erich Krewet; for a copy of the file the author thanks Dieter Nelles.
[304] Richard Krebs's expatriation file, secret telegram, signed Thomsen, Washington, May 31, 1941.
[305] See Expatriation File, The Chief of the Security Police and the SD, Berlin, 23 June 1941, Schnellbrief.
[306] Deportation Hearings Protocol, 17.4.1941, p. 80.
[307] Enemy alien .
[308] Deportation Hearings Protocol, 17.4.1941, p. 80.
[309] Enemy Alien Krebs, 26.2.1943, Message from J. Edgar Hoover to the Head of the Enemy Alien Control Unit, Edward J. Ennis.
[310] "Additional suggestions", script suggestions, undated (from the estate).
[311] Isaac Don Levine: Mitchell, pioneer of air power. New York: Duell, Sloan and Pearce 1943.
[312] Richard Krebs to Dorothy Donnell Calhoun, 31.1.1942 (from the estate).
[313] New York Times, 10.5.1942; Los Angeles Times, 16.5.1942.
[314] On "ABC of sabotage" and its distribution by the US Navy, see Richard Krebs to Roger Baldwin, Ellis Island, 29.11.1942.
[315] National Archives, Washington, Enemy Alien Control Unit, file Erich Krewet, 146-13-2-12-71. In the following quoted as Enemy Alien Krewet.
[316] Biographical information about Erich Krewet here and in the following from Enemy Alien Krewet, Enemy Alien Krebs, Nelles: Widerstand und internationale Solidarität, p. 256 ff., FBI files Erich Krewet and CIC, statement about Erich Krewet.
[317] Public prosecutor's office at the Hanseatic Higher Regional Court, 20.2.1934, criminal case against Popovics and comrades for preparation for high treason, copy for the defendant Otto Gustav Kemnitz, p. 7 f., for the copy of the indictment the author thanks Dieter Nelles.
[318] Enemy Alien Krebs, report Burling, p. 10.
[319] Enemy Alien Krebs, Burling report, p. 8.
[320] 61Nelles: Widerstand, p. 257.
[321] Enemy Alien Krewet, letter from Edo Fimmen to E. Rix (pseudonym of Krewet), Amsterdam, 26 June 1938.
[322] See Harvey Klehr/John E. Haynes: Communists and the CIO. From the Soviet Archives. In: Labor History 35, no. 3 (Sommer 1994), S. 442–446.

[323] Enemy Alien Krewet, FBI-Report, Los Angeles 7.7.1942, statement about mother-in-law, p. 5, statement about Bridges, p. 11.
[324] Enemy Alien Krebs, Burling, p. 13, Burling refers to the FBI as proof that Krewet was not a Communist; quote from the report of March 16, 1943, p. 15.
[325] "Valtin Agent of Nazis", Daily Worker, 26.11.1942.
[326] Quoted from Daily Worker, 22.12.1942, p. 7.
[327] Expatriation file, 16.1.1943.
[328] Letter of 29.11.1942, Ellis Island (from the estate).
[329] Three-page manuscript "Who's who" (from the estate). From the content it follows that it was written by Richard Krebs on Ellis Island for a friend who was out there looking after his interests.
[330] Enemy Alien Krebs, Report Burling, p. 10.
[331] Ibida ,FBI Report on Richard Krebs, p. 24. Translation
[332] Ibid, Burling report, p. 14.
[333] Ibid J. Edgar Hoover to Attorney General, 2.2.1943.
[334] Ibid, report signed Collier, 16.3.1943, p. 18ff.
[335] On Ellis Island see Richard Krebs: "Memorandum on the liquidation of a pro-nazi organization on Ellis Island" (from the estate) and the article "Charge 4 Aided Fronter Bishop", New York Post, 15.7.1943 (Bishop was head of the Nazi organization on Ellis Island); quote from CIC, 28.8.1943, Headquarters Camp Upton, New York.
[336] Jan Valtin: Castle in the Sand. New York: The Beechhurst Press 1947, p. 494 f.
[337] CIC, 29.3.1944, Headquarters Camp Upton, New York.
[338] CIC, 12.2.1944, War Department Intelligence Division.
[339] Jan Valtin: Children of Yesterday. New York: The Reader's Press 1946.
[340] Margarete to Richard Krebs, 25.3.1946 (from the estate).
[341] Estate Richard Krebs to Hugo "Peps" Krebs, May 11, 1946.
[342] Abigail Alderman in conversation with the author.
[343] 15.4.1949 (from the estate).
[344] Rohrwasser: Stalinismus, p. 208.
[345] From the estate.
[346] Jan Valtin: Wintertime. New York: The Beachhurst Press, 1950.
[347] From the estate
[348] CIC, statement about Wollweber
[349] CIC, April 13, 1950, Personality Information on Richard Krebs, last page.
[350] Roger Baldwin to Richard Krebs, 30.1.1950 (from the estate).
[351] "Dear Bill", 8.3.1950 (from the estate).
[352] Don Levine to Richard Krebs, 10. 10. 1950 (from the estate).
[353] Rohrwasser: Stalinismus, p. 209
[354] Hugo Krebs to Clara Medders, 10.1.1951, Bremen (from the estate).
[355] Clara Medders to John Schaffner, 14.5.1967 (from the estate).
[356] Clara Medders to Billy and Jane, 29.1.1951 (from the estate).
[357] CIC, Office Memorandum, 30.1.1957, Subject: Book »Out of the Night« by Jan Valtin (Richard Krebs) »Re: Albert Walter«.

INDEX

A

Abramov-Mirov, Alexander Lasarevitsch.... 23
Adams.. 87
Alexander 23, 86, 215, 216
Andresen, Kitty 144, 147
Anja, Frau von Leo 102
Anton....... see Wollweber, Ernst, sAnton aka Wollweber, Ernst 77, 99, 100, 123, 124, 125, 127, 128, 129, 146, 221
Appel, Jan 22
Appelman, Mike................................... 146, 147
Atschkanov, Grigori 28
Avatin, Michael .. 30, 31, 32, 36, 99, 100, 113, 133, 144, 145, 146, 147, 216, 219

B

Baldwin, Roger .. 192, 194, 203, 207, 223, 224
Bandura 27, 28, 29, 32
Barbusse, Henri... 104
Bareck, Max 80, 158, 222
Baum, Vicki... 53, 81
Bayerlein, Bernhard H. 215
Beilich, Hermann 113, 114, 115, 116, 117, 119, 128, 140, 141, 150, 220
Bek-Gran, Robert 162, 163, 167, 169, 190, 222
Bem, Alfred .. 59, 65, 133, 137, 140, 146, 147, 171, 217, 218, 220, 221
Bem, Danuta Alfredowna 137
Billy 183, 207, 225
Bismarck, Otto von 8
Bloch, Ernst 172, 223
Bond, Richard.. 202
Borgersrud, Lars.... 93, 94, 214, 216, 218, 219
Borowiak, Paul .. 118, 119, 215, 216, 217, 218
Brandler, Heinrich... 25
Bready 15
Brecht, Bertolt... 140
Bridges, Harry 190, 224
Brüning, Heinrich 70
Buck, Pearl S... 172
Bukharin, Nikolai Ivanovitsch 48, 75, 104, 137

Burling 187, 188, 190, 193, 194, 195, 220, 224

C

Cash, Jonny.. 39
Chisholm.. 46
Cilly .... see Caecilie Krebs,
Clausewitz, Carl von 35
Conrad, Gert.................................... 127, 136
Cook, James 8
Cooley 194
Cooper, J.F. 6, 8

D

Darwin, Charles 126
Daul-Sisters...25, 215
Deter 69, 150, 152, 153, 158
Deutschmann 108
Dimitroff, Georgi 169
Dorothy...184, 223
Dose 122
DuBois, W.E.B. 201

E

Eastman, Max....................................166, 194
Ehrenburg, Ilja 201
Emmerich, Julius 186, 187, 188, 193
Engels, Friedrich 35

F

Felix, Hans................................ 4, 156, 157, 215
Feuchtwanger, Lion.............................62, 140
Fimmen, Edo 96, 138, 142, 151, 152, 157, 158, 189, 190, 224
Finkelstein, Sidney 201
Firsov, Friedrich......................... 48, 216, 218
Fitsch................................see Krebs, Hermine
Ford, Henry.. 182
Foss, Leif O. 88, 93
Fouché, Joseph.. 125
Foxworth 179, 182

Franco, Francisco 2, 4, 115, 121
Frank, Hans 132
Fred 59, 86, 198

G

Gehrke 50, 51, 217
Gertrud 221
Gitlow, Benjamin 160, 166, 182, 222
Goebbels, Joseph 56, 170
Goethe, Johann Wolfgang von 104
Goodstein, Morris L. 177, 192
Göring, Hermann 162, 183
Gross, Dr. 55
Günther, Hans. F. K. 126
Guttmann, Kenny 27

H

Haffner, Sebastian 10, 214
Hahn, Edwin F. 38
Halvorsen, Arne 94, 219
Hardy, George 84, 85, 86, 87, 88, 219
Harris, Abigail 167, 171
Harry 3, 86, 190
Haynes, Earl 180, 218, 224
Haywood, Big Bill 32
Hearst, William Randolph 167, 172
Heckert, Fritz 90
Heinzelmann 80, 110, 111
Heitmann 130, 138
Helms, Paul 127
Henley, William Ernest 210
Herma .... see Krebs, Hermine
Herma that is Krebs, Hermine ... 56, 113, 114, 186, 189
Heydrich, Reinhard 127
Hitler, Adolf . 16, 49, 52, 56, 62, 69, 78, 89, 90, 91, 94, 95, 96, 100, 101, 105, 111, 117, 118, 126, 131, 132, 134, 135, 149, 161, 162, 163, 165, 167, 171, 176, 181, 182, 184, 186, 188, 189, 195, 196, 198, 201, 205, 213, 218
Holstein, Martin 106, 114, 150, 220
Hoover, Herbert... 5, 165, 179, 180, 181, 182, 195, 223, 224
Hoover, J. Edgar... 5, 165, 179, 180, 181, 182, 195, 223, 224
Hugenberg, Alfred 51
Humbert-Droz, Jules 48

J

Jahn, Hans 151, 153
Jane 207, 225
Jensen, Martin .. 100, 101, 105, 134, 136, 137, 138, 139, 140, 141, 145, 146, 147, 148, 149, 158, 160, 167, 202, 214, 219
Jensen, Richard 100, 101, 105, 134, 136, 137, 138, 139, 140, 141, 145, 146, 147, 148, 149, 158, 160, 167, 202, 214, 219
Jeschke, Hans Felix 156, 157
Jung, Franz 22, 73, 75, 218

K

Kamenev, Lew Borissovitch 48, 137
Kaufmann, Bernd 18, 215, 220, 221
Kemnitz, Otto 134, 221, 224
Kesselring, Albert 204
Knüfken, Hermann . 21, 22, 23, 27, 28, 36, 69, 72, 73, 74, 75, 80, 142, 143, 144, 151, 152, 153, 154, 156, 157, 158, 189, 210, 215, 216, 217, 218
Knüfken, Sonia 74
Koestler, Arthur 121, 164, 165, 175, 221
Korsch, Karl 172, 223
Koschnick 77
Kraus, Peter 94, 108, 115, 125, 128, 131, 132, 134, 139, 144, 145, 152, 154, 161, 220, 221
Krebs, Annemarie 7, 198
Krebs, Conrad 40, 52, 103, 127, 136, 168, 175, 199
Krebs, Eric 155, 171, 199, 200
Krebs, Hermine 53, 54, 71, 81, 90, 91, 95, 103, 112, 113, 114, 115, 116, 117, 119, 120, 128, 129, 135, 136, 141, 147, 148, 156, 157, 159, 160, 161, 162, 193, 198, 200, 202, 206, 210, 218, 219, 220
Krebs, Hugo jun. 6, 7, 8, 9, 18, 25, 76, 135, 136, 156, 157, 198, 218, 224, 225
Krebs, Julius 7, 131, 135, 180, 186, 193
Krebs, Martina 135, 157
Krebs, Pauline 7, 11, 16, 135
Krewet, Erich 65, 146, 147, 179, 181, 185, 186, 187, 188, 189, 190, 193, 194, 223, 224
Krivitzki, Walter 164
Kuusinen, Otto 146

L

LaFarge, Oliver 173
Lambert, Ernest see Avatin, Mi- chael30, 99, 143, 216
Lamm, Staffan 74
Lamont, Corliss 201
Larsen, Axel 102, 127, 137
Lehmann, Kurt 152, 153, 158
Lenin, Vladimir Iljitch 17, 20, 22, 35, 36, 45, 46, 47, 87, 108, 125, 137, 164, 209, 215
Leo 88, 102
Lewis, Sinclair 31
Liebknecht, Karl 77
Ludendorff, Erich von 8
Luxemburg, Rosa 17, 77
Lyons, Eugene 165, 166, 180, 194

M

Magellan, Fernão 8
Maier 122
Malamud, Charles 166, 192
Mandel, Ben 166, 167, 192, 223
Marx, Karl 17, 25, 34, 35, 45, 76, 218
McGlynn, Elden P. 35
McNamara, Jim 41, 216
Medders, Clara 200, 205, 206, 207, 225
Mehlen 209
Meinhart, Carl 111
Melchior, Otto 105, 109
Mink, George 80, 218
Mitchell, William 183, 223
Müller, Heinrich 133
Münzenberg, Willi 50, 51, 61

N

Napoleon 125
Nelles, Dieter 75, 115, 142, 210, 215, 218, 219, 220, 222, 223, 224
Nettkau, Karl 111, 220
Neumann 106
Nickel, Egon 61
Nickname of Krebs, Hermine 3, 5, 53, 156, 157, 160, 161
Nikolajczik, Ede 38, 68, 79, 216, 217, 218
Nørgaard, Erik .. 102, 105, 113, 127, 139, 141, 148, 153, 214, 220, 221, 222

O

Obermüller, Rudolf 111
Olson, Culbert L. 177, 191
Orlov, Alexander 215

P

Peps .... see Krebs, Hugo
Persson, Gunnar 92
Pietrzak, Franz 150
Pontopiddan, Eiler 154
Price, Arthur L. 43, 51, 52, 54, 162, 217

R

Radek, Karl 137, 164
Raikoff, Ilja 99, 100
Rankins, Gil 40, 41, 44, 45, 216, 223
Rasmussen 113
Robeson, Paul 201
Roe 173
Rohrwasser, Michael 149, 200, 214, 217, 218, 224, 225
Rolland, Romain 62
Roosevelt, Franklin D. 165, 171, 180, 185
Ross, Herbert H. 192
Rost, Friedrich 162
Rübner, Hartmut 19, 215

S

Saefkow, Anton 127, 128, 129, 136, 221
Samsing, Arthur 88, 93, 102, 144, 147
Schaar, Karl 124, 221
Schaffner, John 184, 206, 207, 225
Schelley, Adolf see Bem, Alfred
Schmedemann, Walter 122
Schopenhauer, Arthur 126
Schubert, Hermann 59, 66, 67, 68
Seeckt, Hans von 25
Seifert 50
Semprun, Jorge 49, 50, 125, 217, 221
Serge, Victor 18, 215
Siebert, Wilhelm 146, 147
Smith, Jessica 201, 223
Sperber, Manès 164
Stalin, Jossip Vissarionovitch .... vii, 35, 46, 47, 48, 57, 61, 63, 69, 70, 75, 83, 104, 120, 142, 143, 150, 163, 164, 166, 167, 170, 171, 178, 183, 194, 195, 201, 218

Stampfer, Friedrich 178, 205
Stöver .... see Krebs, Hermine,
Streckenbach, Bruno 132, 133, 134
Stroheim, Erich von 175

T

Tarver, John 87
Tastesen, Paul 124
Thälmann, Ernst 25, 47, 90, 106, 117
Thingstrup, Hildegard 101, 102, 103, 104, 105, 106, 109, 110, 111, 112, 118, 127, 137, 171, 220
Thomas, Sam 6, 17, 44, 140
Thompson, Fred 86, 219
Thomsen 180, 223
Toller, Ernst 17
Trautzsch, Walter 117
Traven, B. 14, 163
Tucholsky, Kurt 163

V

Volkersen, Hildegard .... see Thingstrup, Hildegard

W

Walter, Albert .. 20, 24, 28, 29, 31, 34, 44, 58, 65, 66, 67, 69, 71, 78, 86, 101, 117, 118, 119, 133, 141, 164, 171, 175, 209, 210, 215, 216, 220, 225
Warnke, Helmut 79, 218
Watson, Mary 163, 164
Wells, H. G. 172
Wessel, Horst 123
Wieke 71
Wilhelmine 198
Williams, Robert 105, 109, 110
Winchell, Walter 175
Wist 122
Woile 55
Wollweber, Ernst ...... vii, 76, 77, 78, 101, 103, 104, 105, 110, 113, 114, 115, 116, 119, 128, 130, 134, 138, 139, 140, 142, 143, 144, 145, 146, 147, 148, 149, 150, 151, 152, 153, 154, 158, 165, 167, 171, 183, 202, 203, 210, 214, 218, 219, 220, 221, 222, 224

Z

Zetkin, Clara 48, 82

Made in the USA
Monee, IL
12 November 2022